CW01497365

WELCOME TO PORNOLAND
by
RIC PORTER

Original publication in 2010 by Ric Porter

KDP Edition Published in 2019

Copyright © Ric Porter 2010

Cover artwork by Jonathan Ghostely 2012

ISBN 978-1-4467-1980-0

The author can be contacted via www.ricporter.com

This book is a work of non-fiction, based on the life, experiences and recollections of the author. In some cases, events have been changed, exaggerated or re-worked for the purposes of entertainment or narrative progression.

IDENT BOOKS is an imprint of Vident Media

www.identbooks.com

IDENT BOOKS

WELCOME TO PORNOLAND

With grateful Thanks to everyone who, knowingly or un-knowingly, appear in this book and who have helped me along the road to Porno-Land. And to all the many friends who have played an equally important part in my journey but who, for various reasons, do not appear. Thank you.

INTRODUCTION

Like most young guys, I'd look at a porno mag or watch a dirty video and wonder where on Earth they made these things, and with who? I didn't know anyone who was a porn star and neither did any of my mates. Were sex films and magazines all put together on some mythical island somewhere called Porno-Land? Up until recently I think that's how most blokes thought. But then along came high street lap dancing clubs, amateur internet web cams, couples-friendly sex shops, and suddenly it was OK, even trendy, to say you were in some way involved in the porn business; almost everyone knew someone who (at least knew someone who) was a lap-dancer or an amateur model in their spare time. Along came Ben Dover and Seymour Butts who, with their regular appearances on cable TV and articles about them in men's magazines like *Loaded*, made it all very clear that they were just ordinary blokes like you and me who had the best job in the world – they made sex films! And the girls they filmed and shagged? Were they really innocent little nobodies that Ben Dover picked up on the street and sweet-talked into porno stardom, or were we all being conned by hardened professional models and actresses? At the end of the day, who cared? The viewer would happily suspend his belief because he wanted to think that it was all real – that nympho bimbo babes were there to be picked up right on the street where he lived and not in mythical Porno-Land after all!

I'm going to blow the lid off the whole British porno business and tell you how it really happens, to who, how much they get paid, and who gets to go home with the girls afterwards! I know because I've been there! I've visited Porno-Land and this is my postcard home.

Chapter One:
NO CONDOMS, NO COMMITMENTS

I was lying on a bed in a luxuriously furnished apartment situated just off Park Lane in London's West End. It was the early 1980's and I was in an apartment that was apparently frequently rented out to the Three Degrees, Prince Charles' then favourite pop group, whenever they were in town. I switched on the radio, stretched out and closed my eyes.

Kraftwerk's '*The Model*' was playing on the radio, and in another bedroom just down the hall, a beautiful young girl was spread-eagled naked in front of two fully clothed men who were taking photographs of her as she caressed her body for them.

I hadn't met her yet but in maybe another half an hour I would be introduced to her, and have her press her naked body up against mine. Not bad for my first day at work!

Yes I was working! As the spring sun dappled through the lace curtains from the unknowing world outside where guys were busying about their nine to five businesses and dreaming of having a job like mine, I'd be getting naked with a beautiful girl and be paid in cash for the privilege of doing so!

It was a far cry from my usual day-job of managing a local clothes shop. I'd taken the day off 'sick' in order to come here, and for this one day I'd be earning in cash what it would have taken me all week to earn at the shop.

Like most healthy red-blooded guys my age (I guess I was around twenty or so at the time), I was obsessed with the opposite sex so, seeing an advert in a top shelf men's magazine for models (aimed mainly at recruiting female talent of course) I figured that they must use guys too, as many of the photo sequences involved simulated sex between a male and a female.

I reckoned what the hell; I'd give it a try, so wrote to the address given in the ad, sending them my picture and details.

The sexual climate in those days was still fairly relaxed as HIV had not yet reared its deathly head, and the only health hazard in the adult industry seemed to be catching a dose of something mildly uncomfortable but easily curable: a risk one might encounter from picking up a one night stand at a local night-club.

I was young, single, naive and hot-headed. The only thing I felt I was risking was my reputation; what would my friends think if they found out? I figured that if any of them did find out, they'd probably take it all in pretty good humour, laughing with me rather than at me.

My career? Well, as a failed fashion model, actor, and singer, the only future I currently had was managing a back-street rundown clothes shop, which was going nowhere fast, and unfortunately taking me with it!

So I wrote to Mr. 'Bill Bernard' at the magazine company's address and, early one evening about two weeks later, the phone rang. It was a softly spoken Bill Bernard, offering me one day's work doing a simulated sex photo session.

'Do you know Green Street?' he asked.

'Of course' I replied. The only Green Street I knew of was the one near where I lived in a run-down area of London's East End, just round the corner from the sex shop where I'd bought the magazine I saw the advert in.

'No, this one's off Park Lane in the West End of London, near the Hilton Hotel.' Mr. Bernard told me.

'Oh yeah; that Green Street!' I bluffed, 'Sure'. Naturally I was keen to accept his offer of work, and so I planned that, the day before the shoot, I would come over ill at work, so much so that I would have to take the following day off 'sick'.

I turned up at the impressive four storied building near Hyde Park in London's West End the next morning and, still half wondering if maybe this was after all some elaborate hoax at my expense, I rang the doorbell.

After some interrogation over the intercom to establish who I was, a young man came to the door and let me in to an entrance hall that was in itself bigger than my sitting room was at home.

He led me to a room in which a mass of studio lights, cameras, and cables were strewn, and I was introduced to a stocky man with curly dark hair and a beard. He looked to me a bit like a young Stanley Kubrick and called himself Rex Peters although, when he spoke, I recognised the same soft voice of the man called Bill Bernard who I had spoken to on the phone.

Rex (or was it Bill?) introduced me to the guy who had let me in as Dave, and I wondered if this could be porn king David Sullivan himself, as I knew that today's photos would appear in one or more of the many sex magazines that Sullivan then published. It turned out however that this David was no more than Rex's assistant David Antony, an ex-policeman who is now an internationally respected glamour photographer in his own right.

Dave took me to one of the many bedrooms and told me to relax until they were ready for me as they were going to do a photo shoot with the girl on her own first. No problem I thought – having done my share of work as a film 'extra', I was well acquainted with the long hours waiting around to be called on set during filming and, as in this particular case I was waiting to be called on set to pose with a beautiful naked girl, I was of course happy to sit and wait!

When I was eventually called in to one of the other bedrooms, I saw a cute brunette dressed in a short skirt, top, stockings and suspenders lying on a single bed. She was of slight build and, with her hair in bunches, looked like an innocent sixteen year old. I found out later that she was in fact in her mid twenties and the single mother of a young child. This was how she earned the money to support herself and her child.

My first lesson in Porno-Land – don't believe what you see; make-up, wardrobe and camera angles means that the camera lies! Single mothers in their twenties are made to look like innocent teenagers, and possibly the other way round too, if the role required it. Just like an old Hollywood prop, in Porno-Land nothing is real or to be believed!

Bucks Fizz' 1982 single proclaimed '*My camera never lie!*' – clearly they hadn't been to Porno-Land!

Rex introduced us (I think her name was Carol), and then started taking some Polaroid photos to test that the lighting was correct. These were the days before digital cameras and all photos were taken on a roll of 35mm film, with test pictures taken on a Polaroid camera so that Rex could see the lighting and f-stop results immediately, without having to wait for the film to be developed.

Posing sex with a naked girl isn't the big turn-on that most guys might imagine. First off, the most important thing is that the photographer gets the shots he wants, not that you enjoy yourself. Therefore, you mustn't touch the girl in any way that will mark her body, and you mustn't actually kiss her in any way that might smudge her carefully applied make-up. You must contort your body into (often uncomfortable) positions that look good on camera and that don't throw shadows over the girl's body; the missionary position was out then as all Rex would have seen would have been my spotty back!

What was important was that the girl, not me, looked good – I was merely a human prop for her to pose on and around!

Once the shots were taken, Carol and I pulled away from each other awkwardly and a little embarrassed. In those days, we made soft-core poses. No sex was actually taking place, and yet we were to look as if we were having a wild and raunchy session! A little acting and clever photography was required!

The laws in England at that time, or rather, as I later learned, the rules dictated by the major distributors of so-called 'top shelf' magazines in the UK, were such that, in a sex magazine, one could show a couple having sex as long as either the man wasn't erect or the camera couldn't see it!

With oral sex, neither parties tongue was allowed to actually touch the other's genitals but must always be a few inches away. Similarly any insertable object could only be a few inches away from female genitalia but never seen to be touching or entering. Sex magazines in the USA were at that time littered with shots like this, although a man was allowed to be photographed with an erection in America unlike their British counterparts who were only ever allowed to have semi- limp, semi-hard dicks, reinforcing the stereotypical cliché of British males as being limp lousy lovers who would rather have a nice hot cup of tea than a nice hot babe.

This type of shot (posing a few inches away) was known at that time as an 'American' shot, as was a girl holding herself wide open for the camera. This was also known as showing 'pink' for obvious reasons.

By the end of the session, which took maybe forty minutes of carefully positioning myself to Rex's direction, I was left with a feeling of sexual frustration; I had been allowed to pose and touch this naked girl but at the end of the shoot we both got dressed and that was it. She hadn't touched me or done anything to help relieve my frustration.

While Rex re-set his camera equipment in another room, I was introduced to yet another model; a blonde American girl called Cindy who was apparently on vacation from her job in the U.S. Police Force!

My next photo-shoot was with her, themed loosely around me being her hairdresser, initially combing her hair and ending up in what was becoming familiarly frustrating posed sexual positions.

Finally another photo-shoot with me and both girls, themed loosely around my being a door-to-door shoe salesman. All these shoots were done in a progression of the action, much like a photo story would have been done for 1970s teen magazines *Jackie* or *Oh Boy*, of which I had appeared in a few in my time as an aspiring model. The difference here of course was that we were all getting naked and pretending to have sex!

I was intrigued to see that both Carol and Cindy were exceptionally pretty and, far from looking like tired old slappers or tarty hookers, were in every way wholesome pretty girls that anyone would have been proud to introduce to their mother! Did this then belie the idea that many men have that all women doing porn are somehow bimbos, tarts, not intelligent, or not the kind of woman one would want as a girlfriend?

Well, obviously, girls chosen to appear in porno shoots are done so because they are good looking, as clearly a guy would rather see a pretty girl naked than an ugly one, so that alone would suggest that the female performers are going to be, in terms of beauty, a cut above the norm.

Why then would these two good looking girls, one a U.S. policewoman and one a young mum, get involved in a line of work where they rub up against not only other girls, but also men whom they have never met before – and do it on camera for all to see?

Some of these girls enjoy the attention and the limelight, such as it is. They may originally have wanted to become fashion or catwalk models, will certainly have the looks for it, but are maybe too large busted or too short, and so they do 'glamour work' as the next best thing; a way that they can still feel that they are involved in the professional modelling world.

Some girls may dream of being the next topless 'Page Three' pin-up sensation like Jordan, Jodie Marsh, Sam Fox, Linda Lusardi or Melinda Messenger, getting out of the rut of their small-town provincial life and flying abroad on all-expenses paid modelling shoots, mixing with celebrities, marrying footballers or appearing on reality TV shows, in *OK!* Magazine and becoming a household name; that's a kind of fame isn't it?

It's not however as easy to get on Page Three as one might imagine and, despite what one might think, not wonderfully well paid either, as girls will tend to want to do it for the exposure and the prestige. At the time I did my shoot with Rex Peters, a photo-shoot for Page Three was only paying about fifty pounds, and the girls chosen to appear on Page Three still had to eat and pay their rent of course, and so they may have done the tackier men's magazines, and gone from topless to nude, from nude to open-leg, from open-leg to 'American' and, then sometimes, from 'American' to full-on hard-core.

An 'easier' route, or fast track to media fame these days would be to simply have your photograph taken falling out of a night-club with very little clothing on, on the arm of a well- known footballer or soap star, or to flash your boobs on national television in a reality

TV series.

There is also a type of model who, in total opposition to her 'brainless bimbo' counterpart, is an independent strong- minded girl who often starts doing glamour work as a considered decision in order to beat the system and the dole queue; a way of simply using men to get out of the squat and earn money to pay back her student loan, have a great night- life and buy cocaine.

These girls are very sure of themselves, hassle and tease the photographers for more work and more money, and scorn the stupid old bastards that buy the dirty magazines in which they appear. These girls were a product of the media-savvy 90's, and used the adult business to get on in life, rejecting the business either when they'd had enough or had moved on in their career.

Other girls unfortunately get too involved in the glamorous lifestyle of being a model; free membership to all the top London night-clubs, potentially big earnings, shoots abroad, introductions to celebrities, endless champagne, drugs, and parties. These girls would stay in the business long after the time when they should have moved on, in order to keep feeding their addiction to the wild lifestyle for, like drink and drugs, working in the sex industry can become very addictive and no matter how hard one tries, or how genuinely one wants to make the break, getting away from that rock'n'roll lifestyle, seeing yourself on the covers of magazines, and going back to working nine to five in a local supermarket or factory just doesn't become a viable option anymore. In the words of the Eagles song *Hotel California*: '*You can check out any time you want, but you can never leave*'.

American porn star Ginger Lynn Allen once said that 'the fame, fortune and everything that go along with it were so overwhelming, I stayed in (the adult industry) for about two years, and made seventy films'. And she has since made a comeback, returning to the screen again after several decades, as an older performer.

After we had done the 'shoe salesman' shoot, Rex broke for lunch and, while we were eating brought in sandwiches, a blonde haired guy in his mid twenties arrived.

He had startlingly blue eyes and rock star good looks.

After a brief whispered conversation with Rex, he was introduced to me as Lindsay.

'It's Ric isn't it?' he asked as he shook my hand, looking straight into my eyes. I was impressed that he knew who I was, and that he had remembered my name, recognising me from a letter and photo I had sent to the English hard-core production company Videx in an attempt to get work.

At that time an English company making hardcore sex films was a rare thing indeed; almost a contradiction in terms.

Videx were openly advertising their films in the belief that they had found a loophole in the UK legal system. Video at this time was a relatively new medium, and the laws regarding obscene and uncensored movies only related to those made on film, not video.

Despite this however, the director of Videx Films, Mike Freeman, was currently serving a jail sentence and Lindsay, one of Freeman's regular stars, was starting up on his own, utilising Videx's equipment and mailing list to do so.

Mike Freeman had in fact been involved in making porn films since the early sixties, shooting 8mm and 16mm 'loops' for distribution around the world.

After serving time in prison in the late sixties Freeman had been plotting how to re-invent his career in porn upon his release.

My understanding is that Freeman had paid £4000 each for two business modules at Mipcom Trade Exhibition in France to set up

Videx and that, like many other British companies at that time, was refunded 50% from the Board of Trade.

The Obscene Publications Squad soon caught up with his activities however and arrested him again. Needless to say however the Board of Trade weren't taken to court with him over their part as his financial assistant!

Lindsay Honey was the long-term partner of Linzi Drew, one time editor of the British edition of the international men's magazine *Penthouse*, as well as star of innumerable soft-core glamour videos and magazine shoots in the 1980s. She had also appeared in the Ken Russell film *Aria* and had posed for an album cover for Pink Floyd's Roger Waters. Honey himself is now far better known worldwide as Britain's most successful international male porn star/director Ben Dover with countless adult awards and DVD sales to his credit.

At that time however he was simply a musician involved in the glam-rock band La Rox, which was fronted by Ian Mitchell, an ex member of the 70s glam rock band The Bay City Rollers, and Lindsay's partner Linzi was then far better known than he was.

La Rox were in fact all down the road in another luxurious apartment (this one apparently frequently rented out to the Bee Gees when they were in town), filming a hard-core sex film for Videx loosely based around the band and what happens when Ian's (on-screen) sister gets kidnapped. Starring Ian Mitchell himself, and directed and produced by Honey, the film was called *The Rock'n'Roll Ransom*.

Apparently they had been let down by a couple of models, and Lindsay wanted to know if he could 'borrow' some of us for the following two days.

Would-be actors getting cold feet at the last minute or just not turning up at all on the day is a common occurrence in the sex business, the idea of being a porn star sometimes being preferable to the reality of actually trying to be one. Rex had originally stressed to me on the phone the importance of not letting him down on the day, and had made me re-confirm that I would turn up. It was common practice in those days that a member of the film crew would stand in and have sex with the model on a shoot if an actor failed to turn up or simply couldn't get a hard-on on the day.

The female lead in such cases would have no say in the matter and indeed, the girl wouldn't usually know who her co-star was anyway until the day of the shoot, or sometimes even the actual moment of filming the sex scene with him, so a last- minute stand-in wouldn't make any difference to her. These days models are told prior to the shoot who they will be working with and male leads on hardcore shoots have to provide up-to-date HIV and STD tests (as do female performers), but in those early pre-AIDS days, things were very different!

With Lindsay was a bubbly blonde Australian girl called Nicola, who was the female lead in his film.

She had come to England in search of who she said was her occasional boyfriend but may only have been a groupie's crush, the then relatively unknown Robert Smith of the pop group The Cure, and Nicola was staying on in the UK, working illegally while she looked for him.

Honey were letting her sleep in the Videx offices and giving her some pocket money in exchange for her services performing in as many films and with as many people, male or female, as he chose.

It was an arrangement which suited her and obviously suited Honey and Videx very well as they didn't need to pay her a specific fee per job.

So, like a piece of Videx's property, Nicola was now traded with Rex as part of the deal that Lindsay had struck; Lindsay could hire Rex's models for his film, if Rex could borrow Nicola there and then to do a photo-shoot.

And so the deal was done. I joined Nicola and Carol for another photo-shoot threesome, which once again turned out to be more like real work than the enjoyable sex activity one might believe it to be when viewing the end result.

This shoot was in the bath and I was a little wary at first of taking part as the bathroom was a mass of electrical cables and video lights. I knew that electricity and water weren't a great combination and I wanted to live to shoot another day! But the lure of getting in the water with Nicola and Carol was enough in the end to make me take the plunge, and of course Rex and Dave were very careful in making sure that any electricity was kept well out of the way of the bubbles.

When the day was over, we all got dressed and waited to be paid.

Rex had waited until now to tell the girls and myself about the next couple of days work with Lindsay. First he took Carol and Cindy aside and asked them if they were OK to do a hardcore movie for Lindsay, and then he invited me in and asked me if I was OK to do it; a sex scene with no condoms and with no emotional commitment to my co-stars; a simple sex for cash on camera deal.

In just twenty-four hours I'd gone from being a poorly paid shopkeeper to being a (comparatively) well-paid porno actor. I felt as if I was on my way and that Britain's answer to Ron Jeremy or John Holmes had arrived; watch out Porno-Land – you have a new resident moving in!

Chapter Two:
SCREEN VIRGINS & FLUFF GIRLS

I continued being 'sick' from work for the next day and drove back to Green Street in my old second hand Wolseley car with an audio tape of sexy stories that a mate had given me playing in the car. Read by a breathy female with the kind of voice you'd expect to hear these days on a sex phone line I thought it was just the thing to keep me 'in the mood' for the day's 'work' ahead.

This time I was freely buzzed in when I rang the doorbell to the apartment down the road from the one Rex had been using. There was none of the cautious questioning on the intercom that I had experienced with Rex.

The whole scene was in fact totally different. The entire apartment was filled with young men and women who all looked like they were either members of a rock band (many of them in fact were) or were their groupies.

There was a constant supply of snack food and alcohol. Loud rock music blasted out from a decent music system and people sat around talking, laughing, drinking wine or beer and generally having a good time. The whole scene was like being at a pretty good party – except that the sun was still shining, it was only ten in the morning, and there was a day's work ahead.

Most of the day was spent, as before, in sitting around and waiting, while other scenes were being filmed in one or other of the many bedrooms.

While I waited to be called on-set I drank some wine and chatted with Nicola. She was staying with all the main 'actors' and crew at this location for the duration of the shoot, and told me that, the night before, she had got very drunk and fallen naked through a glass coffee table in the apartment. She had been rushed to hospital in a black taxi, needing several stitches to her rear.

The taxi driver, making conversation, asked her what her job was.

'I fuck for a living!' she had coolly replied. I bet he had wondered just what kind of tip he was going to get!

Around lunchtime, a cheery middle-aged man arrived with a giggly young Chinese girl on his arm. He was known simply as 'Kent', and was a familiar face in the business. A college lecturer by profession, he also acted as an agent, supplying new girls to photographers and directors, as well as making the occasional on-screen appearance if the mood (or the girl) so took him.

He had called in for no apparent reason other than to ogle Lindsay's girls, and to drink his free booze.

Ian Mitchell was the only Irish member of the all Scottish glam rock band The Bay City Rollers, joining them on April 1, 1976 at age 17 as a replacement for co-founder Alan Longmuir. He only stayed in the band for seven months however, leaving in November 1976.

'We've all got a raise, lads!' he shouted out as he caught part of a news item on the big TV flickering away in a corner of the main sitting room. He and the other members of his new band La Rox were all signing on the dole between gigs, and on TV the Chancellor had just announced a raise in the level of unemployment benefit in that year's Budget.

As he sat there, on the dole and yet sipping champagne, a girl on either arm, being given cash to have sex on film, I reflected on how little I was earning working flat out every day in the clothes shop and concluded that a life in porn seemed a far better option!

In *The Rock'n'Roll Ransom* I was supposed to be a member of Ian's band. Nicola was playing Ian's girlfriend and, as such was obviously scripted to do several sex scenes with him. Unfortunately Nicola really annoyed Ian, and he didn't get on with her at all.

Consequently he wasn't performing too well sexually with her, and so Lindsay was having to rewrite her scenes all the time (she had to be employed doing something, remember as Lindsay was getting her effectively for free!).

Lindsay asked me who I'd prefer to work with, possibly thinking that, if I was with someone I actually liked, unlike Ian and Nicola, he might get a far better scene. I chose Cindy, as I was already familiar with her from the previous day.

'Oh, I thought you'd have chosen Jane' he mused, referring to a quiet Irish blonde girl, 'It's her first time doing it on camera – she's a 'screen virgin''.

As on the previous day, the action is for the director, and not for one's own enjoyment. Add to that the fact that one is having sex in the glare of two two-thousand watt lights, in front of a bunch of fully clothed guys who have various technical jobs (sound-man, camera operator, production assistant etc), and that the whole time one has to bear in mind where the camera is to make sure that it is getting the best shot, and it is soon apparent that this really is simply a job of work in many ways like any other.

Much like a Hollywood movie star who spends a long time waiting around and then has to perhaps act in an unnatural way, making sure that they don't muff their lines, look directly at the camera and at all times 'hit their mark' while seemingly doing it all naturally, there was clearly more to this job than just simply being able to have sex in front of a camera. For one thing, one had to be able to have sex to direction; to carry on

at a particular pace for maybe forty minutes or so, and never ever climax before one is told to!

Also the girl doesn't really want to be doing this with you; she probably has her own boyfriend at home and is blanking you out of her mind and simply thinking of the money. In short, sex in front of the camera isn't the heaven you think it's going to be – it's strangely not like you're really having sex; it is unfortunately just like a job! An unusual one I grant you, but a job nonetheless!

I also found it strange that, when called upon to consciously ad lib for the benefit of the soundtrack, I automatically fell back on all the old clichés I'd ever heard, badly dubbed and woodenly performed, in old 70's and 80's porno flicks; 'Take my big dick, you filthy whore!' etc. Did I really talk like this when I was having sex for real? Does anyone? Of course not, so why was I now?

Spouting bad porno under hot studio lights, we broke off to take a break between sex positions.

Bad sex, bad acting; maybe being a porn star wasn't all it was cracked up to be after all!

Lindsay wrapped a big bathrobe around me and escorted me to the kitchen to get some orange juice.

'Lots of Vitamin C.' he advised, 'That'll keep you going'.

'How was it?' one of the girls asked as we came out, assuming that we'd finished shooting the scene.

'We're not through yet' Lindsay informed her, 'He's a long stayer, this one.' That made me feel good; girls love guys that can keep going don't they?

'Too much of a long-stayer!' put in my co-star, raising her eyes heavenward, 'I was doing all I could to get this scene finished, so we could go home!' – Oh well, maybe not!

After our orange juice break, we were back in the bedroom, carrying on; more positions, more clichés, more faking reality for the camera.

As anyone who has ever seen a hard-core porn movie knows, the male star not only has to be able to get hard quickly, and maintain his erection with the stamina of an athlete through a variety of sexual positions, many requiring the physical versatility of a double-jointed gymnast but, at the crucial moment, he has to cum on cue and be seen to do so – usually all over his co-star!

This is the time-honoured tradition of hard-core movies. Little has changed over the decades. In more recent years, female directors like America's Candida Royalle have been more sensitive to portraying the realism of a loving sexual relationship, where men don't suddenly pull out of their partner at the point of orgasm, exclaiming 'Eat my cum, bitch!' This however was no such film.

The male climax shot was, in the early days of hard-core, called 'the money shot'. It proved that nothing had been simulated or faked, and was the one important uncensored shot that the punters wanted to see; the proof of the pudding; the shot that sells the film and brings in the cash; the money shot!

It was said that Berth Milton, publisher of the legendary Swedish hard-core magazine *Private*, would make it very clear to his male models that if they couldn't manage to cum (and cum on cue so that the cameras got the best possible shot) they quite simply would not get paid, no matter how well they had performed all day. Seasoned American porn stars made sure that they maintained a particular diet in order to make their sperm look better for the camera; more thick and gooey. American porn star Ron Jeremy was legendary in the business for being able to cum on cue if he was given a ten second countdown. Did I feel under pressure to deliver? You bet I did!

However I had gone past the point of climax. I was numb and there was no way that I would be able to deliver the all- important money shot.

Lindsay was very understanding. In hard-core work the guys are sometimes treated with more respect, understanding and pampering than the girls they star with as I guess the girl can always fake her pleasure but, if a guy gets tired, pressured or pissed off, it's all too obvious and, on a shoot where time is money, it is important to keep the male star happy, hard and capable of providing that all important 'money shot' on cue so that everyone can go home on time. In this respect shooting a hard-core adult movie is no different from any other kind of movie; everyone's on a wage and basically everyone just wants to get the job done, get paid and go home.

And so the 'fluff girl' was called for.

On an adult film set the fluff girl had a very important role. She was employed purely for her talents at orally stimulating the male stars back into business when they began to wilt. The female stars themselves were not expected to have to deal with such things; it's enough that they acted and fucked on film – they shouldn't have to be really turning the guys on as well! A professional stud will be expected to do that for himself.

In the early days of porn film-making the fluff girl was rarely ever seen in front of the camera, but nowadays there isn't usually the budget to employ someone extra just for that purpose, so the job of 'fluffing' goes to whoever is the most game girl on the set.

So who do you think was Lindsay's 'fluffer'? No prizes for guessing it was of course the girl he didn't have to pay anyway – Nicola!

The crew left us alone for a few minutes but all Nicola did was start talking to me about Ian, telling me that she really fancied him, had been a big fan of the Bay City Rollers in her early teens and, even though this shoot was shattering all her illusions about him, she would still really like to get it on with him even though he'd made it very plain that he found her very annoying.

Normally of course 'getting it on' with someone might mean that you'd like to have sex with them. Ian and Nicola had of course already had sex several times but, in the world of porn, that happens even if you hate the sight of each other, and meant no more than a handshake does in the real world. In fact in porn, as I believe is the case with prostitutes, intimate gestures that are considered offensive are kissing and touching, not sucking and screwing. In the real world one may kiss a stranger on the cheek but never dream of putting one's hand up her skirt. Like some topsy-turvy looking glass world that Alice might have stumbled into, here in Porno- Land the complete opposite was true!

I was still struggling to provide Lindsay with the required 'money shot'.

I knelt beside Nicola but, because of the powerful hot lights, I was sweating profusely and droplets of perspiration dripped from me and landed on Nicola's body. Eyes closed, and feeling something warm and damp on her body, Nicola assumed the obvious and started moaning 'Oh yeah Baby; That feels so good!'

Only in Porno-Land do girls scream out in ecstasy when men sweat all over them! It was a million miles away from anything I'd ever experienced in the 'real world' and yet it was all happening right here in Central London.

Lindsay wasn't prepared to waste any more time or videotape on me to see if I could produce anything other than sweat, claiming that he already had more footage of me in this one scene than he did of Ian in the entire film, and Ian was supposed to be the star, and so my money shot and the finale of my scene with Nicola was now to be 'stunted'.

Chapter Three:
STUNT DICKS & MONEY SHOTS

If Lindsay was making a hard-core film, he hated to have to fake any of the shots so, while I got dressed in disgrace, he hunted around in the sitting room to see who else could perform the money shot in my place.

This was my introduction to the 'stunt dick'.

The stunt dick's role, like the fluff girl, is to sit around waiting for the moment when a guy can't fuck or cum. He then strips off and fucks or cums in the main actor's place, the camera shooting very tight on his cock, so the scene can be easily edited in with shots of the real actor's face groaning pleasure. Much like a stuntman or a body-double in a more mainstream feature film, the stunt dick stands in anonymously for the real star, and the audience never guesses that it isn't the main actor doing all the action himself.

Adult film companies these days can rarely afford to pay someone just to sit around like some perverse and decadent understudy, waiting for his moment to stand in. Reliable guys are the most difficult thing to find in the adult film world anyway, so a guy who can get it up, do the business and cum on cue won't be sitting around stunt-dicking but will be much in demand as the leading player himself.

Usually on small budget video shoots, a member of the crew will stand in as a stunt-dick for the wilting star, and so get the additional 'perk' of a free blow-job from the female lead.

Curious though it may seem to the average man in the street who may dream of doing porno, surrounded by beautiful eager young girls, it is a very different story when one is actually on the set surrounded by a bored looking fully dressed crew, hot studio lights, and expected to perform to direction for over an hour on command. Most guys either can't get it up at all, wilt after a few minutes or cum immediately. None of which is any good to a porn director trying to amass a lot of sexy footage from all angles to make into a decent sequence. Don't forget that, although the on- screen time of an average sex scene may only be seven to fifteen minutes, the couple on-screen will have needed to have been at it for probably an hour or more in order for the cameras to get enough action from all the different angles needed to edit together a decent scene; just like in the real film business, a crew may take all day recording what will finally edit down to perhaps only a few useable minutes or even seconds in the finished film. A good adult film director will want a ratio of 3:1 when he gets into the edit suite; ie: three times as much footage on film as he will actually use in the edit. This way, he can pick and choose and use only the best shots in his edit.

It is the most difficult thing in the world to find studs who possess the magic combination of good looks, a natural acting ability and an ever hard, good sized dick, whereas there is no shortage of young girls ready and willing to take off their clothes and fuck like bunnies in front of a video camera. And girls can always just do it – if they're not really in the mood, then a little lube will always help. If a guy can't get it up however, all the lube in the world won't make any difference – he'll just have a more slippery 'soft-on'!

So Lindsay needed to find someone to 'stunt dick' me, and that was how the man called Kent came to have more involvement in *The Rock 'n' Roll Ransom* that day than he had expected.

'Come on, Kent,' Lindsay persuaded, 'You're always wanting to get in on my films. Well, this is your chance'.

'Yes, but I don't look anything like him.' Kent protested, 'I'm of a totally different build'.

'Listen,' Lindsay reassured him as he helped him undress, 'Don't worry – It'll be a very tight shot '.

Naked except for his socks, Kent and I compared torsos. I was younger, slimmer, and with less body hair. We were basically nothing like each other. Still, the money shot had to be filmed, and Kent was there!

Wasting no further time and dismissing all of Kent's protests, Lindsay set about lathering up a shaving brush and shaving Kent's thighs to match my less hairy ones.

This done, Kent padded from the bathroom in his socks.

No time for introductions, Kent got astride Nicola while I stood out of shot with the microphone so that I could moan and groan appropriate noises as Kent climaxed on my behalf. At least the voice on the soundtrack if not the body would actually match.

My scene over, there were only two things left to do: have a Polaroid taken for Lindsay's files so he could bear me in mind for any future work, sign a model release and get paid.

Rex would always try and give me a cheque advising me to 'say you sold something privately to avoid tax'. Lindsay on the other hand gave me cash and suggested that, if I wanted to hang around, I could go out with everyone to a club later on.

'Neat!' I thought, 'I'm having sex for cash, and now I'm getting a rock'n'roll social life thrown in too!'

The model release is the all important piece of paperwork on any shoot which gives the producer or photographer the right to use your image in his work. It has your genuine signature on it and bears your real name and details. Should there be any problems later on (like you had a change of heart the next day), this is the piece of paper that will mean the producer will still have his film; it will stand up in a court of law.

In the next scene that Lindsay was to film, Carol and Jane were to creep through into the en-suite bathroom and, after undressing each other, have sex in the sunken bath with... for no apparent reason whatsoever... an enormous cucumber!

Why would anyone keep an enormous cucumber in a bathroom? Well this was Porno-Land after all, and a characteristic of sex films then and now is the lack of any logical reason not only for plot, but also as to how sex props like dildos, vibrators and enormous cucumbers pop up in locations like bathrooms or behind sofa cushions for no apparent reason whatsoever.

When Lindsay went to the cucumber prop department, known as 'the fridge', he found his cucumber cut in two with the middle section missing.

'I don't believe this!' he roared, 'Where's the fucking prop gone?'

'What's up, mate?' asked Ian, wandering up and munching away at a salad.

'The fucking cucumber!' Lindsay told him, 'Somebody's cut it up'.

His words trailed off as he watched Ian fork a juicy chunk of cucumber into his mouth.

'It's only a fucking vegetable, Linds. Calm down, mate' he grinned.

The girls held the cucumber so that their hands covered the break in the middle of it and, after it had been inserted for a little while,

Lindsay cut it down even more so that this time, when their hands covered the break, it looked as if the entire length had gone deep inside, with just the very end sticking out.

The scene was nearly over when Jane declared that she needed to pee. Inspiration hit Lindsay.

'Hold on,' he said, 'and we'll film it!'

Squirming around, she desperately held on while they searched around for a piece of glass through which to film so that there would be no risk of getting the camera lens wet.

All the guys in the room got very excited at the prospect of filming a 'pissing scene'; somehow it seemed very kinky and bizarre.

'Crazy isn't it?' Lindsay commented, 'After all the sex we've been filming, everyone's getting turned on by a girl going to the loo! Compared with some of the things we've shot (champagne bottles and cucumbers used as sex toys, gang- bangs and threesomes) this is probably the most natural act we've filmed yet!'

Nevertheless Lindsay too was quite excited and, claiming that he had suddenly got very hot, he began to strip off, revealing his huge penis (he has a dick that's almost a foot long), barely concealed by a tiny pair of women's pants.

'Are those girl's pants?' I asked, bemused.

'Yeah, I'm wearing Linzi's.' he replied, 'They're much more comfortable'.

Ian glanced at me smirking. This was nearly twenty years before David Beckham confessed to occasionally wearing his wife Victoria's underwear, and Ian clearly thought that Lindsay must be a secret transvestite!

'I can't hold on much longer' Jane said and the crew got themselves set up. The camera was at ground level, with Jane straddled over it.

A square of clear glass was placed over the lens, so that the girl could pee directly towards the camera lens.

'Here we go' she warned, and let go.

'Fantastic!' cried Lindsay, watching the video monitor intently, one hand fondling Linzi's briefs. 'What a shot! The glass over the lens was an inspired idea'.

'Yeah, but not totally foolproof!' answered the cameraman, wiping his face!

Inspired by this new idea, Lindsay began plying Nicola with lots of mineral water so that she too could do a 'pissing scene'. Nicola however was less than keen on the idea; 'It's body waste' she argued, 'Not even pure'.

She then tried to persuade Lindsay that if she did do it, she should do it playfully rather than sexually; 'Like children would – in a game'. Clearly in Porno-Land even children's games are thought to be all about things like pissing!

Eventually, as time went on, Lindsay decided that the shoot was running too late, and that any new ideas would have to be cut.

Ian and one of the long haired rockers who were hanging around the location did their scene next, having a threesome with a young girl in the bath. The two guys gave each other high five over the girl at the end.

'Now we're blood brothers!' Ian joked. The girl got out of the bath, wiping her face, and Ian immediately got in and began to leisurely soak himself.

He took the whole experience of blue movie making a lot less seriously than Lindsay, and just enjoyed himself. And that attitude is perhaps the key to survival in this industry for, apart from getting all the technical things correct, how can one really take too seriously an industry where the photography of the emission of various bodily fluids is the criteria for a successful shoot?

During the afternoon a beautiful black girl arrived in a grey fur coat but, before settling herself in, she took Lindsay aside and had a quiet word with him.

It turned out that she was on her period and didn't know if it would still be OK for her to do her scene. Lindsay reassured her that of course it was, and cheerily called out to all the guys lounging around in the main sitting room: 'OK, which one of you guys doesn't mind a bit of blood?'

Not knowing what the girl had just discussed with Lindsay, I wondered for a moment if he was recruiting guys to break in a virgin!

One of the waiting studs who had been bragging all day of his sexual prowess said that he wouldn't mind doing it, and went off with Lindsay and the girl in the fur-coat to do his scene.

He should however have kept his earlier boasting to himself as, after only about fifteen minutes, he came out fully dressed.

He had lost his erection almost immediately and nothing could be done to get it back.

Lindsay burst into the room, visibly distraught.

'We haven't got a cum shot with this black girl yet.' he stormed, 'Which one of you guys aren't needed to do a cum shot later, and could do it with this chick?'

It turned out that there were only two guys left who had already done their scenes, and so could risk coming off now as a 'stunt dick'.

Time was of the essence, so they both went into the bedroom where the black girl was waiting, still in position, doggy style, on the bed.

Remember that it is never up to the female 'star' to get you hard; that, as a professional, you do for yourself.

And so , standing naked side by side, the guys both tried to get hard and save the day like a kind of perverse version of the Cavalry. Lindsay popped his head round the door.

'We've got to get a cum shot soon.' he said, 'Maybe it would help if I got Nicola in to give you a hand?"

Ian loudly voiced his opposition to this idea; I had forgotten that he couldn't stand her.

So the two guys stood there naked beside each other, with eyes closed, trying to get themselves hard while, ironically in the adjoining bedroom, a naked sexy girl was waiting.

Neither of them were able to perform under these circumstances however, and so Lindsay was forced to compromise his artistic integrity and fake the cum shot.

Complaining at how much he hated having to fake this, he got busy preparing a mixture of water, egg white and icing sugar. These days a well known brand of indigestion mixture is used instead to very realistic effect.

Filming the girl's rear in a big close-up, the fake sperm was dripped onto her body from above and didn't really look too unrealistic after all. Shortly after this, the girl reappeared from the bedroom, fur coat back on, and left the house. Since arriving, she had spoken to no-one but Lindsay, had been offered as a sex partner to a man who couldn't fuck her, been offered as a object for two other men to try and cum over, had a mixture of icing sugar and egg white smeared over her rear, and been paid for the experience – only in Porno-Land!

Lindsay's crew got ready to film the last scene of the day; the general party into which all the other sex scenes would be cut together in the edit.

To make it look like a real rock'n'roll party, Lindsay brought out a small mirror, with some lines of white powder on it. I'd never taken any kind of drug before and was a little unsure what to expect. I watched what the others did and followed suit, snorting a line up my nose. It was awful: my nose just felt blocked, uncomfortable and sore. If this was cocaine, I thought, I was better off without it!

'What the hell's the attraction of this stuff?' I asked Ian quietly.

'Well, we've got to do it for the camera,' he answered, nodding in agreement with me, 'Be all right if it was the real thing eh?'

It was only then that I noticed more 'coke' being cut up – out of a packet of Ajax cleaning powder! The coke was of course just a prop. Like everything else in Porno-Land, including the sex, nothing was quite what you thought it was.

Lindsay was a talented musician and had actually toured with the Bay City Rollers as their drummer. He had recorded a beautiful cover version of the old Ronettes classic *Be My Baby* as a duet with Linzi Drew to be released in conjunction with the release of the finished film, and the following day he was filming a sequence in the recording studio where Linzi, Ian and himself were supposedly laying down the track.

My career in the sex film industry would be very short-lived at only two days unless I could wangle another day or so working, and so I suggested to Lindsay that, as I was playing the part of a guitarist in their band, wouldn't it be appropriate if I was there the next day as well?

Lindsay whole-heartedly agreed but said there just wasn't enough money in the budget to pay me for days when I was only doing 'linking' shots.

I couldn't really afford any more time off work unless it was worthwhile financially, and so I decided to enjoy the rest of the evening before returning to the normality of selling clothes the next day.

Everyone was going off to a late night drinking club, the St. Moritz, down the road in Soho, where a scene featuring a striptease act had been filmed the previous day. I offered to give Nicola a lift there in my old Wolseley which, when I got outside, had a puncture! Lindsay helped me change the wheel, and Nicola and I set off.

The line between reality and fantasy becomes blurred working on an adult film. What had seemed an acceptable norm in the sexually oriented daytime was clearly not suitable behaviour in the evening of normality. On the short journey from the house to the club, I played Nicola the sexy audio tape I'd brought with me in the car assuming that she might find it a bit of a turn-on.

The real world however is different from Porno-Land, where every girl has readily open legs, and an equally open mind to all sexual suggestions. Nicola laughed at my tape and, after letting me buy her a drink when we got to the club, spent the rest of the evening ignoring me and chasing after Ian.

I guess this should have taught me one important lesson: while working in the adult industry, never allow yourself to get fooled into believing the scripts. At the end of the day nobody works, no matter how good the job, for anything other than the pay cheque; to feed their children like Carol; to pay for their vacation like Cindy and Nicola, or to further their careers and find a better lifestyle for themselves like Linzi and Lindsay.

Modelling in porno is a tough job, but it is just that, and the sex kittens remain on the celluloid when the shooting's over and the make-up comes off.

I suppose there are exceptions; the odd housewife fulfilling some private fantasy in front of the camera, the guy having a last fling before he settles down, but these are not the norm.

The girls in Porno-Land are not all nymphomaniacs who genuinely crave your body in an orgy of passion off-screen as well as on. They are ordinary girls trying to earn a buck doing an extraordinary job.

I should have learned this all-important lesson then and there, but hey! I'd just joined the ranks of Ron Jeremy, Rocco Sifredi and John Holmes and become a porn stud! So why should I listen to that angel on my right shoulder when the devil on my left was urging me on to go for the next job that would bring me back as soon as possible to this weird and wonderful place called Porno-Land?

Chapter Four:
THE X-RATED MOUNTAIN

Back in the humdrum routine of selling clothes I decided that if I could get enough work in the porn industry, I would leave my job and survive on that kind of work alone. Well I only needed one or two days work a week to equal what I was earning working all week long in the clothes shop!

And a couple of weeks later the phone rang again, and Rex's softly spoken voice asked me if I was free to do another shoot for him, a video plus some stills.

I arrived at the North London address by ten o'clock to find Rex and Dave busying around as before, and I was introduced to a new guy; a big bearded red haired man with an enormous beer belly and a facial twitch which made him look as if he was constantly winking at you, something I would have thought was particularly off-putting to some of the female models! His name was Clive and apparently he was Rex's video technician. He kept calling Rex 'Peter' and I found out then that Rex Peters' real first name was in fact Peter and not Rex. Like many people in the porn business he had given himself a false name just as an actor or a singer will have a 'professional' name (Cary Grant was really Archibald Leach and Elton John was really Reg Dwight!). I didn't know whether Rex wanted me to know that I knew his real name was Peter or not and so I spent half the time that day calling him Rex and half the time calling him Peter to see which name got me the best reaction.

There already seemed to be a lot of other people milling around; girls in various states of undress and make-up, and a couple of other guys in the kitchen making toast and coffee, one of whom was Roger, a young guy about my own age and with similar looks. Rex seemed to be treating him with a lot of respect and asking his opinion on various aspects of the shoot. It turned out that he was in fact a journalist for the music magazine *Smash Hits* who had, as a bit of extra work on the side, written the script for Rex/Peter's video and that, as a writer's perk, was also going to appear in it!

The other man there was a guy called Ernie; older than any of us, in his early forties. He was a resting actor from Yorkshire, filling in between parts with a bit of porno. It turned out that he had been staying at Clive's house the night before and that Clive's girlfriend had taken a fancy to him, and kept him up half the night having sex, something that Rex/Peter found very annoying. But whether this was because Ernie was too shagged out to perform properly, or because there had been some sex going on that Rex/Peter had missed out on, I wasn't too sure.

The first scene was with poor knackered old Ernie and a young girl called Nikki.

After the shoot was over, Ernie came back to one of the bedrooms to rest while Rex/Peter and his crew of Dave and Clive set up for another scene.

'I couldn't really get into that', Ernie confessed meekly, excusing himself for what Rex/Peter had clearly regarded as a poor performance, 'But to me it's not sexy; it's just another job, you know; just another job.'

And, as he wasn't involved in the rest of the day's shooting, the job was over for Ernie, and that was the last I ever saw of him – a resting actor, of small parts!

During the lunch break Nikki began to get more and more worried about her return to work the next day. She worked in a post office in Scarborough and was afraid that they were going to sack her for taking the time off to do this shoot.

I told her not to be so concerned about a boring job in a post office and, to back up my reassurances, I began to tell Rex/Peter that I was thinking of leaving my job at the clothes shop and going full time in the porn business.

Instead of the encouragement I expected, he told me not to be rash, as work in this business was never guaranteed. However, if I really did make the break and found it hard going, he would try and find me some work in one of the sex shops owned and run by David Sullivan, who was employing Rex/Peter to do the photos and videos on this shoot. The photos would appear in the many then Sullivan owned adult magazines, and the videos would be sold exclusively through his shops.

I was a little disappointed with Rex/Peter's reaction to my news. I guess I'd naively expected him to more or less place me on his payroll as a full-time stud for all his productions, and offering me the possibility of working in a shop, albeit a sex shop, was little more than I was doing already!

After all, shop work was the very thing I was trying to get away from!

During the afternoon, while Rex/Peter was busy getting the next shoot set up, I sat and chatted with Nikki. She seemed very worried what Rex/Peter's reaction would be if he found us together chatting as he got very annoyed if any sort of relationship was formed through work – he felt responsible for his models while they were on his shoot – well, either that or possibly he didn't like the idea of any model getting it on with anyone on-set other than himself? I wasn't sure which!

Nikki and I were in one of the bedrooms talking about all this, and I was wondering if Nikki was trying to flirt with me although, like Ernie, any 'work' with Nikki was just a job to me too, albeit a very enjoyable one, when I heard Lindsay arrive. The next moment I could hear Rex/Peter looking for Nikki (presumably to introduce her to Lindsay to see if he could do another 'trade'). Just like a scene from some old comedy farce, Nikki jumped into the wardrobe, telling me not to say where she was, in case Rex/Peter was annoyed with her for being in a bedroom alone with me! Rex/Peter stormed in and I dutifully sat on the bed and told him that I hadn't seen Nikki for ages. He left the room but then a couple of moments later he burst back in again and began opening all the cupboards and wardrobes.

Nikki fell out of the wardrobe she was hiding in and Rex/Peter marched her out, telling me off as he did so like some prudish old school ma'am. The door closed.

A moment later the door re-opened and Lindsay stood there. In the background I could hear Rex/Peter telling Nikki off for flirting with a fellow model while Lindsay grinned at me and wagged his finger in mock anger. The door closed again.

I sat on the bed bewildered until Rex/Peter came back in, explaining that what his models did after work was up to them but while they were working for him they must only get it together on camera and under his direction! I opened my mouth to try and explain that that wasn't what was happening, but he just carried on, reminding me that he was a very influential producer in the business, in a position to put a lot of work my way and, particularly if I was really going to leave my job selling clothes, it would be a good idea to stay on the right side of him. He made it sound as if he had the power to give me a livelihood in Porno-Land or to make sure that I would never work again.

In the adult business, people like Rex/Peter and Lindsay do seem to wield a lot of power but it's only really because of the contacts that they themselves have made over time. The business is relatively small and most models get their work by word of mouth. If a few influential directors or photographers put the word around that certain models are bad news, they won't get too much work for a while.

Conversely of course, those very same directors and photographers are just as reliant on the goodwill of the models to choose to work for them for, of course, without the best girls in front of their cameras, they too are out of a job!

Just like a big-time movie director in old Hollywood however, I imagined Rex/Peter wearing jodhpurs and strutting around with a riding crop shouting directions through a megaphone like Cecil B. DeMille.

I wanted to get paid that day and I wanted to work for Rex/Peter on other occasions, so I decided to keep my head down, my mouth shut and just get on with the job.

But unfortunately it didn't last long. Rex/Peter was sending Clive out to buy some batteries from a local shop and, as I wanted to get a snack, I left with him. On the way to the shop however we passed a pub. Despite all the clues in Clive's huge beer belly and red nose, I didn't really realise that this might prove to be too great a temptation for him.

'Come on' Clive urged, winking away at me, 'We've got time for a quick one. It won't take long'.

'Are you sure?' I asked dubiously. Rex/Peter had seemed very insistent that we hurry back but, as Rex's video technician, I assumed he knew

Rex/Peter much better than I did – at any rate he knew that his real name was Peter, which was more than I did! And so we went in.

We were about half way through the second round of drinks when Rex/Peter burst in.

'I thought I'd find you here!' he raged, literally dragging Clive out, his drink unfinished, as if he were a naughty schoolboy caught smoking behind the bike sheds.

'I've come to expect this of you, Clive,' he scolded, 'but I'd have thought you'd have known better, Ric.'

I retreated back to the house without getting my snack, while Rex/Peter stood on the corner, arms folded, watching Clive go to the shop to get the batteries, making sure he didn't sneak back to the pub to finish his pint.

While Rex/Peter was doing a single-girl photo session with a beautiful Caribbean girl called Denise in one of the bedrooms, there was a ring at the doorbell, and magazine boss David Sullivan himself walked in.

A short, stocky man, Sullivan exuded the flashy gold nouveau- rich look of the Essex-boy car dealer; the wide boy who has bought himself a place in polite society with a few dodgy deals.

A self-made multi-millionaire, Sullivan is one of the richest men in Britain. Publisher of *The Sport* newspaper, he has however served time in prison for his earlier dealings in porn.

Whatever one's opinion of him, one can't help but respect him as a very astute businessman, having built up his empire completely on his own, and from nothing.

After getting a degree in business studies, he decided to sell mail order photo-sets. 'Twenty lovelies for a pound' were advertised in bargain hunter publications like *The Exchange & Mart*. Business was slow and so Sullivan upped his offer to 'Two hundred lovelies for a pound.' The orders then came flooding in, although the unsuspecting customer little knew that their 'two hundred lovelies' would merely consist of ten copies of the original twenty lovelies! Well, he didn't say that they'd be two hundred different ones!

Printing and publishing his own adult magazines and utilising the advertising space to promote only his own products meant that Sullivan was from the start never giving anything away to his competitors – not even advertising space!

Realising that he might have difficulty selling his mags through the usual channels, he opened up his own chain of shops to sell them in; the 'Private' Shops. He therefore had control at every stage. His own shops sold his own mags, which only advertised his own products.

So that his publications would be easily accessible to the ordinary man in the street, he opened his shops not in London's Soho where all the other major sex stores were, but in provincial town centres around the country. In almost every town nation-wide there was a Private Shop enabling anyone to buy sex aids and magazines while they were doing the weekly shop at the local supermarket. If the ordinary man in the street couldn't get to Soho, then Soho would come to him! Sullivan had so to speak effectively bought the X-Rated mountain to Mohammed.

His first sex mag was called *Private*, blatantly ripping off the name and logo of the successful hard-core Swedish publication of the same name. Berth Milton's Private Organisation were unable to sue under British law as, being a hard-core title, they couldn't legitimately sell their own title in England anyway at that time.

Other controversially titled magazines followed: *Whitehouse,* named after the morals campaigner Mary Whitehouse (every month Sullivan displayed a naked model who he claimed was also called Mary Whitehouse), and *Ladybirds.* The children's book publisher Ladybird sued and Sullivan was forced to change the name to *Playbirds*, possibly as a reflection that the magazine was a down-market *Playboy*.

Of course there was also a successful mail order side to his business, and naturally videos and even feature films followed. Costing just £83,000 to make but generating over £3 million in revenue, Sullivan's first proper feature film was *Come Play With Me* starring, along with an impressive array of British comedy talent, Sullivan's own, and Britain's first, real porn star, Mary Millington.

In the days before Page Three girls and ladettes like Jordan or Jodie Marsh became household names, England had never had any real sex stars in the way that America did.

In the States, the old 'Hollywood star system' survived in the multi million-dollar porn movie industry based in Burbank, just north of Hollywood. As in the days when stars like Monroe and Clark Gable could name their own fee, living the life that only rock stars live today and creating box office revenue simply by having their names on the cast list of a particular movie, names like John Holmes (a casualty of AIDS in the late 1980s), Traci Lords and Candy Samples were as big a star name to their fans as ever Astaire, Monroe, or Jane Russell were to theirs.

Sullivan launched 30-year-old divorcee Mary Maxted in the mid 1970s as Britain's first sex star, giving her plastic surgery and changing her name to Mary Millington, a character he'd invented to be the figurehead editor of one of his magazines.

She was to receive a lot of exposure, doing many personal appearances, and a number of feature films, even including a cameo role in Julien Temple's punk rock tribute to the Sex Pistols, *The Great Rock'n'Roll Swindle*.

However, Mary was emotionally disturbed, took a lot of drugs, shoplifted, and worked as a prostitute.

Mary committed suicide in 1980, clearly finding her lifestyle, being constantly hounded by the public and the police alike, just too much to bear.

Aged just 33, Sullivan's own version of Marilyn Monroe had followed her 'double M' namesake to an early grave.

Sullivan's business continued to thrive however as he blatantly ripped off the titles of the most popular hard-core European sex magazines including *Color Climax* and *Swedish Erotica*.

Duplicating genuine covers from these magazines onto poor quality paper, he would then put the worst of his own soft-core material inside, shrink-wrap the magazines so that no one could see the contents until after purchasing, and then sell them expensively in his shops as the original article.

Did anyone complain? Well, if they did they were then in the position of admitting that they were trying to purchase illegal hard-core material. It was a customer 'Catch-22' situation that Sullivan fully exploited to his advantage. Allegedly, he would advertise an expensive 'Women and Animals' magazine in his publications, and then despatch to buyers a copy of *Horse and Hound*, the up-market (and perfectly legal) society magazine for the country living hunting set.

If anyone complained, he ignored their complaints. If they continued to complain, he would send out an official looking letter explaining that he was unable to sell anything pornographic on the subject of women and animals as the law currently prohibited it and that, if the customer continued to write to him requesting such illegal material, he would have no alternative but to pass their details on to the police. This was usually the last he'd hear from them.

Sullivan devoted a huge budget every month to advertising his perfectly legal titles in as many of his competitor's magazines as he could.

Needless to say, *Color Climax*, and all the other magazines he was ripping off were, like his dissatisfied customers, none too happy about his exploits.

They decided to answer his advertising by doing some of their own. However, they were not allowed legally to advertise their hard-core product anywhere here in England. The British soft-core magazines couldn't touch their advertising knowing that their product was the real thing, yet they would happily accept Sullivan's advertising knowing full well that his was not the genuine article! The magazines couldn't afford to turn away Sullivan's enormous advertising account.

'Catch-22' indeed!

Sullivan was banned from advertising his newspaper *The Sport* on television due to its explicit content, but he could always find a way round things. Being a racehorse enthusiast, he bought three racehorses and called them The Sport, The Daily Sport, and The Sunday Sport, ensuring that the names of his publications were mentioned by the commentators on every televised race that they entered!

David Sullivan tottered into the sitting room on his specially stacked platform heels, to see how his photo shoot was going. Rex/Peter introduced him briefly to everyone and together they disappeared into one of the master bedrooms for a private discussion. A few moments later Rex/Peter appeared on his own and informed Denise that David would like to see her – alone.

He was paying her wages and she wanted to work for him again. Sullivan is known for his 'blow-job or no job' policy and, not really being in any position to refuse, she averted her eyes from the rest of us and walked into the bedroom, closing the door behind her.

At the end of the day, Nikki slinked towards me.

'So do you have a girlfriend?' she asked breathily

'No' I replied

'I don't know why' she answered, 'I'd give you my phone number anytime.'

'Great' I said, holding out my hand. She took my hand, shook it, and left, without of course actually giving me her phone number!

Everyone went off home no doubt to their respective partners. I once again went home alone. I was quickly learning that Porno-Land could often be a very lonely place, and one where the only true winners are those that look good and are comfortable in their role. Anyone slightly out of sync, for whatever reason, like me or Ernie, would go home alone feeling awkward and wrong. Porno-Land was seemingly a place for only perfect looking people who could perform all day and go to sleep at night dreaming of more perfect sex to come.

Chapter Five:
IN THE DRIVING SEAT AT LAST

The phone hardly rang with any further offers of work. So I was re-thinking my porno career. It had often occurred to me during all the shoots I'd so far experienced that the people who worked regularly in the business (i.e: every day), the people who were really making the big money on a regular basis, and those who in the long run had the most fun and socialised more regularly with the porn stars themselves, were in fact (surprise surprise) those on the other side of the camera; the director, producer, cameraman, agent, video technician, lighting guy, and even the video editor! In short, the people who were really making the movies, and not the kids who were simply making it in the movies for a paltry daily rate – I guess much like the 'real' film industry.

It is a common occurrence in the American porn industry (again, much like its Hollywood counterpart) for its actors and actresses to progress onto roles behind the camera screenwriting, producing, or directing, after a successful on- screen career. Ron Jeremy, Randy West, Candida Royalle, John Leslie, and John Stagliano are just a few examples of this.

Normally of course they do so after having spent years already building up a reputation in front of the camera. I now wanted to become a Rex/Peter or a Lindsay myself. So what if I'd only been at it for a few months? I was working in England, in a sexually repressed climate; I didn't have the career opportunities that my American counterparts had!

I decided that it would be a smart career move, if my days hamming it up in front of the camera were indeed over, to learn the ropes on the technical side; become a cameraman, editor, maybe even direct!

As luck would have it, I saw an ad in my local paper – a small- time video production company were looking for a trainee.

They were mainly making corporate training films and shooting weddings, but it was an opportunity to learn those all important skills of camera work and editing that I could then utilise by transferring them to my more interesting choice of profession!

They happily took me on as a trainee and, while I was in training with them, I continued to write to any companies I saw advertising in the sex magazines, and hassled any contacts I had already made in the industry.

I wrote to the Color Climax Corporation in Denmark, and one morning received a phone call from Rupert James, who was then their English language editor.

Initially he seemed quite interested in me but I blew it by proudly stating that I'd worked for David Sullivan.

I'd forgotten that Sullivan was a taboo name in their organisation, after his callous exploitation of their titles and logo to his own highly profitable ends.

But even though work with them never materialised I soon felt, through my experience with the local video company, that I had a sufficient grasp of camera technique to embark on my own porno epic!

My idea was to keep everything very simple. I would film it directly onto ordinary domestic VHS videotape, with no titles or credits, and sell it by mail order as a kind of 'home-shot' amateur style video. I knew that there was a big market for 'readers' wives' type material, and this way my budget was kept right down to the bare minimum, which suited me fine because, as a trainee at the video company, I wasn't earning a fortune.

Having been learning about script writing and story-boarding at work, I thought that I'd better write a 'script', not knowing that most 'home-shot' style gonzo porn is planned on the day (indeed the very minute) of the shoot itself.

So I wrote a proper script based around a guy and his young eighteen-year-old girlfriend who decide to do a home movie in order to make a bit of extra money.

The script, such as it was, went like this:

SCENE ONE: INTRO.

Fade up to reveal pretty girl, drink in hand. She introduces herself, and explains that because she and her boyfriend are short of money, they have decided to make this home-produced videofilm. She hopes we enjoy it.

SCENE TWO: LOUNGE.

Cut to close-up shot of boyfriend. He coolly orders the girl to strip. Camera pans across to girl standing in the centre of the room.

Music Overdub. Girl performs strip tease to the camera.

Finish on close-up of a red rose. Music ends, and while still focused on the image of the rose, we hear the sound of running water.

SCENE THREE: SHOWER.

Cut to close-up of girl's hand (red painted nails) leaving the tap, after having just turned on a shower.

Camera pulls back to reveal the shower cubicle, and pans round to reveal the girl in a bathrobe looking into the mirror, and fixing her hair up.

Close-up of her hands untying robe belt. Robe falls open (still in big close-up), revealing belly button.

Girl slips robe off her shoulders. From behind we see her naked shoulders and back.

Long shot of bathroom, taking in shower (with water still gushing out; this is the only sound), and girl standing legs apart, the robe fallen at her feet. She is looking into the mirror, still fixing hair. She wears a pair of tiny white briefs.

Close up of her legs and feet. The pants fall around her ankles. She steps out of them. Following her feet, we see her step into the shower.

This scene is inter-cut with shots of another young girl walking down the road. Cut to close-up of her hand ringing the doorbell.

SCENE FOUR: HALLWAY.

Cut to interior shot of hallway (facing front door), and boyfriend walking past camera, and answering front door.

He casually greets the new girl (she is obviously a close friend of his girl-friend), and informs her that his girlfriend is in the shower.

'She won't be long' he says 'Go on through if you like'

SCENE FIVE: SHOWER.

Cut back to interior bathroom (facing door). We see the

door open, and the new girl quietly slips in obviously un-noticed by the girl in the shower.

Shot of girl in shower, soaping herself, and then a third hand joins in. Girl turns, startled, and then smiles encouragingly.

New girl gets out of her jeans, and into the shower in just her pants and T-Shirt (which, when wet, cling to her figure).

In the shower, they soap and caress each other's bodies.

Fade to Black.

SCENE SIX: KITCHEN.

Fade up on original girl in kitchen, smiling to camera. Music Overdub. She is dressed only in a blue and white striped apron. She does various domestic kitchen activities, showing off her body (bending over to cooker, etc), and lots of suggestive movements are made with phallic kitchen objects (cucumber, banana, pan handles, etc).

Finally, looking in the fridge, she finds a carton of whipped cream (the type that squirts out of a can ready whipped and fluffy).

The music fades, as a wicked look spreads over her face.

SCENE SEVEN: BEDROOM.

Cut to the boyfriend fully clothed and lying on top of the covers in the bedroom. He wears a pair of jeans, or trousers, and a shirt which is not buttoned, thereby revealing his chest, and stomach. He is having an afternoon nap.

The girl quietly enters with the can of cream and, kneeling on the bed, slowly squirts a little cream onto his bare chest. He jumps awake startled, and then smiles, realising what's going on. She smiles up at him, licking the cream from his chest.

She does the same to his stomach. Close up shot of her sliding his fly down, and easing his jeans down his legs. She pulls the waistband of his pants away from his body, and squirts some cream inside. We then see her head hunched over his lap, but nothing is visible, or explicit.

The guy (now naked) then rubs cream onto the girl's body, etc.

They then make love. This will be very artistically shot, with limbs arranged to produce erotic and interesting shapes. During this scene, both bodies will be covered in baby-oil, and sprinkled with a little water to give that look of hot sweat.

At the end of this scene, as the guy is supposedly reaching his climax, we cut to a shot of the canned cream squirting out onto the girl's body and face.

Fade to Black.

SCENE EIGHT: LOUNGE.

Slow, moody music begins.

Fade up to reveal either the girlfriend or her friend dressed as a schoolgirl, beating time on her open palm with a short bamboo cane.

She moves around sensually in front of the camera for a while (behind her is a plain coloured wall, or drape).

Cut to shot over her shoulder of the rest of the room; it looks like a living room, and relaxing on easy chairs, with cans of lager, glasses of whisky, etc, are her boyfriend and several other men. It is apparent that this girl is performing a private strip tease for her boyfriend and a few of his mates, along with her f riend the other girl, who also sits in the 'audience', enjoying the show.

During the course of removing her school uniform, she moves

amongst the guys and, taking one of their beer glasses, pours the contents over her breasts etc.

This scene is inter-cut with close-up shots of her lips, pouting kisses, her eye winking to the camera, etc.

Eventually, she ends up on the lap of the other girl.

Music ends.

Voice-over of girl (as at the beginning) saying that she hopes we enjoyed the film.

Fade to Black.

I thought I had it all planned out really well. I even got a friend who was a professional musician to write some original music for the shower scene. He was also keen to get involved in the shoot itself as he was a bit of an amateur camera buff.

My boss at the video company where I now worked was going on holiday, and I knew this to be the ideal opportunity to make full use of all the professional production equipment for my own shoot while he was away.

All I lacked now were the models! Where would I find two young girls willing to act out my little scenarios for a maximum of £50 each, which was all my very limited budget could afford?

When I had been working at the clothes shop I'd met Jim, the manager of one of the other branches; a tough little Scot in his early thirties. He had a passion for sex like almost no one I've known since.

I gave Jim a ring, and asked if he knew of any likely girls. He told me 'No sweat!' He didn't know of any right at that moment but he'd find me a couple – just as long as he could star in the film as well. I said it seemed reasonable compensation for his trouble – and that meant I had my male star! I then sat back, and waited for his call.

It didn't take him long at all, and he was as good as his word. Not only had he found me two young blondes (both eighteen; one a night-club dancer and the other an office secretary) who shared a flat together, but he'd also sorted out a location for me: a friend of his had an ideal bedroom with mirrored walls, a king size bed that swung on chains from the ceiling and an en-suite shower. And we could use Jim's house for the two strip routines, and the kitchen scene.

'How did you get hold of these girls?' I asked him, amazed.

'Simple.' he replied, 'They came into the shop, and I just asked them!'

A simple enough strategy, but one that I must admit had never worked quite as effectively for me! Jim was definitely worth knowing. And all he wanted in return was to be the stud in my film.

I went out and bought a fresh red rose, the biggest banana I could find, a can of whipped cream, and a couple of bottles of wine... oh yes, and a blank VHS video tape!

The chef's apron, old school tie, and bathrobe I supplied from home. Any producer would have been proud of me – the budget spent for my epic was so far astronomically small!

On the day of production I got £100 out of the bank and went to pick the girls up from the office in London where one of them worked.

I planned to film through the evening and maybe into the night; it would take as long as it took!

One long night's filming and I'd have a forty-minute video that I could sell! Not a bad shoot-to-edit ratio I figured, certainly not by Hollywood standards anyway, where it could take three to six months to produce a seventy minute feature film. But then again, this production was far from being anywhere near Hollywood standards!

In the afternoon I went to the video office where I worked. It was all locked up and with my boss away. I let myself in and started loading up the company van – lights, power leads, tripod, camera, monitor, recorder, microphones, spare bulbs and fuses – the new Spielberg of the porno world was ready!

I climbed into the driver's seat, and set off to pick up Martin (my musician friend and today's camera assistant), smiling at the irony of the company motto emblazoned across each side of the van: "*You Name It And We'll Film It*"!

Chapter Six:
BANANAS, CREAM AND APPLE PIE

Martin and I arrived at the office dead on time, and parked in full view of the entrance. There was a pretty blonde girl waiting outside yet she made no move toward us, so neither did we – it would obviously have been very embarrassing to have propositioned the wrong girl.

After about fifteen minutes however, I walked across and asked her if she was Jane. She said she was, but hadn't come over to us, as she wasn't sure if it was the right van. I had given her a clear description over the phone, and wondered how many other vans with a filming logo and company motto "*You Name It And We'll Film It*" would be parked up by her office at that time of night!

Jane went in to get her flat-mate Tracy, who turned out to be just that – a flat mate! Whereas Jane was very curvy, and well endowed, Tracy was the exact opposite; quiet, shy, and with a very boyish figure. Still, variety is the spice of life, and I certainly wasn't going to complain; I was, after all, getting my first two actresses at a rate that was next to nothing.

I loaded both girls into the back of the van, and locked them in. It was an old van and I didn't want the doors to fly open accidentally as I went round a bend, but more to the point I didn't want the girls to have a change of heart and try and get out en-route!

We set out on the road to Kent, where Jim lived, just as the sun was setting and, for a moment, stopped at traffic lights, I thought we would still be in London by midnight. The engine stalled, and resolutely refused to re-start. Cars behind began honking, as the lights changed from red to green, and back to red again.

I sent up a silent prayer to whoever the patron saint of porno might be. I would have hated for a policeman to come along at that moment as I didn't want to try and explain my position driving a van that wasn't mine, full of expensive video equipment that wasn't mine, with two girls locked in the back with a bag containing lingerie, wine, and a schoolgirl uniform on our way to Kent to do some filming; 'Oh, just a home movie, officer, you know!'

Fortunately I didn't have to worry. The van spluttered back into life, and we kangarooed off down the road on our way to that well-known Kent filming location that was known as 'Jim's house'!

Much of the wine had already been consumed in the back of the van by the time we arrived, but we all drank most of what was left and made small talk, as Martin and I set up.

After getting the camera ready, and approving Jane's outer and under wear, we shot the first scene.

I told Jane to think of a name that she felt comfortable with to use as her name in this video (she chose Natasha), and to explain to the camera how, as she and her boyfriend were going through some hard times financially, they had decided to do this 'home video'. I wanted her to use her own words rather than give her a word-for-word script to learn as I thought it would come over more naturally.

She did great. One take and it was 'in the can' as they say. The only reason we could have done with another take would have been to compensate for my inexperienced and wobbly camera work.

Next we shot Jim in close-up, ordering her to strip. And then, the strip itself. We put some music on the stereo (*Sexual Healing* by Marvin Gaye), and Jane started to dance provocatively around, discarding garments as she did so.

'I'm not going to stay here and watch her strip off.' announced Tracy, and went off to the kitchen. I could tell she was less comfortable than her uninhibited flat-mate, who giggled and retorted 'I'm only doing this 'cos I'm pissed, you know.'

She poured herself another glass of wine, and carried on.

I kept my eye glued to the black and white viewfinder of the camera, while Martin squatted on the floor beside me, his eyes firmly fixed on the small colour video monitor.

Finally, naked and clutching the rose that I had brought along as a prop, she covered her face, giggling 'I can't believe I've just done that.'

We all congratulated her, and she went off to the bedroom to get changed for the next scene which, for the sake of our convenience in filming, was actually to be the last scene of the film – the one where Jane (or 'Natasha' as she now was) strips from the school uniform in front of a huge crowd of her boyfriend's mates.

Unfortunately my budget hadn't allowed for any more actors to be the 'huge crowd', and it was now getting quite late to start ringing round Jim's mates, so the first compromise of the production was reached – Natasha would strip in the lounge in front of a huge crowd that consisted of... Jim and Tracy!

First of all we rehearsed the end of the scene where Jane falls into Tracy's lap and then once again we put some music on the stereo (*Sexual Healing* by Marvin Gaye once more). Dressed in an odd ragbag of a school uniform (my old school tie, Jim's old cardigan, Jane's blouse and skirt, and Tracy's black beret), Jane danced around, teasing Jim and Tracy, and finally stripping down to the bare essentials.

The music ran out before the strip ended but Martin kept time by beating on top of the monitor with his hands and continued to hum the melody until the strip was complete.

Jane ended up on Tracy's lap as scripted, but the moment I said 'Cut', she jumped up and ran behind the curtain to modestly hide her nudity, not realising of course that behind the closed curtain was a plain glass window, overlooking the front garden and therefore providing a great view of her rear for any of Jim's neighbours who happened to be passing!

Next we filmed Tracy's first on-screen appearance, where she knocks on the door and asks Jim if Natasha is in. Not particularly difficult one would have thought, but I was about to learn my first all important lesson about making porno – never include more scenes than necessary which require the girls to act in any way at all.

Once outside the front door Tracy couldn't hear me yell 'Action' and so didn't appear on cue. We subsequently told her to go outside, count to ten and then knock. Tracy promptly went outside, counted about three, and then opened the door herself.

A third take got it right however and Tracy's seemingly difficult screen debut was 'in the can'.

Martin and I rearranged the camera and lights in the kitchen, and Jane put on the blue and white striped apron for her 'cream scene'.

It was nearly midnight by now and, having drunk quite a lot of wine on an empty stomach, Jane was fast losing the few inhibitions that may have still remained.

She seemed naturally quite an extrovert girl, but with the can of whipped cream she became really quite rude, rubbing it all over her body, and virtually devouring the banana, sucking and tonguing it, sliding it up between her breasts and between her legs.

'I've never had so much fun in a kitchen before.' she giggled, moving the banana seductively around under the apron. 'Me neither!' Jim commented.

Unfortunately I couldn't use any of the ruder action, as I wanted to keep the film soft enough to sell as the equivalent of an 18-rating in England. I hadn't sought any actual legal advice and didn't know quite frankly what I could get away with in hoping to sell adult videos mail order, so I was veering on the side of caution and keeping the material fairly soft.

After a while of letting Jane just get on with it as it was all going so well, Jim reminded us that it was already gone midnight. He'd gone to a lot of trouble to set up the shoot at the other location and didn't really want to keep his friends waiting any longer than necessary.

The bedroom/shower that we were going to use were apparently above an American style bar owned by a friend of his who, needless to say, wanted his own payment in way of a copy of the finished film.

So we 'wrapped' the kitchen scene, Jane got cleaned up and we all packed up ready for the move to the second location.

The last few late night drinkers were just leaving as we arrived at the Bar/Restaurant and, after brief introductions, we were shown upstairs to the bedroom.

It was ideal. A huge bed swinging on four solid chains dominated most of the room, while floor to ceiling mirrors occupied most of the walls. I didn't realise at the time the problems that can be caused by reflections when filming against mirrors, and consequently I appear, camera in hand, in the background of most of my footage.

Martin and I set up the lights and camera while Jane got back into her apron as, in the edited film, this scene was to follow straight on from the kitchen scene previously shot.

Tracy crouched in one corner of the room. It had been a long night for her so far; she had been here for nearly five hours, and done nothing yet but be part of the 'audience' for Jane's schoolgirl strip. Oh yes, and walk through a door (badly). Tracy was becoming more and more introverted and bored and I couldn't help but recall my own experience waiting around all night to film my scene with Joe in Long Lane, except that now I was looking at it from the other side of the camera.

But I couldn't worry about Tracy now, as we only had a few hours to go before we should be heading back to London, and I still had a lot of filming to do.

The owner of the Bar/Bedroom hung around for a moment or two but, when he saw all our professional equipment as Martin and I busied around getting everything set up, I think he felt a bit in the way; he made a comment of how it looked like a T.V. studio, and went back down to his Bar. I suspect he probably expected something altogether more tacky; the equivalent of some seedy guy in a raincoat turning up with a cheap home movie camera with no film in it! But oh no – we were professionals! We were the future of the British porn industry! We meant business, and we were making a serious sex movie – albeit straight onto domestic VHS!

Jim lay on the bed as if asleep, and Jane crept in and surprised him with the cream.

Jane unzipped Jim and squirted cream onto him, uttering the line that was to become my working title for the film: 'Mmm...Apple pie!'

I moved around them with the camera hand-held, Martin following me about with the recorder unit, as this was in the days before all-in-one camcorders, and an umbilical cord linked my camera to the

VHS recorder. Tracy meanwhile sullenly sat in the corner and watched the monitor.

After a while the bar owner and some of his friends tried to come in and watch the action but Jane took me aside and whispered that, while she didn't mind Martin and I being there, she did object to a group of voyeurs getting a free show.

I had a discrete word with the guys and they agreed to leave until we'd finished. I guess they could have insisted on staying; after all, it was their apartment and I wasn't paying them anything for the use of it, but I'm glad that they were more sensitive to the situation.

I made a few attempts to keep the look of the scene sensual rather than blatantly crude, as I had planned in the script. I rubbed baby oil onto the bodies of Jim and Jane, and arranged their limbs in artistically pleasing shapes, much to the scorn of Martin however; we all knew why we were there – to make a dirty movie and, despite my attempts to insist I was doing something arty, deep inside I guess I knew it too.

It was now gone one o'clock in the morning and Jim was tired. Eventually I had enough footage, and we finished the scene according to the script. I laid down on the bed and shot Jim's face from Jane's point of view as he pretended to cum, and then I shot over Jim's shoulder, from his point of view, while he squirted the cream out of the can and all over Jane's face and breasts.

It looked great, and funny as well as obviously the viewer wasn't expecting to see Jane get covered in UHT cream! Jane licked her lips, and gave a sexy wink to the camera as I manually faded to black and we all got ready for the very last scene of the night; the two-girl shower scene.

While Martin started getting the equipment set up, I filmed some 'cutaways' in close-up of Jane licking her lips, winking, etc, to possibly cut in to the various scenes already shot if needed. It's always advisable to shoot loads of 'safety cutaways' in case, when editing later, you suddenly find that something doesn't cut together smoothly, most likely because of continuity problems, and an extra shot of something is needed to 'cut away' to, and thereby make the edit look seamless.

I put a soft-focus star filter over the camera lens to make the shower cubicle look misty, and in order to transform any droplets of water into tiny stars of light. I was still striving to turn this piece of ultra cheap porn into an artistic masterpiece!

I turned the shower on and set the temperature, checking with Jane that it was OK for her – I still remembered my scalding experience in the bathtub while working for Rex/Peter.

As per the script, Jane parted the bathrobe revealing her belly in close-up, and the robe then fell around her ankles. Her white pants followed, and she walked to the cubicle and climbed in, twisting her body under the spray.

Finally, at three in the morning, it was Tracy's big moment. She was still very unsure, but Martin and I tried to make her feel pampered and special, and hoped that the experience didn't feel too sleazy for her.

Dressed in a white T-Shirt and tight blue jeans (ironically, the own-label brand from my old clothes store), she first peered around the door in true voyeuristic style as she watched Jane showering.

I then set up a big close-up shot of the zipper on Tracy's jeans. Her red painted nails reached down for the zipper and, watching the monitor, Martin suddenly shouted out as the zipper, thanks to my filter reflecting the light, turned into a little silver star at the top of her fly. It looked absolutely gorgeous, set off by the deep blue of the denim, and the red of Tracy's nails.

'Beautiful! Slowly, slowly.' I enthused like some slightly crazed director, as she started to unzip, 'Try and keep that lovely star!'

Tracy of course, not seeing what the camera saw, hadn't a clue what star I was talking about and must have thought I really had gone mad.

I wondered if, at the end of the day, anyone who bought this tape would notice my pretty star either, or appreciate all the hard work I'd gone to, to try and maintain some artistic integrity. Indeed, would anyone even care?

Tracy stepped into the shower in T-Shirt and pants and the two girls immediately began giggling, and fooling around.

Martin and I told them to take it more seriously and try and be sensual with each other, but it obviously wasn't easy for them; they were flat-mates and office girls, not hardened lesbian porn actresses!

Tracy's T-Shirt clung to her tiny figure, and it looked very good. Unfortunately, their 'acting' was not so hot. They were joking and noisily camping it up in a far from erotic way.

From behind me Jim motioned for Tracy to remove her pants. She didn't expect this so soon and was visibly embarrassed as she gingerly took them down.

She was now very still and quiet, her face a burning crimson. All the joking had now stopped. Jane pulled Tracy's wet T- shirt over her head, while Tracy, now naked, stood quietly, her cheeks matching the colour of her nails.

Her small quiet body contrasted well however with Jane's lively buxom one. Jane moved around the whole time, throwing her head back and moving her hands over Tracy's body. It looked great but I still couldn't get an awful lot of useable footage from them; the chemistry just wasn't there.

And so, after a short while I manually faded the camera to black and announced that the long night was over, and that we were 'wrapped'!

Tracy quickly stepped out of the shower, and covered herself with a huge towel. Jane stayed in there, however, to clean up; she still needed to wash all the cream, oil, and sweat from her body.

'Well done.' I told Tracy, kissing her on the cheek, 'You did great.'

'I didn't think I was going to have to strip off completely.' she grumbled, eyes downcast.

'I know,' I said, 'But be fair; you've hardly done anything tonight compared with Jane.'

Tracy nodded and went off to dry her hair.

Martin and I packed up all the equipment, thanked Jim for everything and, at four o'clock in the morning, nearly twelve hours after we'd kangarooed out of London, we all piled back into the van to head for home.

I gave the girls the one hundred quid, advising them to share it out between them as they thought fit. Martin opted for travelling in the back, and Tracy sat up front with me.

'I don't want to do anything,' Jane warned Martin as he climbed in, 'I'm really tired, and just want to sleep, O.K?'

Tracy slept too for most of the journey until, arriving back in London, I dropped them both off at their home.

Tracy said she was going to take the day off work, and sleep. Jane said she was going to go straight into work, after some breakfast.

They both asked me who was going to see this film, and I reassured them that it was only going to be sold mail-order, and that it would have a very limited release, so it was very unlikely that any of their friends or relations would see it.

I returned all the equipment and the van back to the office, and went home with my first 'master' tape of 'rushes'.

It had been a very exciting experience. I began to understand the power games that Rex/Peter had occasionally liked to play. I'd got quite a kick out of being the one calling the shots and directing the action. I'd now got a film that could, in theory, sell for years to come as this kind of material rarely dates; films are still on sale today that were shot ten or twenty years ago!

And all this for my small outlay of £100. Not bad, I mused. The Actor had turned Producer/Director. Now he had to turn Editor, and then Salesman and Marketing Manager if his small investment was to show any kind of healthy profit!

Chapter Seven:
HIGH HOPES AND CRAZY DREAMS

Perhaps not surprisingly, I never heard from either Tracy or Jane again.

Still never mind; Jim had plenty of other girls and often rang with the offer of a new prospective starlet that he'd chatted up in his shop.

However, until '*Apple Pie*' was bringing in some return, I didn't have any more money to spare.

So I set about editing my masterpiece, and very crudely too by today's standards. I borrowed a friend's home VCR machine and, linking it and my VHS recorder together with an ordinary RF aerial lead, I simply 'crash-edited' the film by copying the original footage, assembled in the right order, onto the 'edit master' tape – which was just another ordinary VHS!

Pretty hit and miss, but it seemed to work well enough, and I felt pleased to find that I hadn't forgotten anything crucial in the filming – all the scenes seemed to cut together perfectly.

Thinking (incorrectly of course) that, as I was to be selling the film mail order and not in shops, it wouldn't matter if I used copyrighted music, I put together an impressive soundtrack consisting of George Benson, Marvin Gaye, Bob Geldof, Barry White, and Lou Reed. Quite an enviable score in a feature film, let alone in my low budget effort!

However the only bit of original music (the guitar piece that Martin had written for the shower scene) caused a real problem! Editing with domestic VCR's, I only had one audio track to play with, and I needed the sound of the running shower water, as well as the guitar solo to be heard.

In professional edit-suites there are multiple audio tracks to use, mixing them all together in the edit suite, but of course I didn't have such luxuries, so I sorted it out by having Martin play his guitar sitting on the toilet seat in his bathroom with the shower turned on behind him, while I simultaneously recorded both sounds live, directly onto the tape!

Finally, *'Apple Pie'* was ready for the public – but the public didn't of course yet know of its existence! How to make people aware of this exciting new product? I would obviously need to advertise. And for that, I would need an address for customers to write to – and a business name of course.

I didn't want to use my real name, as I still wasn't sure if I was acting totally within the law, even though I couldn't really see any difference between selling *Apple Pie* or a home movie of my cat to the general public – neither would be illegal hard- core footage and, if someone wanted to buy it, then surely such a transaction between two adults wouldn't be a crime?

However this was still in the 'grey area' days before the law demanded that all U.K. video releases of any kind required the approval of the British Board of Film Classification (the BBFC) – and at the very hefty price to the BBFC of over £10 a minute! To get a forty-minute film legally certificated would have cost me well over £400!

Going for the cheaper option, I decided to just try and sell home produced copies via a small ad, and so I signed a contract with an accommodation address service, and then went to open a bank account under an assumed name.

I was very surprised to see just how easy this was to do, and it is perhaps to the shame of one of the major High Street Banks that they let me just walk into one of their branches with no proof of identity whatsoever and open a current account (complete with auto cash card, and cheque book) under the highly suspect name of Mr. Dick Harrd, and with an address that looked very suspiciously like an accommodation address, which of course it was.

My accommodation address reference number was 1242, so I put my address down as apartment number 1242 which, in a Country where apartments rarely go above the hundreds, let alone into the thousands, should surely have raised some degree of suspicion.

But no! And then there was my name! I was going to say I had a foreign father or something if my surname was queried, but the girl behind the counter didn't bat an eyelid.

'And what do you do for a living, Mr. Harrd?' she asked, filling out the form.

'I'm a video cameraman' I answered, truthfully.

'Oh yes?' she responded, looking up momentarily with a smile, 'What sort of films do you make?'

'Oh, business films, weddings, you know; that sort of thing' I answered, again truthfully.

'Not naughty ones then?' she laughed. 'I wish!' I laughed with her. And it was as easy as that!

I placed some small ads in the top shelf men's magazines and in David Sullivan's *Daily Sport* newspaper, and pretty soon the orders began to trickle in.

Every time I had a batch of orders, I'd borrow my friend's VCR again, and run off the copies for my growing list of clients, sending them out in the plain slipcases that the VHS tapes had come in. No fancy packaging, no box cover picture; just the unmarked tape.

Being unsure as to the legal position, I kept a list of all my customers under the heading 'Members List'. I didn't know if there was some loophole in the law that might make it more acceptable to sell this kind of thing to listed members of a club rather than to unknown individuals. At any rate I thought I'd take no chances, and list all the names and addresses as 'members' just in case. This list also gave me an ever-growing database of people interested in adult videos that I could then mail-out to with details of my next epic when it was available.

I got some amazing letters, many addressed personally to 'Natasha' or 'Lisa' (as Tracy had decided to call herself), asking them to send their panties, or asking if they would do another video, performing more explicit (and sometimes pretty disgusting) sexual acts.

I also received some very touching letters from people who had been ripped off in the past (perhaps ex-customers of Mr. Sullivan?) thanking me for sending a genuinely 'as advertised' product. I got one letter from an old-age-pensioner who said that he had no living relatives and now wanted to spend the remainder of his life-savings on buying videos that he could enjoy in the privacy of his own home. He used to send me £100 every month and ask me to send him a copy of anything new, and he would always stay at least £100 in credit with me.

It was for people like him that I also started advertising other videos, pirate copies I'd make at home of more professionally produced sex films, as well as hardcore porn magazines which I'd import from Germany and make a very small profit on.

But I'd never rip my customers off. If a product got stopped at customs I'd return their money with a letter of apology, bearing any financial loss myself.

Several customers bought from me time and time again, buying every item I had to offer. It became quite a lucrative little business; a 'cottage industry' that I ran from my kitchen table – with the invaluable assistance of the elusive Mr. Harrd of course!

And so, with his assistance, I strove to take every opportunity to make my little empire grow.

I went to Birmingham to meet the managing director of an import/export company, hoping to get him to put up some money so that I could make a series of high quality erotic films, from which we'd split the profits. However, after several promising meetings, the project was reduced to a proposal that I make just one low budget video for him on the subject of gardening! Eventually however not even this one materialised.

I met with a local strip-a-gram company with the idea of introducing the 'video-gram': a pre-recorded ten minute tape consisting of various dancing strippers fast-cut to a lively music track and with a personalised message inserted at the beginning and end from a scantily clad model.

The strip-a-gram bosses were far from impressed with my demo tape however, which consisted of extracts from *Apple Pie*, and some clips I'd culled from TV shows and a few old videos. Needless to say I didn't get that commission either!

On another trip to Birmingham I met up with the bosses of Yago, then a major mail-order lingerie and sex-aids company who were keen to introduce their own range of videos in promotion of their new leatherwear catalogue, the 'Samantha Spade' range.

Once again, extracts of *Apple Pie* and other odd bits failed to impress and, although I got as far as submitting a very well crafted storyboard, I never heard from them again. Years later I found out that Lindsay had also been approached to quote for the job but that, in the end, it had gone to Rex/Peter as he was able to quote more competitively due to his permanent production set up and his many contacts within the industry.

I went to a mud wrestling show in a large function room above a London pub to meet the organisers, with a view to producing videos of the shows for mail order sale.

I'd never attended such an event before and expected naughty girlies inviting rude and dirty audience participation. I sat in the front row, only to be confronted in the first half of the show by a fat balding man wrestling an equally fat old woman, both (thankfully) covered up in black leotards.

As she was thrown down onto the mucky canvas, mud spattered out from the ring and drenched all of us sitting in the front row. This was not the kind of audience participation I had expected and my interest in filming mud wrestling was quickly cooled off as I scuttled off to the Gents to get cleaned up, and return to watch from a safer viewing point.

I wrote to Halifax based video producer Fiona Cooper to see if I could become her London end cameraman. She wrote back asking for some examples of my work and I sent off *Apple Pie* as the only example of my work that I had, and heard nothing more.

I later learned that 'Fiona Cooper' was in fact a man, and the cousin of 'Yorkshire Ripper' Peter Sutcliffe! Porno-Land is a strange and surprising place – old men pose as young women to sell videos, and audiences pay good money to see fat old women wrestle fat old men in mud.

I started attending various leather/rubber fetish clubs, like Submission and Torture Garden, again with a view to finding some in-road to video work there.

At the clubs, dressed in PVC jeans, a black rubber vest and a Zorro style mask, I was confronted by a wonderfully bizarre assortment of outrageous people, all of dubious decadent sexual preferences.

Old transvestites dressed in PVC French maids outfits rubbed shoulders with amazonian high-heeled leather clad dominatrixes, and submissive Schwarzenegger look-a-likes wearing nothing but tiny posing pouches and spiky dog collars.

Gays, straights, lesbians and transvestites all joined in the evening's fun. It was like one big bizarre happy family and, ironically, there was a much 'safer' atmosphere here than at many mainstream night-clubs where everyone seems only to be there 'on the pull'. People at fetish clubs seemed to accept other people's right to dress and act how they wished, and girls could wander around completely naked if they wanted without getting constantly hassled by men trying to pick them up.

I felt as if I had wandered in from the real world and stumbled upon another parallel world; just as real, but far more dazzling – a compelling cross between a Fellini film and a Thierry Mugler fashion show; strange and enticing, with topless leather clad girls gyrating on the dance floor, while men and women, either semi-nude or dressed from top to toe in shiny rubber suits strode confidently around.

At the first club I attended I stood by the bar drinking in the atmosphere, wearing my rubber eye-mask, and with a leather bullwhip tucked into my studded belt. A topless girl in stockings and suspenders wandered over to me, and started chatting.

I wasn't sure how to react; should I reply 'in character' pretending to be a dominant 'master' (it seemed to me that the dressing up was in its way a form of role-play), or was this girl just chatting to me as if I was a normal bloke? After some brief small-talk she went off to 'find the boyfriend', so I guess that either I wasn't playing my role well enough for her, or she didn't fancy me and had just wandered off to find her boy-friend!

The people at these clubs are after all just real human beings like the rest of us, and relating to each other in a real human way – they were just dressed weirder that's all!

It seemed to me that these clubs are peopled by ordinary folk who 'come out at night', when they swap their daytime business suits for a figure hugging rubber one and, if only for that one night, they live out their fantasies, safe in an environment where everyone else is doing the same and so where no-one else is going to criticise or take the piss; they can wear what they want to wear and be visually who they want to be. But underneath the make-up and the stretched PVC, these are just ordinary people like the rest of us, with normal nine to five existences, fragile self-images, high hopes and crazy dreams.

At another club, I watched as one semi-clad man fondled a nearly nude girl over a pinball machine adorned with a portrait of Charles Addams' monstrous family The Addams Family. I soon became aware of a burly young guy dressed all in leather watching them from a nearby-darkened corner. He gradually edged closer and I assumed that he was getting off watching their public display.

Finally however he came right up, and I was expecting him to ask if he could join in, or maybe to try and arrange a threesome at a later date.

Instead, he exclaimed, small change at the ready, 'Could you hurry up, please, mate? I want a go on that machine; It's my favourite!'

Another time, a middle aged couple from Rome wrote to me, asking if I could make arrangements to have the wife filmed shagging a donkey when they next came to England!

'Or if you can get a big dog and train it, we'll willingly buy the dog from you.' they said. I wondered how on Earth I could 'train' a dog in readiness for their visit? How would I broach the subject to a top Alsatian breeder? Fortunately this proposition eventually came to nothing.

Once, I drove up to Gloucester with Martin (the guy who had done *Apple Pie* with me) to film a young eighteen-year-old girl who was living with a rugged Irishman in his mid fifties in an old run down farmhouse.

On the way there, Martin was in very good spirits, reading hard-core porn magazines and flashing them to passing motorists, but when we reached the farmhouse of schoolgirl depravity, he got 'cold feet' about the whole thing and wandered off to the nearest pub for the afternoon.

The girl looked about fourteen dressed in her schoolgirl uniform, lying on a single bed in a typical teenagers room, with pictures of show-jumpers and horses pinned to the wall. I thought, 'How sweet. Like lots of young girls she obviously likes horses.'

Despite her youth, this girl had been fully inducted by the Irishman into the ways of bizarre sex however. When she found out about my magazine import service, she asked me if I could get her an 'animal sex' magazine.

'Are you into that kind of thing then? I asked.

'Of course.' she replied, 'What do you think all the pictures of horses are doing on my wall?' – clearly I had misjudged what I had taken to be her innocent passion for horse riding!

I got a call from a company called St. James Films of Kent. I'd written after seeing their full page colour ad featuring their new production *The Perils of Mandy*, seemingly about a well developed schoolgirl who got herself into all sorts of (mostly sexual) scrapes. I'd written asking him if they would be interested either in doing anything with my *Apple Pie* material, or in doing anything with some of the new 'models' that Jim had been sourcing for me.

A very genial man named Ken phoned and asked me to meet him in a little sandwich bar in the heart of London's film industry, Wardour Street, in Soho.

I arrived very early with videotape containing various clips from *Apple Pie* and other odd bits I'd shot, along with some photos of prospective models.

I sat down, wondering how I would recognise Ken, never having met him before.

Eating a sandwich, I eyed up a guy sitting alone at another table, toying with a coffee and looking around as if he too were waiting to meet someone. Was this Ken?

I was just about to go over and press photographs of naked women into his hands, when a cheery voice called my name from the door and Ken bounded into the cafe and sat down beside me.

He couldn't stop for long, he explained, but would like to take the tape and photos away with him. He spoke enthusiastically of new productions of which I was to play a major part, and of an exciting business trip he was just about to make to Germany. He'd show my tape to the producers over there.

'We may well find ourselves shooting in Germany soon.' he smiled, 'Your passport's up-to-date I hope?'

I nodded eagerly. 'Dick Harrd International' seemed just around the corner.

So off Ken went with my tape and portfolio of girls, and leaving me with the bill for coffee. I went home feeling very excited about the future and, of course, never heard from him again!

Before I left London that day, however, I called into one of David Sullivan's 'Private' sex shops to have a look around.

One of the videos they were selling, called *Gay Leather Joy Boys*, had a full colour cover photograph of me grinning coyly out at the camera, in the process of removing my shirt!

On every professional modelling shoot, one must sign a model-release form, signing all rights over to the photographer, and once that is signed, one's image can be used in any way the photographer or the publisher chooses, coupled with any text, and to depict any sexual preference... and for decades to come! So from that day forward, the world was to think I was a 'gay leather joy boy'!

Then I looked along the rack and saw, on the cover of a shrink-wrapped magazine called *Screw* (a title that Sullivan had blatantly ripped off from Al Goldstein's best selling American publication) a picture of me and Nicola from the shoot in the bath.

The magazine was in a sealed pack along with two others, the cover photo being the only one you could see (obviously the best picture; the other two mags were probably the usual ultra soft rip-off material from the early 60s).

I took the pack over to the bored looking guy at the cash desk.

'£10 for the pack, mate.' he said, looking up briefly from the paper he was reading.

'What if I only want to buy one of these mags?' I asked, 'Do you sell them separately?'

'No.' he answered simply, '£10 for the pack, mate.' and he went back to his paper.

I thought for a moment.

'Look, I'll be straight with you.' I ventured. He cast sullen eyes up to me again.

'You see, this picture? It's of me. I'm the guy in this magazine! I only want it as a souvenir, as I'm in it, see?'

I grinned at him and winked in what I took to be a 'men-of- the-world' sort of a way.

'So can't you separate them? That's me, you see?'

The salesman's face broke into a grin. 'So that's you?' he said. I nodded. 'That's great!'

I smiled.

'I thought I recognised you – you're on *Gay Leather Joy Boys* too, aren't you?'

My smile froze. I nodded, hoping that it might improve my chances of getting the deal I wanted.

'It's still £10 for the pack, mate' he said, his face returning to its former stoniness.

He went back to his paper, and I paid £10 for the pack.

Attending the local pubs that had lunchtime strippers, I'd try to act like a big-time film producer, sitting in the front row with a cheap cigar, even though I didn't smoke, and watching the girl's strip with what I hoped would be taken for a professional eye. The other men all leered, and nudged each other over their beer.

Occasionally, if I were very impressed by one of the girls, I'd seek her out afterward. She was usually hanging around having a drink with her boyfriend, minder or driver.

Once I approached one of these minders; a big solid man with a boxer's face and closely cropped hair.

I gave him a friendly smile, sitting down opposite him with my pint.

'She's good; the girl you're with; very good.' I assured him in what I hoped seemed an authoritative and influential manner.

Perhaps he was deaf. He acted as if the chair opposite him had remained unoccupied. I leaned across the table in a more conspiratorial manner.

'I'm in the business actually.' I confided, slipping one of the business cards I'd had printed in a cheap machine at a supermarket across the table to him.

'The video business, you know. Does the lady do any modelling at all... as well as her exotic dancing?'

For the first time there was a glimmer of understanding in the old man's eyes.

'No.' he answered flatly, his gaze clouding over again, excluding me from his world.

'Well,' I persevered, 'I'm planning a big movie soon in Germany, and...'

'Just fuck off, mate, OK?' he barked at me.

'Oh right.' I said, jumping up and spilling my pint, 'Well, you keep the card, eh? You never know; should she change her mind... or something.'

He sat there impassively, my card lying where I left it, in a puddle of spilt beer.

I nervously retreated back to the bar and, when the next stripper came on, I joined the leering, nudging lads clutching their pints and hiding at the back.

Chapter Eight:
HE WHO HOLDS THE CAMERA

Eventually I was ready to make another production of my own. I had now bought my own camera and could legitimately borrow lights any time I wanted from the video company I worked for.

John, a shy Jewish friend of mine, said that I could use his house as a location if I wanted. So I phoned Jim to see if he had any new girls that might be willing to do a shoot for me.

On top of working in the shop, Jim was now operating a visiting massage agency called 'Body Talk' on the side, and yes, he said there was another young girl that he'd chatted up for me.

Geraldine was eighteen, and looked like the then popular ice skater Jayne Torvill, and he'd been ribbing her that she wouldn't really do it for £50 when it came to the crunch. Well, the crunch had come.

He told me that he'd arrange for her to meet me at my local train station at 2pm on Saturday so I rushed over to John's on the Saturday morning with the camera equipment and props to get everything ready. My old school tie made another appearance (as I planned to make a 'schoolgirl' style video this time), along with a vibrator, and a pleated school skirt that I'd bought in Marks and Spencers 'for my niece', and this time I also had a stills photographer on stand-by to get some proper photographs to accompany the video.

I got everything ready and then sat down to wait for her arrival.

Two o'clock came and went, as did three o'clock. I didn't have a contact number for Geraldine and so, assuming that she had chickened out, I packed up all the equipment and returned home.

I was about to learn one of the all-important lessons of working with glamour models, bethey amateur or professional – they are always late! They work on 'model time', which can be about two hours behind the rest of the world!

Half an hour after unpacking all the equipment back at home, John phoned.

'She's just rang me.' he said, 'And she's at the station now!'

I repacked all the gear as quickly as I could, phoned the photographer and told him to meet me at John's again, and then drove off to the station.

Sure enough, Geraldine was there, and she did look like a young Jayne Torvill. We drove to John's house and I had a look at the clothes she'd bought with her. I was hoping to get another couple of scenes shot as well, so I could build up a programme along the lines of Fiona Cooper, who specialised in single girl sequences of girls often dressed in schoolgirl uniform.

We got set up and I filmed one sequence in John's bedroom, with Geraldine stripping off from her mock schoolgirl uniform.

The photographer I'd called in snapped away, as did John, as getting his own pictures was his 'payment' for the use of his house as our location.

After this sequence, we set up in the lounge and John served us all tea and biscuits.

He smiled at Geraldine, handing her a cup of tea and obviously not quite knowing what sort of small talk to make.

After all, he'd just seen this girl, who he'd only just met an hour or so earlier, naked with a vibrator in front of him!

'Well!' he said at last, after smiling meekly at her for a while as she sipped her tea, 'Do you do this often, then?'

The photographer and I swapped glances. Such a remark is the last thing one says to a nude model, even an experienced one, much less one who is doing it for £50, and virtually on a dare!

Next we got Geraldine stripping off and posing on top of John's old upright piano, an heirloom from his grandmother who had been a member of the legendary World War Two all-female Ivy Benson Band.

'Mind the piano! Mind the piano! It marks easily!' John chanted, hopping about like a demented character from a Woody Allen film, as Geraldine climbed aboard in her white stilettos.

After this scene was shot, it was getting quite late in the day, and Geraldine had to catch the train back to Kent. I had two scenes, with photos, 'in the can', and I took Geraldine into John's kitchen to pay her.

'We said £50 right?' I checked.

'Well, whatever you think I was worth.' she answered, obviously trying for more. I explained that my budget could only afford £50 and so, although I thought she was worth much more, that was all I could pay her.

I gave her a thank-you peck on the cheek, and got ready to take her back to the station.

'I must admit it wasn't so bad after all,' she said on the way; 'I was ready to do much more for you than I did.'

I let the remark pass, but who knows? – for £50, could we have all gang-banged her if we wished? She had obviously been keen to fully fulfil Jim's original dare!

I drove her to the station, and saw her safely onto her train home to Kent.

So the 'Dick Harrd Video Company' now had a new title for its mail order catalogue: *Young Girl Piano Lust!*

I now had about 150 names on my mailing list, which I thought was pretty good going for my humble endeavours. Many of my customers bought everything I had to offer, so selling a new title was relatively easy, and I had renamed Geraldine 'Young Jane' after her look-alike similarity to Jayne Torvill.

I even became an employer, taking on John's girlfriend part- time to photocopy my list of titles, stuff them into envelopes and mail them out to new and existing customers. She used the public copier at the local library as I didn't have one of my own. She would sometimes have to wait in line to use it, while students and pensioners made use of the library copying facility before she could get to the machine and, with a quick look round to make sure that no-one could see what she was doing, pull out from a plastic carrier bag my home-made pages of badly typed copy, illustrated with photocopied pictures stuck on with glue. It was all a very amateurish set- up, but this was after all in the days before desktop publishing, and I certainly couldn't afford to get professionally produced leaflets designed and printed.

I found that my involvement in adult material proved quite useful when bartering with friends and acquaintances.

I was now living in a nice rented flat and, when my landlord found out how I was making a living, he suddenly became quite matey and was even uncharacteristically understanding about the back rent I owed him – as long as I provided him with a tape or two of hard-core video entertainment!

I gave him a couple of imported titles from Copenhagen or Germany, and he went away happy. Next week however he was back full of complaints; fuzzy picture quality, too many lesbian scenes, not enough big boobs, etc, etc. In one week he'd changed from someone with a 'wink wink, nudge nudge' interest in what I was doing into an experienced connoisseur of international pornography! As the old saying goes: 'everyone's a critic'! He began to turn up more and more regularly, always sniffing around, wanting to borrow tapes and virtually undressing all my female friends with his eyes, assuming that any girl I happened to know must automatically not only be in the sex business, but a nymphomaniac prostitute as well! I learned my lesson after this experience, and vowed to keep my new profession to a low profile, only ever admitting to filming weddings if anyone asked.

A company called Ultravision International wrote to me, asking if I'd be interested in selling my mailing list to them, as they were promoting Vision X, a new video they were releasing featuring the amazing (and completely faked) ultra large breasts of a Miss 'Tina Small'. According to their letter, the office manager was called Mr. E.N. Stitz. I immediately became suspicious, remembering a Spike Milligan T.V. character called 'E. Norma Stitz' (' enormous tits'), but phoned them anyway. I told 'Mr. Stitz' that I had a large mailing list, and he said they were willing to pay me £1 per name.

'How large is the list?' he enquired, 'We're only interested in purchasing fairly substantial ones.' 'Oh yes' I said proudly, 'There's 150 names on mine.' There was a silence on the line.

'Well, we're really looking to buy lists of at least one thousand addresses.' he informed me, '150 is hardly worthwhile to us. Or to you financially, is it?'

To me at that time, the thought of getting paid £150 for just passing on some names was very worthwhile but I didn't want to make myself look any more small-time than I obviously already had, so I answered 'No, I guess not', and hung up.

I continued to write to all the companies advertising in the adult magazines, and one day I got a phone call from a man called Tom who ran a specialist adult video company based in the East End of London, called Bizarre Films.

He told me he was planning a sado/masochist video shoot and I of course showed interest in being involved. I tried to persuade him to use me as director/producer, liberally name-dropping Rex/Peter, and Lindsay, as if I still worked every day of the week with them. In truth I hadn't even been in touch with Rex/Peter for at least a year.

A few days later, Tom rang to tell me that he had found another production company to do the job but that, as it was to be a two camera shoot, he was interested in using me as second cameraman. I arranged to meet him the following day to discuss details.

That night I went out to celebrate the possible job, and when I returned home there was a missed call from Rex/Peter on my home phone.

Strange, I mused, to hear from him after all this time, but went to bed thinking no more about it.

Next day I met Tom in his office and he briefly told me about the film, what equipment I'd be using and, after a cup of coffee, he ushered me out of the office, and into his car.

'We'll go to the studio where we'll be shooting.' he said with a twinkle in his eye, 'And you can meet the rest of the crew.'

He was very hesitant about telling me any more, and I was soon to find out why. We arrived at an anonymous run-down studio in North-East London, and Tom took me through a maze of empty abandoned corridors to a little office.

As he opened the door I heard a familiar softly spoken voice call out: 'Come in, Tom... and Ric.'

I entered, and came face to face once again with Rex/Peter.

He sat behind a bulky video-editing desk and grinned at me. I'd been stringing Tom along that I'd done lots of work for Rex/Peter as a professional cameraman rather than simply as a model.

To his credit however, Rex/Peter was very discrete. He didn't say anything until after Tom had left us alone together to discuss the technical details for the shoot.

'Well, Ric, I hear you've become quite a wizard with a camera since I saw you last.' he said.

I grinned sheepishly. I couldn't fool him. I was to be second unit cameraman for him, but he knew exactly how long I'd had any experience of video work. I was still very green, and I had a lot to learn.

He was very good to me however, treating me like an apprentice and taking me under his wing, throwing me titbits of advice about lighting, camera angles and editing.

Rex/Peter had moved Clive, and his edit suite into the studio building for the duration of the shoot in order to continue his work editing other productions, while this shoot was underway.

The office was obviously usually empty and had purely been hired for the duration of the shoot. It was very bare; just a basic table and chairs, with the edit suite complex of videotape

machines and monitors sitting on packing crates. In those days, no editing was done on computer, and an edit suite consisted of a couple of TV sized monitors, two huge professional VCR machines, and a bulky video controller, all linked together by long thick cables.

While I was there, Rex/Peter contacted the telephone company to try and get a phone line put in to one of the offices. Clearly he only wanted a line in there for the few days he was shooting (this was in the days before mobile phones) and didn't really want to have to pay out on any kind of long- term contract, so was thinking of giving them a false name and leaving before any bill came in.

'It'll be a business line' he had told them, and they must have asked him, 'What name?'

Just as he had perhaps taken his own pseudonym (Rex) from the world of show business (Rex Harrison?), he now once again delved into the world of mainstream entertainment for the company pseudonym. Possibly he thought of early memories of cinema (James Fox) and radio comedy (Kenneth Horne), to get inspiration for his company name.

And so a meeting with a representative from the phone company was arranged, and Rex/Peter hastily scribbled 'FOX- HORNE FILMS' on a piece of note-paper, and told Clive to go and stick it on the front door by the bell.

'What with?' Clive asked. Rex/Peter turned his eyes heavenward.

'Use your brain, Clive.' he snapped, 'This has got to look professional – it's our company sign!' And with that, he handed Clive the scribbled note-paper and a roll of sticky tape!

When the phone company representative arrived, I could tell that she was understandably suspicious of renting out a new line to a company that seemingly had all it's assets (one edit suite) sitting about on wooden packing crates. 'We've just moved in.' Rex/Peter explained.

'And how long do you intend using this office?' the girl asked, 'You don't seem to have moved a lot in yet.'

'What?!' Rex/Peter stormed, 'We're here for good! Look – we've got all this equipment here; thousands of pounds worth of equipment, this is. Do you honestly think we'd have all this here if we weren't seriously moving in?'

Against all odds, he eventually persuaded the girl into giving him a phone line, and she started to fill out the obligatory form.

'What is your company name again?' she asked

'Fox-Horne Films.' Rex answered confidently

'And you are?'

'James Fox, and this is my partner Kenneth Horne.' Rex answered, motioning to Clive.

'Well, if you'd both like to sign here, please.' the girl offered the form to 'James Fox', who signed his name and then held out the pen to 'Kenneth Horne'.

'Sign here, Clive.' he said

'All right, Peter.' Clive answered, and went to sign his name on the form as Clive.

A shadow of confusion briefly passed over the girl's face, as she hastily pulled the form away from them. Needless to say, they didn't get their phone line.

The main set for the film consisted of enormous black plastic sheets, which were draped around the studio walls in folds, and lit moodily with red, green, and blue lights.

As this was a sado/masochist film, various implements of torture had been fastened to the walls, ceiling and floor, and old Hammer Horror film posters were added for good measure.

The story involved a young girl troubled by recurring nightmares of satanic torture, who is persuaded by her female guardian to visit a specialist doctor. She is then escorted by two male nurses to a hospital ward. But on the other side of the door to this ward was the nightmare dungeon of her strange dreams. The male nurses turned into wild sadists dressed only in leather loincloths, and the girl was strung up and whipped, while witnessing three other young girls being administered similar punishments.

The 'doctor' reappears as a masterly Devil worshipper, and his leather clad female assistant, after receiving a good whipping herself, is finally unmasked and revealed to be the young girl's guardian.

A script worthy of a place in B-Movie history!

I spent the next evening helping to 'dress the set' with all the relevant items of torture, and then went off with Clive to the nearest pub for his customary 'couple' of pints.

The following morning we began filming, and Rex/Peter set up a monitor by his feet with a 'feed' from my camera, so that at all times he could see what I was filming as well of course as checking his own camera image through his viewfinder.

It is more common these days, with video cameras being so much more affordable to all, to use two cameras on most adult shoot, but it was a rare occurrence in those days to do so on anything but the most lavish of productions, expenses usually being kept to the bare minimum. But on a shoot such as this, where the artistes taking part were actually in physical pain, an exception was made because, as the shoot progressed, their bodies would clearly get more and more marked due to the whipping, thus making retakes for different camera angles impossible as the continuity would never match.

After filming the initial doctor/patient scene (which was shot in one of the many empty offices in the building), we moved into the main 'stage' area for the rest of the two-day shoot.

And what of the 'actors' involved? Well, one really was a keen S&M leather fetishist, who frequented kinky clubs and acted out S&M scenarios in his private life. He obviously took to his part with relish, and whipped one poor girl until she screamed out, begging him to stop. She was another young single mum, taking part in the film to earn a little extra money for her baby. Another of the girls, chained to a wall, had her huge breasts tied tightly with thick white rope.

The young blonde heroine of the film was the wife of one of the male torturers and, as the filming progressed, she became increasingly distressed, until we had to break while her husband cuddled her and calmed her down. Through her tears, she explained that it was all just too much for her; the whippings, the horrific images on the posters adorning the black plastic walls. She knew it was only acting but couldn't help being effected by it; after all, the beatings were real enough!

The girl playing her guardian was similarly affected. She sobbed loudly as she was whipped, her tear stained face being the final image of the film. I can assure you that no special make-up was needed to produce either the tears or the look of wretched humiliation on her face; it was all genuine enough.

Technical disaster almost struck however during the first scene we shot in the 'dungeon'. With all the electric power consumed by the high wattage video lights, a main fuse blew and the entire studio complex was plunged into darkness.

Clive really came into his own, and was immediately on the case, running around torch in hand and, within fifteen minutes, unable to locate the mains fuse unit, he was pulling extension cables through from another part of the building that still had power, and re-plugging everything up. Lights and cameras burst back into life. I was very impressed; it was as if Clive had managed to produce electricity for us out of nowhere.

Filming wasn't easy however. Rex/Peter had never before worked as a freelancer for another director, and Tom himself was very much in control in that respect, leaving Rex/Peter playing 'second fiddle' as assistant director.

Many times there was a clash of the two 'De-Milles', as Rex/Peter and Tom both attempted conflicting directorial input.

Needless to say however, Rex/Peter eventually always won, and directed the film his way. It was his equipment they were using and so he persuaded Tom that he knew best. A case of he who holds the camera calls the tune!

As usual, I was trying to keep a distanced professionalism from the models; something I've always done throughout my career in the adult business, with the result that while the rest of the crew have been involved in getting free blow-jobs and 'director's perks', I was always maintaining a noble disinterest... but always going home alone!

Rather than gaining respect for this attitude however, I usually ended up as the laughing stock of the models. They knew they were there for sex, and that the crew were usually getting off on it as much as the other male models. Some girls took it almost as an insult if they weren't flirted with by the director, and almost all certainly preferred the crew to 'call a spade a spade' and not politely pussyfoot around why we were all there.

During the lunch break the model who had been manacled to the ceiling (doing it for her kid) and another girl made a rush for me while I had my hands full with sandwiches and coffee, and tried to 'de-bag' me of my trousers. I was rescued by Rex/Peter who was of course in his element trying to keep two 'naughty submissive slaves' in order.

The video finished, it was eventually released as *Slaves of Desire*. It had a wonderfully bad 'Hammer Horror' style soundtrack of ominous organ music.

In my opinion, although only a video release, it ranks as a cult porno classic, along with all those 'so bad that they're good' type B-Movies.

I was billed in the credits as Ricardo Morales, and Rex/Peter renamed Tom as Ed Ake (headache) for his role as production manager.

Chapter Nine:
THE PROSTITUTE AND THE SCHOOLGIRLS

After he'd finished editing *Slaves of Desire* Rex/Peter phoned, asking if I was free for a couple of days. He had rented a huge apartment in Brighton where he then lived, as a location; an old Edwardian house similar to the ones we filmed in near Park Lane in London.

Rex/Peter wanted to use me as a production assistant (i.e.: general dogsbody) to see how we got on together, with a view to offering me possible further regular production and editing work. This of course meant that I was to work unpaid for the trial period. But I didn't much mind the idea of that; it would be a pleasant couple of days by the seaside in Brighton, and I was still keen to learn all I could from a real professional as to how adult films were made. If it meant I could form an on-going business relationship with Rex/Peter, then maybe I could leave the mainstream video company that I still worked for and make porno my full-time career.

On the first day in Brighton we went straight to the location house where we shot a series of girls 'auditioning'. This meant that they were doing simple striptease routines to music, and Rex/Peter let me film one all on my own. I wanted the girl to strip really slowly and seductively, still striving to make my stuff look tasteful and arty, but Rex/Peter told me to hurry it up and get on with it. The poor model was obviously confused by our conflicting direction, not knowing whether to strip slowly and seductively or just yank her pants off as quickly as possible for the camera.

The next day, a husband and wife arrived from London to do some filming with us. The wife, Paula, was to do a hard-core two-girl sequence with a local girl called Deborah while her husband was going to clearly enjoy the display as we filmed it.

Deborah was actually a prostitute who got to know Rex/Peter through renting an apartment from him to use as her workplace, which was above the lock-up shop where he kept his copying bank of video recorders.

We set up at the hired location, a huge double bed dragged in from the main bedroom now dominating the centre of the sitting room.

First we filmed a short sequence of Deborah on her own, and then we shot the two-girl sequence.

Two girl, girl/girl or girl-on-girl are the industry terms for a lesbian shoot, boy/girl that of a standard heterosexual sex scene, and solo or single girl that of a masturbation scene with just one girl. A model is always expected to quite simply do a lesbian scene without making any kind of fuss. Like Queen Victoria believing that lesbianism didn't exist, people in the sex business somehow consider lesbianism to be so inconsequential as not to be any kind of problem for a female performer, almost as if it somehow can't really be genuine if it didn't involve a male cock! The same train of thought however does not seem to enter a director's mind when dealing with male performers. Nobody would expect a guy to just do a gay scene as if it were no big deal, simulated or not, and yet every girl is expected to do the equivalent simply as a matter of course.

In the adult business as far as guys are concerned, straight is straight and gay is gay and the two will rarely ever meet. Girls get it on with other girls as a matter of course, but naturally only ever for the voyeuristic pleasure of heterosexual men.

In fact, male gay work is a completely separate business within the adult industry. Guys who shoot or appear in heterosexual movies do not generally also do gay work, or if they do, they keep it quiet. Only in Europe is there more of a cross-over with a number of bi-sexual studs doing both types of work, even within the same film. And of course in America there is the legendary Jeff Stryker, who became very rich by unashamedly appearing in both gay and straight films.

Due to the obligatory exposure to lesbian acts with female performers however, whether real or simulated, many female models do in fact go on to share genuine lesbian relationships in their real lives, or at least some become actively bi-sexual in their private lives, while many remain of course simply good actors!

Some of course are gay or bi-sexual to start with, and enter the business as a way of finding uncommitted sexual encounters with other women, in much the same way as many men do when making the decision to become a porn model in order to have a lot of uncommitted hetero sex.

Our 'two girl' sequence turned out really well. Both girls seemed to be really into each other, and didn't need to have to act too much for the sake of our cameras.

For the most part during the sequence, I moved around operating a small hand held high-powered lamp, which Rex/Peter called a 'cooze light' or 'pussy light', and which was used specifically for throwing light on the shadowy genitalia when the camera moved in for a close-up.

It was pretty late when we finished shooting the scene, and it was the end of my two-day job. The couple from London and myself just made the last train home.

There was of course no mention of payment to me and, although I was happy to have helped him out on this occasion, I determined that if there was to be a next time, then I would try and get some payment for my work.

I had passed my number on to Deborah and, about a month later, she phoned me at home and asked me if I wanted to visit her in Brighton.

I drove there in my old Wolseley, not quite sure whether this was a 'date' or just a nice social evening with a friend.

We went for dinner in a charming candle-lit bistro, and Deborah told me of her life and her plans for the future. She told me of her regular clients, the 'nice old gentlemen' as she called them, who paid her over £100 to spend just an hour or so simply cuddling and chatting. These were her favourites, not the pervy ones who treated her like dirt to be abused.

She intended to stay 'on the game', supplementing this with some occasional amateur modelling work, for another year, maybe two; just until she had saved enough money to fly off to a warmer climate (I think she fancied Spain), hopefully fall in love, and settle down to enjoy the money she'd made, with nobody knowing how she had earned it and pointing the finger. Maybe she'd have children, and start a new life for herself away from all the problems she had here in the UK.

After dinner we went back to her apartment for coffee, but it was around half midnight that I realised that the evening was going to end with just the coffee. Deborah had simply thought that I was a nice guy, and had wanted to see me for an evening of friendship, and nothing more. I guess, for a sex worker like Deborah, genuine friendship with a guy, with no ulterior motives, is possibly a rare thing.

So I gave her a peck on the cheek and told her that I had to be getting back to London, and she didn't come on to me or insist that I stay.

I never saw Deborah again, although she phoned me several times just for a chat, and even wrote to me once, enclosing a photo of herself in which she looked just like any other ordinary girl, smiling out at me, dressed in sweater, jeans and sneakers.

Years later, when I was once again working for Rex/Peter, I discovered that Deborah was in fact being treated for cancer when I knew her and that, as a consequence, a year or so after I had last seen her, she had died, alone in Brighton, never achieving her goal of having children or reaching that island in the sun.

*

A month or so after my visit to Deborah, Rex/Peter phoned and asked me if I'd like to help him on another film he was doing. I tried to make it clear that this time I wanted some payment, and he in turn tried to convince me that he was doing me a favour by giving me some kind of 'porno work experience'. I wanted to keep on Rex/Peter's good side, as I wanted to continue my involvement in the British porno industry and, as such, he was presently my only real contact!

The planned filming job was to be a two camera shoot like the S&M one, as this one was to feature spanking, and Rex/Peter asked if, as the location was a London town house and he lived in Brighton, could I hire a second camera from a well known London hire company on his behalf, and bring it with me on the day. I said that of course I would, and Rex/Peter then asked me to pay upfront for it as well, and he'd settle up with me on the day.

I wasn't getting paid for the work, and now I was also going to be laying out my own money in advance! Oh well, I thought, in for a penny as the saying goes! So I agreed.

Not quite judging accurately the scale of professional video equipment however, as opposed to my own little VHS filming rig, I went to the central London hire company on the train, only then to be laden down with several huge and heavy silver aluminium flight cases, containing foam packed camera, separate recorder, and metal tripod with separate wooden 'spreader', each item individually packed in its own heavy duty case.

I stared at all these boxes transfixed, my mind racing; how was I to get them all back home from Central London with no car? I couldn't get them all on the train on my own. How much would it cost for me to get a taxi all the way back?

Would all these boxes and cases even fit in one taxi?

It was all going horribly wrong. I was laying out my own money in an effort to make Rex/Peter think I was responsible and capable of organising things for him, and here I was making my first big mistake by casually turning up at the hire company with no transport. I felt stupid! I should have remembered that, even my little VHS rig needed the transit van to transport it all to Kent when I shot *'Apple Pie'*!

An over-eager office junior at the hire company offered to help me load up my 'van'.

'Ah!' I said, 'The van. Yes. It's... er... parked quite a few blocks away.'

'I'll walk it all round with you then.' he offered obligingly.

'No, that's OK.' I said, 'There's... um... so much stuff here; why don't you just help me into a taxi and I'll do it myself.'

'OK' he smiled, starting to carry boxes out into the street and hail a taxi for me.

Not wanting the added expense of a taxi all the way home, I asked the driver just to get me to the nearest underground station.

But then what was I to do?

The boxes were all so bulky and heavy that how would I get them from the street level down the steps and into the station on my own?

If I went down to the train in two trips, hideously expensive video equipment, which was not mine, would be left unattended on the street, and maybe stolen. But how would I get it all down there on my own in just one journey?

Fortunately a passing tourist came to my rescue. Asking directions to some famous London landmark (just a short walk up the road), I told him that the quickest way to get there was on the train and, as he was going down to the platform anyway, would he mind carrying a couple of my boxes for me?

Full of gratitude for my help, he was only too pleased to oblige, and so I managed to get on the train! I only had to get out of the station at the other end and climb into another taxi for the short ride home.

So far, with equipment hire costs, train and taxi fares, my 'work experience' was proving very expensive indeed. I only hoped that I would indeed get the money back from Rex/Peter on the day of the shoot.

Next day, when I turned up at the location, my little old car groaning with all the equipment boxes, I found Rex/Peter, Clive, a make-up girl-cum-production assistant and a number of models already busying around unloading boxes, getting changed, setting up, etc.

Rex/Peter had been specially commissioned to shoot this 'schoolgirl spanking' film for a foreign production company. The fetish of spanking, corporal punishment, and bondage is regarded as a very

'English' fetish and so maybe that is why the commissioning company had chosen an English production company to shoot it for them. Historic British schools and stately homes are always favoured as locations for such films but, in this case, clearly on a low budget, a modest terraced town house was what Rex/Peter had chosen as the location!

First of all, we filmed some scene-setting material of the model who was playing the role of the schoolgirl's mother, in the kitchen making tea.

I recognised her as the same girl who had played the guardian in the *Slaves of Desire* film. She clearly seemed to be getting typecast as a parent/guardian figure!

Around mid-day we set off with just one camera to do all the exterior filming. The two models playing the 'naughty schoolgirls', although both over eighteen, were slight and very youthful in appearance. Even more so with little make-up on, their hair in bunches, and dressed in short school uniforms, complete with white knee high socks and blazers.

We went to a nearby playing field, where Rex/Peter set up his camera and Clive set up the portable monitor in order to check the picture, covering both it and himself in an old dark rug, to shield the monitor screen from the bright sunlight. This gave him the appearance of one of those old-fashioned stills photographers hidden under a black cloak. I expected a big puff of smoke at any second!

The female production assistant slated the beginning of each take with a traditional clapper-board, snapping it shut after announcing the title ('*School Report*') and take number to the camera.

I asked Rex/Peter why she did this, as we were only shooting with one camera at this point and videotape records both sound and vision onto tape simultaneously unlike film where sound and vision are recorded separately, the snapping shut of the clapper board providing the synchronisation point for the editor to match the sound and vision.

'It's a tradition carried on from the film industry.' Rex/Peter replied, as if in his past he had regularly worked on all the great British movies.

In fact porno filmmakers and low budget corporate video makers alike love to use traditional filmic terms and references as it makes them feel as if, by association, great cinematic techniques will rub off onto their productions. They also believe that, by doing this, their actors will take them more seriously, and that their work will become serious screen fare rather than an odd wank film or some dull sales training piece. One corporate filmmaker I worked for once even said that there was no real difference between himself and Steven Spielberg:

'We both just point a camera at someone and turn it on.' he commented!

While Rex/Peter filmed the two girls chatting in the field, the cool breeze causing their short skirts to rise up to reveal their underwear, a helicopter flew around overhead from the local Territorial Army Base. It circled and then flew over again a little lower. I'll bet the Army boys had their binoculars finely focused on our activities! But not for long, as we all soon set off to the local high street, to film the girls running down the road, only to miss the last bus home.

Getting this shot involved Clive standing on the corner watching out for the bus to come along and then cueing the girls to start running.

By the time the girls got near the bus stop, the bus had usually sped on past the Request Only stop, and so gave us the desired shot of the girls missing the bus. On several occasions however, much to the annoyance and confusion of the bus driver, the bus stopped and waited for the two hurrying schoolgirls, only to have them then stop and, giggling, wave the bus on!

Next came a scene which showed the girls 'father' at his place of work. He was meant to have a supervising job of some kind, but Rex/Peter hadn't actually any work location fixed up.

Driving along, we came to a building site and, after a few words with the site foreman, Rex/Peter pointed to the schoolgirls and their 'Dad' and, with a smile, filmed some shots of the girl's 'Dad' wandering around the site, hard-hat on, supervising the workers.

'How did you wangle that one?' I asked him afterwards.

'I told them we were filming a programme for children's television about different types of jobs.' Rex/Peter explained; 'Piece of cake. They were happy to let us film!'

I had to hand it to him; he had no qualms about saying whatever was needed in order to get the shots he wanted. The builders no doubt thought they were going to be on TV soon, whereas in fact all they would be on was a hard-core spanking video on sale abroad.

Back at the house, we had lunch and Rex/Peter checked through the script. Yes, he actually had one! It may surprise you to know that most of the bigger budget adult films made, certainly by the bigger production studios like Private, Vivid etc, are properly scripted in the usual way, although few are actually story-boarded.

The script for this particular 'epic' had been approved by the people who were putting up the money for this venture.

'They've already paid me a thousand pounds upfront.' Rex/Peter smiled, 'So I think I can trust them'. A thousand pounds in those days was indeed quite a lot of money!

The plot was as follows: the two young girls were sisters and, playing around on the way home from school, they miss their bus, lose their mid-term reports, and get their uniforms into a very dishevelled state. Their mother scolds them severely, telling them that they'll have to answer to their father when he returns home from work.

After inspecting the two girls, the Dad sends them up to get ready for bed with no supper, and to wait for him in their room.

The man playing the father turned out to be none other than Kent, the man who had stood in for me as my 'stunt dick' on Lindsay Honey's *Rock 'n' Roll Ransom*.

'Hello' I ventured, 'I met you on *Rock 'n' Roll Ransom*.'

'Oh yes, I remember that film; what a nightmare!' he answered, 'I had to stand in for some poor bastard who couldn't get it up!'

He obviously didn't recall exactly who I was, so I didn't remind him.

It turned out that he was involved in casting a scene for the erotic U.K. video company Electric Blue the next week and needed a handsome young guy to work with American big boob superstar Candy Samples. I offered my services, and he said he'd give me a ring about it. 'Great!' I thought, I'll get to work with a real American porno legend!'

Needless to say, he never phoned.

Rex/Peter and I moved all the camera equipment upstairs to film in the girls' small bedroom as they got undressed, and then on to the bathroom, as the girls washed and got ready for bed.

Rex/Peter's camera was linked by a long 'CCU' cable to a heavy mains operated video recorder, which was situated downstairs with a huge 'Grade One' Barco colour video monitor of which Clive was extremely proud. Clive himself operated the record/pause switches of the recorder on the direction of Rex/Peter via a 'talk-back' system, the sort commonly used by television crews in live studio multi-camera shoots, enabling the director to talk to the camera operators without himself being heard on the shooting set.

The use in this situation however, was for Rex/Peter to keep shouting down to Clive to 'pause the tape', 'roll the VTR', 'are you recording?', 'have you paused?' and 'get a move on, you fat lazy bastard'.

We filmed the two girls taking off their clothes in the bedroom and then, naked, they went into the bathroom to splash about together in the bath. They were warned to beware of the live electric cables in the bathroom, and I remembered my experience on my very first shoot with Rex/Peter; except that now I was the one giving the warning.

After getting changed into cute pink and white cotton pyjamas, the girls went into the master bedroom, where their 'father' and 'mother' waited for them.

'Dad' reprimanded them severely, and then conferred with 'Mum' as to what their punishment should be. They decided on a severe spanking each, followed by six of the best with a leather strap.

Kent however was very reluctant to slap the girls too hard, unlike the enthusiastic actor of *Slaves of Desire*. And so, Kent's spanking began very half-heartedly indeed.

'Come on, Kent,' Rex/Peter encouraged, 'You've got to do it for real; the kind of people that buy these films can tell the difference, you know. It mustn't be faked or they simply won't buy it'.

So Kent gave both girls a thoroughly sound spanking, and then gave each one six of the best with a thick leather strap.

Once or twice the filming had to stop due to the girls' crying out that it really did hurt too much, whereupon Rex/Peter would cuddle them briefly and reassure them that there were only two, three, or four more strokes to go, and that the quicker they got through it the quicker it would all be over and they could go home.

And once or twice the filming had to stop while Rex/Peter shouted down to Clive to get a move on or to put his headset back on – Clive kept taking it off as he said that it made his ears sweat! The talk-back system was unnecessary anyway as the house was so small that Rex/Peter's shouts were quite loud enough to be heard without the aid of any talk-back system. But Rex/Peter had paid for the talk-back and, just as he insisted on using the clapper-board, he obviously thought that that was how professional films were made, and so he was determined to use it and Clive just had to put up with having sweaty ears!

As a compromise however, Rex/Peter kept his headset on but spent most of the time actually going to the bedroom door and simply shouting his instructions down the stairs to Clive anyway.

So spanking continued and eventually, after the girls were sent to bed, Kent then took the strap to their 'mother' too to teach her a lesson in trying to intervene and undermine his authority. All outrageously 'non-p.c.' stuff of course by today's standards, and indeed pretty unacceptable I suppose even then, although it wasn't really until the early 1990's that the porn industry world-wide started adjusting it's traditional on-screen attitudes to women, albeit by very slow degrees.

At least nowadays girls too are shown to be actually enjoying themselves as willing participants in sex and not merely as playthings for men's pleasure alone. Directors like American ex-porn star Candida Royalle with her Femme Productions, and porn star Annie Sprinkles have put the female perspective on film, while arty film-makers like Michael Ninn and ex-Playboy video director Andrew Blake started to set a trend making magnificent soft-focus porn pretty enough for couples to accept and watch together.

In Britain, female directors like the excellent self-publicist Anna Span have also put porn with a female perspective very much both in the available market and in the media.

As sex comes out of the closet and becomes more socially acceptable, changes in porn attitudes necessarily follow. But it will take a long while before there is anything like a real equality on screen. Women will no doubt still be wearing sexy lingerie and high heels for men's pleasure, and pouting bimbo-like for a long while to come yet.

During the 'mother's' spanking, the owner of the house returned from work (it now being about 7p.m.). I'm not sure that she was fully aware of the nature of the film Rex/Peter was making, so he asked the woman playing the mother tactfully to 'try and scream a little quieter' if she could.

However not long after this, in response to the sound of Clive bumbling around downstairs, Rex/Peter shouted down at the top of his voice:

'Come on, Clive; hurry up changing that tape! There's a girl getting spanked black and blue up here for God's sake!' – Very tactful!

When it was all over, Rex/Peter settled up with me in cash for the equipment hire, I packed all the equipment back into my car (it was down to me to return it to the hire company), and gave one of the models a lift home. She lived in a North London squat with her boyfriend and, on the way, I told her that I too was making my own films and took her phone number for future reference. It's very easy to meet models when you're involved in this business but, unless you're the director, producer or casting agent, their phone numbers are not usually going to be passed round to you.

I never, for example, got the home telephone number of any of the girls I'd worked with while modelling but, as someone of some influence; someone who could actually get them work, it was altogether different. I spent two days once, working with one model who thought I was just a hired hand but, when I gave her my business card (which at that time carried the name of *Penthouse* magazine on it) she spent the rest of the shoot sticking to me like glue and flirting with me outrageously.

The adult industry is surprisingly small world-wide: everyone knows everyone else who is doing anything worthwhile, and so girls' phone numbers get traded around between directors and producers internationally. There are surprisingly few people (models, photographers, and film-makers) in this business, and that's why a particular model can be seen time and time again in magazines, and on numerous video programmes world-wide.

New girls are hard to find, and new photographers or film- makers working on any kind of professional level are even rarer. Of course there are plenty of amateur photographers around who pay girls to model for them privately, and many girls get their 'bread and butter' money doing just this, but the adult industry per se is very incestuous; a small 'family' of models and photographers working closely with each other time and time again and looking after each others' interests.

After dropping the young girl off at her squat I drove home. It was late and I was tired. It had been a long day and tomorrow I had to get up early and return all this hired equipment.

One lesson I had learned from this particular 'work experience' however was that this time I wouldn't be returning the equipment on the train.

Chapter Ten:
A SEX MANIAC ON HIS OWN

By the following winter I had come to realise that if my new line of business was to expand successfully I needed financial backing, and I needed partners.

With an old mate of mine, Mark, I set about planning a series of productions for mail order sale, made in the same way as '*Apple Pie*' but with more specific themes; big boobs, mud wrestling, outdoor flashing etc.

I wrote to Rex/Peter asking him if he'd be interested in backing us financially, and he phoned back keen to arrange a meeting.

So one wintry morning, Mark and I drove down to Rex/Peter's apartment in Brighton, the window wipers flexing back and forth flicking the soft flakes of snow off the windscreen.

I had decided that I would now address Rex/Peter simply as 'Peter'. I had learned from both Clive and Deborah that Peter was his real name, 'Rex' being the name he had decided to work under for his porn productions, a 'nom-de-porn' as British porn director Jack Bedford once called these 'made up for porn' names (as opposed to a nom-de-plume). Also I now felt that I was dealing with the 'real man' on a business footing, and so was finally in enough of a level position with him to call him by his real name, 'man to man'.

The meeting itself was very properly conducted, although Peter spent the first hour going through the video orders that the post office had delivered to him that morning in a big sack from his forwarding post office box address.

He complained when a customer hadn't included the extra one pound required for postage and packing, deposited all cash orders securely straight into his wallet, and proudly showed us the letters of praise that he had received for his product. I think he was trying to establish in our minds that he could be a powerful and wealthy backer for us and that we should be proud to be associated with him.

We then sat round in a little circle with Peter and his secretary Jean, an older woman who had acted as the production assistant on the *School Reports* film.

Jean took down the 'minutes' of the meeting and occasionally commented on our ideas: 'I think there should be more videos that women would enjoy.' she said.

'Do you mean with men in?' we asked.

'Oh no, dear; sexy lesbian videos.' she replied with a twinkle in her eye.

We all nodded thoughtfully, and then continued our discussion about videos aimed at men.

'Well, boys,' Peter finally asked us, his smile broadening, 'How much can you two put into this venture?'

'Only about £400' we answered quietly. 'Well, £800's O.K.' Peter began, 'No, no, not each!' I interjected, 'Between us!' Peter's expression only momentarily fell.

'Businesses have been set up for far less than that,' he encouraged, 'What we have to do is set things up correctly. You'll need a name; let's see... Ric and Mark... something like R.M. Supplies will do.'

Peter's own business name at that time was G.S. Supplies. 'I know the business inside out,' he continued, 'I know what the public want and they want as much big boob stuff as you can make.'

Peter's business at that time was particularly specialising in big boob material.

'Then maybe a messy tape, and a schoolgirl tape; three tapes a month; that's not unreasonable is it? If you boys can produce three films a month, sort out all the models and locations, then you can hire my camera and all the filming gear, hire my editing suite here in Brighton (I'll give you a good competitive rate), and then you can sell your films through my mailing list, paying something toward the admin costs of course. I'll do all this for you, and we'll split the profits three ways. Fair enough?'

Mark and I looked at each other and nodded dumbly. We weren't businessmen. We were young and wet behind the ears. We nodded our heads into a deal where we had to arrange all the models, do all the filming and editing ourselves, pay Peter for his equipment, pay Peter for his editing suite, pay Peter for his office facility, and in return he would add the films that we had made to his own mail-order catalogue – and take a third of all the profits.

Just then Clive arrived from the copying bank down the road, and while Peter went to answer the door to him, Jean leaned over to us.

'Listen,' she hissed, out of Peter's earshot, 'Think hard about this, boys. Don't do any deals with Peter until you've really thought all this through.'

She sank back into her seat just as Peter returned with Clive in tow.

'Hello.' Clive beamed, his nervous twitch making him wink and blink at us.

Peter went off to another room to get Clive what he had called in for and, while he was gone, Clive crept closer to Mark and I and, breathing alcoholic fumes over us, he too warned us against doing any business deals with his employer.

What were we to make of this whispered mutiny amongst the G.S. Supplies crew?

We didn't make anything of it, but just sat back and sipped our malt whiskies, courtesy of our generous would be business partner.

Peter showed me a copy of *Slaves of Desire*, and proudly showed me an edit he'd done of the strip routine he'd let me direct when I'd stayed over before; the one I'd wanted to do slowly, and he'd insisted I hurry it up. I had thought that my sequence had been quite good in itself but Peter had added all sorts of video tricks and effects, normally only called upon to help an editor out of a tricky situation, or to spice up a dull pop promo.

'See,' he told me proudly, 'With clever editing one can make even a boring sequence look good!'

Later on, as Mark and I got back in our car to go home, Peter shook our hands, told us he'd get Jean to send us a copy of the 'minutes' and bade his new business partners farewell.

I later heard that Peter's apartment was at that time allegedly under constant police surveillance. Whether this was true or not I never knew, but I have since wondered just who the boys in blue might have thought Mark and I were, and just what crooked multi-million pound porno deal we were all shaking hands on in the car park that night – if they only knew!

Mark and I stopped off on the way home in a little snow covered country pub and had a pint and some food.

'Well, what do you think?' I asked Mark. We both agreed that, although the partnership might work very well, it was very odd that both of Peter's employees had tried to warn us off doing business with him. If this was how his loyal employees acted, what did his business competitors think of him?

Our suspicions were confirmed when, with the 'minutes' which arrived by post a day later, was a hastily scrawled note from Jean, again warning us to think twice before taking on any partnership with Peter.

And so we wrote to Peter explaining that we had thought everything over and decided not to accept his business offer after all, and so R.M. Supplies never came into being.

And consequently Peter not only failed to acknowledge my letter but also failed to get in touch with me at all, despite my regular correspondence both by mail and telephone seeking further work.

Unfortunately for me, as Peter was really my only important professional contact in the business at that time (I had lost Lindsay's phone number long ago), my 'career' in the British porn industry seemed to have came to an abrupt end.

I continued to sell '*Apple Pie*' in a small way via mail order until the introduction of the Video Recordings Act in 1984 when, as the grey areas of legality and certification were tightened up, I withdrew the film from sale, and concentrated on my more legitimate activities of video business; that of filming weddings, corporate films, pop promos, and TV commercials.

Although at one time I'd employed a part-time secretary to deal with my postal orders, I now wound up the 'Dick Harrd Video Company'. I let the account overdraw to the extent of several hundred pounds and then just disappeared with the money, closing the accommodation address from which the account operated.

Dick Harrd had never actually existed. His address was merely a forwarding address. By closing the account while it was in the red, Dick Harrd had technically now become a bank thief as well as an illegal pornographer! Maybe the police are still looking for the infamous Mr. Harrd in connection with his dubious business affairs, but I doubt they'll ever find him, as he never ever existed in the first place.

It seemed as if, just as quickly as I had been embraced into the select circle of those involved in the production of adult material in England, I was now on the outside again, only 'looking in' on that world as a customer, occasionally purchasing adult magazines or videotapes.

Several years passed, and I continued with my legitimate career, building up knowledge and skills as a video cameraman, editor and producer, now working on music videos for the likes of Rod Stewart, Robert Palmer and Duran Duran, as well as TV commercials and travel films.

It was as if my involvement in the world of porno had been nothing more than a flirtatious affair that I'd indulged in as a young man. But little did I know that my old paramour had not yet finished with me, and was all too soon to be wooing me once again with temptations far more compelling than before.

*

Tuppy Owens was an exceptional woman. Having made cameo appearances in porn films in her early days, she now ran Outsiders, a charitable trust set up to help people with physical and social disabilities find acceptance, friendship and love within an openly sexual environment.

Tuppy published The Sex Maniacs Diary each year to raise money for her charity, and also organised the annual Sex Maniacs Ball, an outrageous themed party held in a different 'secret venue' in London each year.

There was always a wonderful gourmet buffet included in the entrance price, and one year a naked girl was served up, laying across a table, elaborately decorated in meat, bread, fruit and creamy desserts. Needless to say, the guests all piled in enthusiastically and black tie was definitely not required as they tucked in, eating the food off her body.

Every year guests were encouraged to dress in fetish or revealing gear, usually associated with that particular year's theme.

Erotic fashion shows and cabaret also formed part of the Sex Maniacs Ball's entertainment, much in the same way that it does at events like Erotica these days. There was often even a sponsored striptease from male or female members of the public. There was also a high-powered disco, as well as live appearances from the likes of sexy singer Danielle Dax and outrageous performance artist and fashion designer Leigh Bowery, who one year was winched down from the ceiling to perform his now legendary enema show.

Well-known celebrities, most notably Boy George, also usually made an appearance.

Money was raised not only from ticket sales but also by inducing party guests to pay a pound or so to take part in various side-show activities such as the Grope Box or the Human Pony Ride.

With the Grope Box, men or women were persuaded to step inside what resembled a magician's cabinet. The door was bolted shut and punters were then encouraged to place their hands through strategically placed holes in the box, and grope the inhabitant, after paying a pound for the privilege.

For the more exhibitionist amongst the crowd, the pound- paying customer could step inside the box him or herself, and be groped.

The Human Pony Rides involved a small pony-trap powered not by a horse, but by a submissive male or female 'slave'. Customers then paid for the privilege of being run around for a few minutes in the slave-powered cart.

The Peep Show was another popular regular favourite, where couples fondled each other while party guests paid a pound or so to peep in at them.

Another favourite was a large bath with a picture of a naked woman painted inside it. A real naked woman stood beside the bath, renting three plastic hoops (similar to those used in a fairground 'Hoopla') for a pound. Customers could throw the rings into the bath and, wherever they landed on the painted image, they were allowed to kiss, lick or touch the real girl in exactly the same place.

The first year that I attended, I felt as if I had stumbled upon some wonderfully depraved and decadent fantasyland. Anyone turning up in ordinary street clothes stood out like a sore thumb, as everyone (men and women alike) were either dressed in kinky leather, rubber, or PVC outfits, or were naked except perhaps for some lacy lingerie, or a solitary leather thong or harness.

The infamous Cynthia Payne was a guest at the first Ball I attended; a wonderful woman with whom I spent a long while chatting. Now more widely known from the successful feature films about her life, *Personal Services* and *Wish You Were Here*, 'Madame Cyn' used to run a brothel in South London, her clients paying for services with luncheon vouchers. She was also at that time standing for Parliament with her own sexually oriented political party. She signed my programme, 'From L.V. To M.P. Sexplicitly Yours, Cynthia Payne'.

At one point during the evening, I spotted organiser Tuppy Owens chatting to two revellers dressed very realistically as police officers. A rowdy naked girl brushed past them cooing: 'Great costume! It looks really genuine!' It was! The two policemen had called in to check that the partying was all legal and that nothing too naughty was going on!

The most worthwhile contact that I made that night however wasn't a sexual one, but a social and a business one. One of the people at the Ball, raising money by having her photo taken with the general public was none other than Linzi Drew, and who should be taking the Polaroid pictures of her but Lindsay Honey himself, who I hadn't seen since filming in Park Lane years before.

'Lindsay,' I ventured, 'Do you remember me?' As before, Lindsay remembered instantly and impressively: 'Ric! How are you?'

He introduced me to Linzi who quite plainly didn't remember me at all, and I asked him how the finished version of *Rock 'n' Roll Ransom* turned out.

'Oh, we had a few problems with that.' he told me, 'Did you ever see the finished film?'

I told him that I hadn't, and he took my address and promised to send me a copy.

He told me that a few of the original camera tapes had been stolen and that, as a consequence, most of the infamous pissing scene had gone, as had Kent's stand-in cum shot for me, the 'blood brothers' in the bath clip, and the entire scene with the black girl who was 'on' and whose cum-shot Lindsay had had to fake.

I must admit that I didn't expect to get a copy of the tape as promises made at a party to some guy you haven't seen for several years are not often fulfilled, no matter how well meant at the time. But I was happily surprised when a package arrived a few days later containing not only a copy of *The Rock 'n' Roll Ransom*, but also a hand written note from Lindsay on headed paper. He and Linzi had moved home since the early days when I first knew him, and so I was happy to now have his new address and phone number.

I rang him to thank him for the tape and he asked me if I knew of a good editing suite he could use. Apparently he had just produced a video entitled *Linzi Drew's Striptacular* and needed to get it edited. I suggested a place I was currently working at, and he not only booked it but hired me as the editor as well.

So once again I was editing naked girls rather than some corporate film, or the pack-shot of a tub of butter!

Whenever I'd worked at this particular edit facility I'd been treated as just another freelancer, but this time I was treated with enormous respect, as our edit was clearly attracting a lot of attention from the in-house staff. Production assistants, runners, and senior editors alike kept wandering in getting us tea, sandwiches, etc; all of course just to catch a glimpse of the on-screen nudity. Lindsay seemed oblivious to all the attention. Working full-time in the porn industry, and living with top glamour model Linzi Drew, I guess he was used to being treated like royalty by the envious Joe Public.

Even the chairman of the edit company himself popped in to check that 'everything was O.K.', his eyes glued firmly on the screen the whole time he talked to Lindsay.

'By the way, how will you be settling your bill?' he asked.

'Cash of course.' Lindsay answered, pulling out a wad of notes, 'Is there ever any other kind of payment?'

I smiled to myself, thinking of all the red tape, thirty day invoices and triple signed company cheques that I was sadly becoming used to. Perhaps I should try and get back into porn again, as the idea of a wad of tax-free notes in my wallet and everyone falling over themselves to be nice to me was very appealing.

We edited the film to what we surmised were the standards of the British Board of Film Classification at that time, but neithe of us really knew what kind of things the BBFC found objectionable. I learned through later experiences with them that the British Board of Film Classification are a rule unto themselves, passing titles like the highly explicit Dr. Andrew Stanley's *The Lover's Guide* with an '18' rating, while rejecting granting a certificate at all (even 'R18', which is only granted to films so strong they may only be sold through licensed sex shops) to mild titles like *Tied and Tickled*, an imported American film in which girls were tied up with their total consent and then tickled with soft feathers until they cried with laughter.

The only 'guideline' the BBFC will ever give you is that one's edited film mustn't "deprave or corrupt". Outside of that 'ruling' it's anybody's guess just what the BBFC will object to, and on what grounds. My only advice is to veer on the side of caution!

Linzi Drew's Striptacular was not released in the end until three years after our edit, as the original distribution deal had fallen through.

This had been done with the same distribution company that had brought the controversial and now banned film *I Spit On Your Grave* to England several years earlier.

The 'Master' edited tape of *Striptacular* had lain in a garden shed for a long while until eventually Lindsay managed to arrange certification and release of it.

By that time I then knew just how puritanical the views of the BBFC were, objecting as they did to anything that showed more than the tits and bums of 'Page Three'. I was therefore amazed to learn that *Striptacular*, edited with no insight as to what should or should not be cut out, had been passed with only two minor amendments!

And that was it. Lindsay paid me and the editing house in cash and once again disappeared out of my life.

I continued editing and filming corporate films, fashion shows, weddings, travelogues, TV commercials, and pop promos.

I'd meet Lindsay and Linzi on an annual basis – every year at the Sex Maniacs Ball and, while his anecdotes of what he'd been doing and the many naked women he'd worked with were numerous, I just smiled and said that I'd been busy too, although I didn't tell him that all I'd been busy doing was filming weddings and not seeing any naked flesh since last year's Sex Maniacs Ball!

One year I told him I was desperate for work, and asked him if he knew of any. He suggested I try stripping.

Under the name of 'Hot Rod' due to his then similarity in looks to the singer Rod Stewart, Lindsay had been a male stripper, doing hen nights up and down the country. He said it was a great laugh and easy money. Linzi interjected however with a story of when he got badly beaten up by jealous boyfriends as he left one particular venue.

I considered the idea of giving it a go, but this was in the days before *The Full Monty* or even the Chippendales; before sex for the girls became as socially acceptable as stag nights and table dancing are for the boys, and the opportunities for a guy to make a good living taking his clothes off in a heterosexual environment just weren't there at that time. Also I didn't fancy having to wrap an elastic band around the base of my dick night after night so that it stopped the blood flow, making it almost black and blue looking, a trick that all male strippers do just before they go on stage so that their dicks look big and thick while still only semi-hard.

And, anyway I didn't run the risk of getting beaten up in my current line of work; the worst I could expect was not to get paid if I fouled up somebody's wedding day film by not including a shot of their aged aunt in the final edit!

So I continued with my video work, always thinking of new angles to try and keep working, determined to make video production my successful career, like an old dog blinkedly gnawing away at the same old bone.

I continued to attend the Sex Maniacs Ball, and one year some friends of mine at a mainstream production company I did some freelance work for, were approached by Tuppy Owens to provide the equipment and crew to film the event, with a view to selling the resulting video to regular Ball guests as an extra fund raiser, and I asked if I could go along as their production assistant, thus gaining me free entry on the night for relatively little work.

In order to blend in with the fetish crowd, the crew had all donned skin-tight rubber diving suits, and one particular member of the crew liked it so much that he has since become a regular visitor not only to the Ball, but to other fetish events as well, always dressing up in skin-tight rubber! I myself wore a rubber vest and skin-tight PVC trousers and spent half the night running around with the cameraman, and the other half just running around socialising.

The following year, I had the idea of utilising my video skills with a fund-raising 'side-show' style activity, and phoned Tuppy Owens to suggest that I arrange and run a 'video confessional' booth, where Ball-goers could enter a small private booth and videotape themselves in any activity they chose, taking the tape home with them as a souvenir; I was sure Tuppy would think this a winning idea.

To refresh her memory of who I was, and to give her assurance that I was a professional video technician, I began by reminding her that I had been part of the previous year's film crew.

'Oh you were, were you?' Tuppy replied curtly 'Well, perhaps you could tell me what happened to the tapes?'

It turned out that after the Ball that night, the tapes had mysteriously disappeared, never turning up for the edit, and consequently never materialising at all into the finished fund- raising film.

By confidently stating that I had been a member of the video crew, I had suddenly become implicated and, without even getting round to mentioning my 'confessional booth' idea, I became deeply involved in searching out the missing tapes. Tuppy took my home phone number and expected me, as her new key contact, to find them.

Through various phone calls I eventually tracked the missing tapes down to the director who apparently hadn't known where to send them or what to do with them, and had simply hung on to them and waited to be contacted.

Tuppy was obviously pleased to get the tapes back but, after having waited a year for them, didn't think I was due any special thanks for merely achieving what should have happened automatically one year before.

And so I bought my entrance ticket as normal that year, and the Ball was missing a video confessional booth.

Chapter Eleven:
LINCOLN, SPAIN AND WANDSWORTH

By the late 1980's I presumed that, due to the Government's 1984 Video Recordings Act, which had severely restricted the proliferation of adult releases in the U.K., and the BBFC's certification fees and rules had proved too expensive and complex for all but the most established adult video companies to deal with.

Consequently the adult shelves in video stores were soon empty for all but a few Electric Blue and Playboy titles. I suppose I thought that the adult business in England was pretty much dead and that, as a consequence, it was not worth pursuing any further work. After all, surely everyone I used to know (Peter, Lindsay, Ken) must all be suffering a bit of a recession of work? How wrong I was!

Eventually my 'freelance' career as a video cameraman and editor began to resemble that of a resting bit-part actor. I found I was 'resting' more than I was working and I ended up shooting very cheap-end wedding videos out of both financial and psychological desperation. I wanted to be able to at least still say I was doing some kind of work as a video cameraman, but I really wanted to be doing something a little more creative and more stimulating than filming another happy couple walk down the aisle.

I finally wrote to Rex/Peter again, reminding him of my capabilities as a cameraman, and as an editor, and asking him if he had any work available for me.

Within a week, Peter responded. He was no longer based in Brighton, but now had a beautiful detached four bed-roomed house in Lincolnshire, from where he ran his production empire.

Of the Lincolnshire village he lived in, Elton John's song writing collaborator Bernie Taupin had apparently written the lyric *'Saturday Night's All Right For Fighting'*! However, Peter's part of it, in a beautiful rambling old farm-house hidden behind some lime trees, was rather idyllic.

He wrote asking me to phone him and, when I did, he explained that he had had a full time editor working for him who had just left to go to Film School, and would I be interested in taking his place? Would I? The next week I hired a car, my old Wolseley having long since given up the ghost, and drove up to Lincoln to discuss the matter.

Peter advised me to ring him when I was in the area and he would give me full directions, but instead I drove straight to what I thought was his office address; 'The Business Centre' address that was at the top of his letter to me.

When I got there however I found an empty locked up building. Ringing Peter I announced I was outside his office only to be told that the address was merely a front, an address from which Peter picked up his post on a daily basis.

From his real business centre, the converted farmhouse where he lived, Peter ran a veritable cottage industry. He would use his house and the surrounding land as a beautiful filming location, and edit his films in his purpose built state of the art editing suite, luxuriously created in one of the converted barns; a far cry from the cramped spare room he used in Brighton, or the 'packing case edit suite' on the set of *Slaves of Desire*.

In another of the converted outhouses, a thirty machine duplication bank continually ran copies of his films ready for sale, while in an adjoining office, members of his immediate family, and of course the ever present Clive, packed the films, sent mail-outs, and handled all the orders both direct to the public, wholesale to shops and distribution companies, and via credit card on the phone.

Peter was working closely with photographer Jim Deans (these days better known for his work establishing the medium of IPTV in Britain, or for his work as porn director 'Phil McCavity'), a tough but talented Scot, while Peter himself now concentrated solely on the video side of things.

Peter employed me on a four day a week basis. I would drive up to Lincoln on Monday morning and work through until Thursday night, when I'd then drive back home to enjoy a three-day weekend. Peter always paid me promptly at the end of every week and for the period I worked for him, I edited various niche themed videos and ironically many of the 'Samantha Spade' films that Peter was now producing for Yago; the very same lingerie/leatherwear company that had turned both Lindsay and me down all that time ago.

To play the part of Sam Spade, Peter had found a brand new girl with enormous boobs and huge aureole. Half Portuguese-Indian and half Jamaican she was an English hairdresser from Chertsey doing the odd bit of modelling part-time before Peter discovered her, changed her surname to Sinclair and signed her up.

Charmaine Sinclair worked exclusively for Peter for a long while before branching off on her own very successful modelling and acting career, where she has since presented and starred on satellite TV station Television X, danced in road-shows around the country and, perhaps most famously of all, had a very well publicised affair with Hollywood screen actor Robert De Niro.

In all the time I worked with her, I found her to be a sweet, friendly and lovely person to know. We had to dub her voice on the Samantha Spade videos however as, dressed like a dominatrix in full leather she looked set to kill – until she opened her mouth, as she had at that time a high squeaky and giggly voice that hardly matched up to her tough image on screen. To avoid the problem of lip-syncing, her on-screen voice was only ever heard as a voice-over expressing her inner thoughts, which was dubbed by an older woman with more sultry tones.

Peter had signed Charmaine under contract exclusively to him, and she was happy to take his advise on everything in building up her modelling career.

Peter was also very generous in his advice to me on production techniques, and so I was happy to find myself finally properly fully employed in adult film work for what was really the first time since I started out in this career. I was editor, cameraman and production assistant for Strand International, the name of Peter's production and distribution company.

But it had been such a long time since I had been actively involved in the industry that I found myself in the same position that my Jewish friend had been when I was shooting the Jane Torvill look-alike at his home. When meeting large breasted model Tracey Gibb for the first time I began to make ridiculously inappropriate small talk:

'Do you do any other kind of modelling then?' I asked awkwardly.

'Yes, I've just come back from the Bahamas on a major fashion shoot.' she answered sarcastically.

While I was working for him, Peter had the great money-making idea of sending out a mail-shot of an explicit but totally non-existent video, taking the cash only orders into a bank account disassociated from himself, sending out nothing and spending the dosh on a badly needed holiday! Unfortunately he chose Clive's bank account as the one through which all the cash would tumble. When however Peter came to total up what he had made and book his flights he found that the account was all but empty – Clive had gone through most of the two grand at the pub with his mates.

I found myself making cameo appearances in several of Peter's films, most notably as a villain in one of the Samantha Spade programmes, where, with some clever editing techniques, Charmaine appeared to literally slash me to bits with her bullwhip!

Peter would book a girl for a couple of days, she would stay at the house and, while she was there, he would shoot two or three scenes with her of various genres, to be used in a number of different videos. Once, when it was one of the sales team's birthday, Peter shot a messy food scene with one of the girls, and then got her to sing happy birthday to him, while she was all covered in cake mix! I think the idea was for him to lick it off her, but he was too embarrassed to do anything other than go bright red!

My time spent with Peter and his family in Lincoln during this time was a very happy one, and I felt as though I was learning a lot about adult production techniques from a genuine master of the game.

Peter was soon making contacts abroad, and particularly with German porno mogul Hans Moser.

Mr. Moser once ran the enormously successful V.T.O. Pictures from Hanover in Germany but, as an undischarged bankrupt, he fronted the company with his wife, model Teresa Orlowski. Thus Moser's company was called Video Teresa Orlowski (V.T.O.), and the Moser millions were officially earned by the 'company boss' Teresa.

However, due to this seemingly convenient legal arrangement, there was nothing to stop Teresa from getting up one morning and literally walking off with the business, complete with name, money and all it's assets. And this, as I understand it, is exactly what she did, leaving Moser with no Company and with no millions!

Hans Moser's genius at creating erotic video programmes of a very high quality was largely due to the fact that he was never afraid to spend money on the latest technology. His production and post-production facilities were frequently updated with the latest Sony had to offer, making his edit suites the envy of many of his broadcast contemporaries, and indeed professional interest had been shown by many of them, including, so I'd heard, Richard Branson's Virgin empire.

Because of his renowned success and reputation, it didn't take Moser long to get enough money invested into his business to set himself back on his feet with another company, Sascha Alexander Productions (S.A.P.) and another young wife to act as front woman/superstar. This time she came from Britain: a young Jewish girl called Sarah Young was given the Moser star treatment of a boob job and star billing in magazines and videos, and Mr. Moser was back in business – The company was dead; long live the company.

Peter was soon doing work for S.A.P. among others, and this new European connection frequently took him away from the day-to-day running of the business in Lincolnshire.

Editing work in the U.K. began to tail off as Peter concentrated on European hardcore and consequently, my services were eventually no longer required.

He moved his entire business to Spain, virtually re-inventing himself from his new base near Marbella.

I worked with him only once more after that, flying out to do some editing for him. But both his business and his lifestyle were now very different.

Peter was much more laid-back in his attitude to both business and life than he had been in England, happy to enjoy the sunshine, the more relaxed lifestyle that Spain offered, and the company of models like British girl Anne-Marie, who he gave a boob-job to, re-named Misty McKane and launched as a new big European sex-star.

While I was out there, Peter recruited a local Spaniard from one of the many bars there to try out as a stud for Misty. The guy arrived at Peter's villa but had trouble getting it up, so Peter left him and Misty alone for a while thinking that would help. While out of the room, the guy got it up, had sex with Misty and promptly came immediately. Needless to say he then had trouble rising to the occasion again for the camera and even had the cheek to ask Peter if he could have some whisky as he thought that a stiff drink might help! Peter was incredulous afterwards, exclaiming that this must have been the best day in this Spanish barman's life – he had come to a luxurious villa, shagged a porn star, had some expensive whisky and then gone home! Peter on the other hand, got nothing whatsoever on film. And as for Misty? Well, I guess it was all part of her new life as a budding porn star!

Peter's day-to-day business back in England was suffering without him at the helm however. His UK tape sales were falling, and I flew back home from working for him wondering how, without Peter around in the UK anymore, I would continue to find work in the British sex industry.

But the adult industry is indeed very small and once you're in it's a bit like an 'old boy's network'. One is privy to all the up- coming model parties at the top London night-clubs, where one can network with industry types on both sides of the camera. One knows which models are around, who are 'bad news', who are contemplating doing hardcore, and who have temporarily 'retired', either through personal choice, pregnancy, or just because no-one wants to work with them.

One also gets to know quite quickly everyone else who is working in the business and, as the adult industry is small worldwide, everyone knows everyone else who is doing anything on a professional level. Word soon gets round on the grapevine of anyone new. Photographers trade models' phone numbers with other photographers, and indeed trade numbers of any new talent on either side of the camera.

And so it was that, through my work for Peter, I met and eventually worked for John Graham, a benign South African businessman now based in the U.K. who was working as a telephone salesman when he set out to shoot and market a topless calendar for his company. In doing so, he saw a buck to be made in glamour photography, and quickly set out to make it, establishing himself as Britain's premier specialist of big boob material, prolifically producing magazine sets, and videos of the biggest busted girls in the world.

Peter was right when he once said to me that there was an insatiable market for big boobed girls. There is, and John Graham found a new way to help satisfy it.

At that time in America there was big business in exotic table dancing, now of course also hugely successful in the U.K. except that, in the U.S., it was an altogether much more glamorous affair. Girls paid top surgeons to give them huge breast enlargement operations, gave themselves a bizarre stage name like Wendy Whoppers, Topsey Curvey, Lotta Topp, Justa Dream and Fluffy Pillows to name but a few, and tour the specialist dance clubs set up around the United States and Canada, performing their 'exotic dance' routines, which were essentially an elaborate form of burlesque striptease, a mixture of exotic cabaret and sleaze where, unlike the U.K. where unknown models just writhe around a pole, well-known dancers (with their own successful fan clubs) performed cabaret acts which featured elaborate costumes, props and often skills such as magic or fire-eating. They also used their enormous silicone breasts to do 'tricks' such as accepting tips from customers in their cleavages. Due to varying American State laws, some clubs only allowed the girls to go topless, while others required them to keep their nipples covered as well.

The girls got a fee for the job, and they also earned a nice tax- free sum in the tips that customers would stuff into their stocking tops, garter belts, or between their enormous boobs. These girls at that time (early 1990s) were earning in excess of half a million dollars a year. They become cult celebrities in their own right, with their own fan clubs and a devoted following of male admirers. The only equivalent in terms of fame here in the U.K. would be the successful tabloid 'Page Three' style glamour models. Due to their ridiculously inflated curves however, these girls would have been more at home on Page Three of David Sullivan's *Sport* newspaper than any of the other British tabloids.

As their earnings from public appearances were so good, they would often only agree to do magazine modelling or video work for the publicity it would attract to their live act, and not solely for the modelling fee. As U.S. porn star Lynn LeMay once said: 'Most of the girls who do videos are doing them for the dancing. They use the videos to make a name for themselves so they can go out and tour – that's where the money is'.

Here then was a vast untapped source of enormously breasted women that nobody was really shooting any magazine photo-sets or video of, and it took John Graham to see the opportunity.

He met the American agents for many of these dancers and arranged a special deal whereby the girls would work exclusively for him as their sole UK representative, doing nude photo-shoots and video sequences that were sold initially only in America through Big Top Productions, and then also in England under the 'Double D' banner, a brand that John himself set up, and then eventually world-wide.

These girls were big. Most of them, their breasts surgically inflated with silicone to three or even four times their original size, looked like a real life version of Barbie or Jessica Rabbit – cartoon caricatures of real women. These blow-up love dolls made of flesh and blood only represented men's fantasy figures however as, with their platinum blonde dyed hair, extra long false nails, silicone boobs, carefully nurtured tan, inflated lips and pubic hair trimmed into a 'landing strip' mohican or heart shape, they were usually about as far removed from a genuinely proportioned natural looking woman as it was possible to get.

John used to hire Peter's edit suite after his trips to the strip bars of America, and I'd be given the day off while Peter worked away, teaching John the basics of how to edit the footage he'd just shot.

Before I went to work for Peter in Spain, after he had moved everything out of his Lincolnshire farmhouse, I wrote to John reminding him that I had been Peter's editor and suggested that maybe I could do some work for him, as work with Peter was now looking pretty irregular. On my return from Spain there was a message from John asking me to give him a ring.

I went to see him at his then modest office in a business centre in Wandsworth, South London. He and his colleague Dave Wells (whose 'nom-de-porn' was Lee Francis, named after his favourite footballer Francis Lee) were just about to launch the Double D video label in the UK with a thirty minute tape of American dancer Traci Topps, as well as in America, via Big Top Video, with a feature length film starring a British porn actor who was to find later success in the U.S. under the name Dick Nasty, called *Mammary Manor For Sale*.

Neither John nor Dave were at that time proficient video editors and so were keen to employ me to cut all their new titles on a full-time basis.

Selling footage of American big boob stars back to the Big Top company in the U.S. seemed a bit like 'taking coals to Newcastle' as the saying goes, but Big Top were more than happy to let this gangly South African businessman do just that, giving him a fantastic deal that covered all his shooting costs plus profit for the American rights only, leaving John free to edit up video versions of the same sequences for distribution in the U.K and worldwide which would all be pure profit for him. And needless to say, while shooting these videos, John and Dave would shoot photo sets which they could sell to big boob magazines all over the world, creaming off yet more profit from the one shoot.

And so began a very long and happy relationship for me with John Graham, during which I edited virtually the entire U.K. Double D video catalogue, along with many feature length films for eventual worldwide video release. John even flew me to New York once just to do a one-day edit for Big Top, who were based in nearby New Jersey.

One of the many feature length films I edited for John was the original *Duke of Knockers.* This film won the American AVN (Adult Video News) 'Best Speciality Tape' Award of 1993 (the porn equivalent of an Oscar). I was amazed, as the film had been shot simultaneously with another feature length movie with the same cast over the period of a week. It was then common practice to hire a location and a group of models and make two or more films 'back to back' to economise on costs, shooting scenes from both movies 'out of context' over the period.

However, little regard had been made to continuity and, when I came to edit *The Duke of Knockers*, I found that I was forced to let dreadfully bad continuity edits slip through. In one scene the main starlet walks through a door wearing one dress, and enters the next room in a completely different outfit! The fact that this film won an award unfortunately goes to show just how little attention is actually paid to the artistic detail of porn films, a fact I have since often recalled when struggling over a difficult edit. I pride myself on being a bit of a perfectionist who will re-do an edit over and over until I feel it is just right – but obviously in the porno world, unnecessarily so. And *The Duke of Knockers* certainly put that into perspective for me.

John often trusted me to 'sort things out in the edit', including a scene that had been completely shot on the wrong camera filter, so that the entire scene had a blue hue over it. Another time I noticed that a number of scenes looked as though John had shot them with a smoke machine on, as there were constant wisps of smoke floating across the lens, giving all the shots a hazy look. The reason however was soon easy enough to guess – John was a chain smoker and had a constant cigarette in his fingers, even when filming, which meant that there were often plumes of smoke drifting past the lens while he shot the sex scenes!

John brought many of his American big boob superstars to England where they graced the front page of Sullivan's *Daily Sport* newspaper. They also got all John's staff not only complimentary entrance to, but also the best seats in, London's Planet Hollywood restaurant and the best London night-clubs, and they stopped traffic as we filmed them flashing their huge boobs outside the London landmarks of Tower Bridge, Big Ben, Nelson's Column and St. Pauls.

Perhaps one of John's greatest coups however was when he hired the specialist make-up artist who had apparently built the 'Alien' for the film of that name, to create enormous 70" FFF breasts out of soft latex, which were glued on to a leggy young blonde whose natural bust line was actually only about a 34A.

It took a full eight hours with the make-up team until these fake latex breasts looked like a genuine part of her anatomy. Then a further eight hours were spent, through the night, shooting two videos and taking several rolls of stills. Everything had to be done in one long session as once the breasts were removed they were unusable for re-attaching and had to be thrown away.

The model danced around rather unconvincingly in my opinion, as the breasts, not being filled with anything but air, were far too light. A woman with genuine 70"FFF breasts, of slim build and with a 26" waist would hardly be able to walk without support, let alone jig around John's studio to music!

But the magazine readers and viewers of the video which I edited seemed convinced, and 'Zena Fulsom' was born, and so successful was she that she went on to make another (hardcore boy/girl) video, and later even introduced us to her younger (and thanks to the same special effects team, equally well endowed) 'sister' – Cindy Fulsom!

When 'Zena Fulsom' did her first hardcore shoot, I wondered how the stud managed to do the scene with a straight face – I had found it hard in the early days to do a scene with a girl who had real breasts, but having to have sex with a girl who was wearing giant false latex ones? I think it would have been a huge turn-off no matter how pretty the real girl inside them actually was.

John Graham's work was very prolific. He churned out videos and magazine photo-sets at a rate of knots, soon amassing more than enough material for the next year and a half – and still he continued to shoot, bringing more women over from America and auditioning new large busted girls from the U.K.

Given, at that time, his very limited studio set, one could be forgiven for imagining that all of America's big breasted women not only shared the same apartment, but all slept in the same brass bed, and all shared a preference for gaily coloured scatter cushions instead of pillows, as John and Dave would shoot one model after another against the same backdrop before changing it.

I soon became aware of other photographer's equally limited sets and quickly began to recognise which photographer had shot what particular photo-set when flicking through a magazine purely by the backdrops or the bed the girl was lying on rather than by a photographer's particular style of shooting.

Very often John's girls wouldn't make enough audible moans of pleasure to create an authentic soundtrack to accompany the videos of them writhing around in mock orgasm, and so I would get which ever model happened to be in that day to do a live voice-over of moans and groans to the video of whatever model had been too quiet, as I edited the pictures together in my tiny broom cupboard of an edit suite.

It struck me on several occasions what a weird scenario this was: I would be sitting at the edit controller, headphones on, with a fully clothed beautiful girl sitting next to me, who I had only just been introduced to. We would both be intently staring at the video image of a different girl, who was writhing around naked, while the girl next to me was breathing orgasmic moans into the microphone. Then I would say 'thanks very much' to her and she would go off to get ready for her nude on-screen appearance, which might be similarly dubbed by someone else a week or so later!

John was soon selling his videos and photo-sets all over the world. Photographer Bob Tanner remembers him speechless with excitement one day after receiving a cheque from Holland for some video footage that had already covered its costs several times over by the sales to America and the UK.

John's big boobed models were particularly popular in Japan where girls of such stature are definitely not the norm. John arranged for one busty model from Prague to be flown over to Japan to be interviewed by the editor of top girlie magazine *Bachelor*. English was obviously not the first language of either party but nevertheless, the interview had to be conducted in English as the resulting video footage was to be sold worldwide. It was almost painful to watch them both struggling to hold a conversation complete with lots of 'I'm sorry?', 'Pardon?', and many misunderstandings. But nevertheless, despite all these minor pitfalls and potential problems, John's business continued to flourish – and I with it.

Chapter Twelve:
THE PORN MACHINE ROLLING ON

While working for John Graham I discovered a big secret to success in this business – learn the skills!

It seemed that everyone wanted to get involved in the 'production' end of adult movie-making and so, in order to bluff their way onto the set and thereby get close to the horny young starlets, they would pretend everything from having shot photographs with Patrick Lichfield to having made movies with Spielberg!

I on the other hand really did know how to operate both a video camera and an edit suite as I'd been genuinely doing just that as my living for almost a decade, learning my trade hands on and from 'the ground up'.

But I actually didn't like to be involved at the production end of things, preferring the 'magic' of putting the programme together rather than the tiresome business end of seeing the girls going through their motions on the day, pretending orgasm when in reality they were moaning off-camera that it was the wrong time of the month for them, or that the shoot was going on too long etc.

If I wanted to get close to a new model, I could easily get her phone number and give her a ring like any normal person.

And so, to a lot of the models passing through John's studio, I may have appeared as a kind of enigmatic figure, locked in a windowless edit room, watching and re-watching their performances but never over-keen to be personally introduced to them or make a move on them. This alone may have made me a more interesting character to meet than the ones who had just been twelve inches from their fannies and possibly spent all day trying to get off with them.

Models are after all people just like the rest of us, and appreciate someone who is interested in them other than just as a piece of 'glamour pussy'.

Consequently some of the American models that John Graham brought over were quite keen to socialise with me after their shoots, although I usually preferred to work late and go home to sleep! I did however get to know American model Tawney Peaks as she made regular trips over to John's studio, and another model Zoryna Dreams even invited me out for the evening to see the rock musical *Forbidden Planet* in London. She insisted on paying for my ticket, buying us champagne in the interval and taking me for a nice meal after the show, which she also insisted on paying for. I then drove her back to her hotel and said goodnight. There was no invitation to come in either for coffee or for anything else and I certainly didn't press it. Much like Deborah in Brighton, I think Zoryna had just appreciated a night out with a guy who was treating her as a real person for once, with interests outside the porn industry, rather than looking at her as some kind of big- breasted 'sure thing'.

Zoryna told me that U.S. porn star Lynn LeMay had had 'a thing' for me when she had recently been over shooting with John, something I had been completely unaware of, locked away in my edit suite! Who knows what opportunities I may have missed out on with any number of well-known porn starlets due to my disinterested attitude?

Danni Ashe flew over to be photographed and filmed by John and his team, and Steve Berlyn, then one of John's photographers, and I went out in the car to shoot some pictures and video of her flashing her boobs around Big Ben, Nelson's Column and all the other great landmarks of London.

Danni Ashe was in the Guinness Book of Records as the most downloaded woman on the Internet. On December 5th, 2000, Danni Ashe recorded the historic billionth download of her image from her website. Her skills at marketing her website, Danni's Hard Drive, has to be admired, as it is more than just her pretty face that has put her where she is today.

Danni's Hard Drive was sold in 2004 to John Morisano and, in 2006, Penthouse Media Group Inc bought Danni.com and Video Bliss Inc. (owners of the website) for $3 million.

According to Wikipedia, Danni is the only woman in the world who has appeared on the cover of both the Wall Street Journal and Juggs magazine!

As a parting gift to us, Danni left her underwear in the car when she left – if only eBay had been around in those days, I'm sure I could have sold them for a small fortune!

I was thrilled to meet big boobed model Tiffany Towers when she came over for a shoot, as I'd become a bit of a fan while editing up her tapes. The video image can be deceiving however as, seeing Tiffany writhing around in solo sequences, I had thought she was tall and willowy. When I got to meet her however I was surprised as how very short she actually was in real life and in fact I had nothing much in common with her and nothing much to say to her, although she did autograph one of her box covers for me as a souvenir.

Meeting your pin-ups literally in the flesh is sometimes different from what one might think, and I soon learned that I actually preferred creating the fantasy in the edit suite to seeing the cold realities of production with all the inherent problems of girls not turning up for work on time, having to disguise the fact that they were on their period etc, or simply seeing the reality that the girls are only putting on the sex for the camera – they're doing it for the money and not for the turn-on, as the viewers would all like to believe.

So I decided there and then that I wanted to specialise in editing rather than in the production side of porn – to create the on-screen magic, because there was no doubt that, for me, it was the creation of the fantasy in the edit room that was the exciting part of film-making; the moment when all the planning, ideas, and hard work prior to that moment finally take form and give birth to the finished product.

There were many people involved in the industry who could 'blunder through' a job, but not many it seemed who could do the job as technically well as if it were a T.V. commercial or an advertising shoot, and even then all those 'blunderers' were all on the production side. The editors were usually the directors themselves who, as it was their film, were the only ones prepared to sit alone in a darkened room late into the night to meet the deadlines, painstakingly piecing the footage together.

Very often porn directors in those days were simply ex-photographers who, like John, saw a buck to be made in video and so turned their hand to it, with little or no technical training in correct televisual techniques.

Rex/Peter was an exception; he took trouble to learn the skills of his trade, and he took a real pride in his editing. My editing skills had been vastly improved after I'd worked with him in Lincoln, and for that I will always be very grateful.

I soon found however that, after I'd been working with John for a few months, other people in the business were noticing his new editor and were quietly slipping me their business cards, seeking out my services as an editor, cameraman or production consultant for their own films. I wasn't doing anything that clever with John's films but, due to the shortage of properly trained editors in the industry, everyone thought I was amazing – finally my career in adult production seemed to be taking off.

A friend of Lindsay's, the international porn producer Bill Wright, who now makes films for *Private* among others under the 'nom-de-porn' of Frank Thring (a name I believe he nicked from an actor's name he saw in the credits of the film *Mad Max*), was introduced to me at a celebratory *Penthouse* party at Peter Stringfellow's Hippodrome night-club, where I was also introduced to Mrs. Moser, Sarah Young, who seemed tipsy and keen to flirt with everyone.

Bill Wright was a curious mix of the intellectual professor – his London flat was stacked to the rafters with old leather bound books – and the worrying pervert. Actually much younger than he looked, he seemed to enjoy playing on the image of being a dirty older man, while also playing on his strong English accent, both of which seems to have got him a long way in progressing his talent as a producer with both the American and the European adult markets.

Following my meeting with him, Bill offered me work as camera assistant and editor on a film he was shooting in London called *Lusting London Style* with European porn stars Christoffe Clarke and blonde starlet Sandrine Van Herpe, along with American porn star Madison Stone, who has since gone on to make appearances in a number of more mainstream movies as well.

John Graham's business colleague Dave Wells was also involved in the film, and Lindsay was cameraman on the job, also playing a cameo role at the end which, although small and verbally improvised on the day, virtually stole the show.

Bill used a very good American lighting director and, with Lindsay on camera, a top international cast and me on the edit, he could hardly fail to produce a good film.

I was to learn from Bill that this was indeed what had made him, and anybody else that follows his dictum, into a good producer. Surround yourself with a talented crew and cast and you can't go far wrong. If the film is a success, it will be you that takes the glory, as it was indeed you that booked the talent that made it such a success! If it fails, then you can blame your crew, blame your cast and move on to the next project, saving face.

During the shoot I met the American lighting director's girlfriend of the time, who was a little known English model called Joanna Gee. After a boob job and a successful move to L.A., she became better known as the porn star Taylor Wane. She has gone on to become a director herself, as well as having made appearances on a number of mainstream 'reality style' American TV programmes.

When we met up with Madison at her hotel for breakfast on the first day of the shoot, she was decked out in a very revealing outfit that had 'Fuck Me' written all over it in black letters. In her brazen American way she told us that, if she did that for a living, people might as well know about it! I was reminded of Australian Nicola in the *Rock'n'Roll Ransom* blatantly telling the taxi driver how she earned her money. Maybe there's something more up-front in one's attitude to life and sex when you don't come from stuffy old England!

We were shooting in a big old house in Greenwich, South London, and toward the end of the shoot, while we were filming a gang-bang scene in the large open hallway, there was a bang on the front door and a voice called out: 'Open up! It's the police!'

We ran around, the models hastily getting dressed while we hid the camera tapes, only to open the door to discover some kids laughing their heads off. They'd seen what was going on through a chink in the curtains and decided to play a prank!

The middle-aged woman who owned the Greenwich house was herself an interesting character. She had been hiring her home out as a location to adult film companies since the 1960s and she often asked for a copy of the finished tape as she clearly had a personal interest in what was being filmed. The look of the place had hardly changed at all for decades, and was full of both priceless antiques and junk shop curios, and it was often difficult to tell which was which when moving things around while preparing a room for a scene, not knowing what one should be especially extra careful with!

Doing the edit for *Lusting London Style* I included out-takes underneath the end credits as they rolled up which, with a cast of French, American and English speaking actors, were quite hilarious in accent alone, as they all struggled to communicate Bill's involved script without fully understanding a word of what they were saying.

I did a good job with the edit however and, on the music soundtrack, even managed to mix in a tiny bit of David Bowie's *Space Oddity* so subtly that no-one ever spotted it was there – and so no copyright fee to pay!

My work with Bill earned his praise to the extent that, on another shoot, he flew me over to Rotterdam in Holland initially to help out technically, although I ended up not only advising on camera angles and lighting, but also doing some of the camerawork and even playing a cameo role of the detective in the film!

I ambled around the Rotterdam docks looking thoughtful and moody in a light downpour of rain and, later on, mouthed a suitably Marlowe-esque voice-over onto tape.

For a great location Bill had booked us all into the Presidential Suite at the Rotterdam Hilton. As I was the only one out of all the cast and crew who owned a suit, the suite was booked in my name. The Hotel staff were told that I was a very special VIP from England travelling with expensive production equipment which must be stored with me in my suite, thus giving us a perfectly legitimate reason to have full production equipment in the suite with us. And, if we just happened to turn it on and make a porn film while we were there, well who was to know?

The day before we moved in, Michael Jackson had stayed in the palatial suite of rooms (huge bedroom, enormous lounge, two bathrooms, vast office, kitchen, etc), and the day after we checked out, The Artist then still known as Prince was moving in. We searched the rooms for any trace of a white sequinned glove but Michael had left no souvenirs. We on the other hand left Prince a pair of one of the girl's knickers as a little present.

The British guy who was the financial backer of this production decided that it would be safer to drive all the camera-tapes back to England with him underneath his car seat, rather than have Bill take them on an internal flight (Bill was then living in Holland) and, of course, he got stopped at the border and the tapes seized by customs officials and never returned. My detective role in the Presidential Suite was therefore never ever seen.

I was however paid off in cash, and drank complimentary champagne on an upgrade on the flight back to England. One of the models on the shoot was somehow convinced that I had put her name forward for the job and so was keen to show her appreciation to me when we got back. I never took her up on this however, and also never let on that it was in fact Dave Wells and not me who had been responsible for her getting the job!

Back in England I was almost immediately involved in another of Bill's shoots: this time at John Graham's studio where Bill, Dave Wells and I shot a beautiful French model that Bill had flown over to the U.K.

Driving us all home afterwards, she had sex with the hired stud in the back seat of Bill's car as we toured around Buckingham Palace to get to the hotel that the French girl was staying at. I wondered if the Queen was looking out at the time and saw what was going on? I guess it would all have made for good Anglo-French relations!

A make-up girl I knew introduced me to Page Three model and David Sullivan favourite Tara Bardot-Jackson, who was contemplating putting together her own video production, *Tara Bardot's Hot Sexy Video Show*. She was doing it in conjunction with her friend, a wealthy ex-public school entrepreneur called Michael, who made his living mainly by producing very British hard-core spanking films for sale in the United States and, via mail order, in England. He also ran a specialist-spanking magazine called *Roué,* and led a very extravagant playboy lifestyle, often throwing wild parties where coke, girls and alcohol all flowed freely in his fashionable London apartment.

He made a lot of money out of his spanking films, as his expenses on them were very low. He would shoot his 'epics' in the same style as I had filmed *Apple Pie*; straight on to ordinary VHS videotape, and editing 'in-camera' as he went. What then came out of his camera at the end of the day was virtually the 'master' tape ready for duplication!

Unfortunately however, when the dates were set for Tara's shoot, I was mostly unavailable, so I did all the pre-production but got my mate Mark to stand in as cameraman on the day.

My pre-production work must have impressed Michael however as I was soon being regularly employed by him as the cameraman on all his spanking films.

I was still mainly employed at John Graham's but it made a nice change from my work there to do a shoot with Michael on my day off. Michael's models were usually young, pretty 'schoolgirl' types with flat chests, and not the inflated amazons that John favoured for his specialist big boob market, so it couldn't have been more different from my work with John.

Lindsay took part in one of these films, happily playing the part of a supposedly well known ageing rock star (typecast?) and spanking a cute Chinese girl in an apartment owned by a runner that I'd met while I was working on a TV commercial.

Far from experiencing a difficult atmosphere on the spanking shoots, due to the fact that the girls were literally getting their hides well and truly tanned, there was always a great sense of silly fun, partly because Michael himself was like a big kid who took only the art of making money seriously. This meant that the girls were always happy to work for him, even though they couldn't show their rears on camera anywhere else for a week or so afterwards due to the red raw markings that they had received. Michael took a great pride in this and would sometimes point out their bums on videos he owned saying: 'Look! They must have shot that one just after they'd worked for me!

But Michael was a great guy at heart – really good fun to be with socially, and incredibly generous both with his money and as a person.

Through him I met a British photographer called John Thomson who was then acting as camera assistant on Michael's video shoots as well as being Michael's personal minder and chauffeur. John was later to become invaluable to me as camera assistant on many of my own shoots as well, eventually becoming a photographer and video cameraman himself whose services I would employ in the future.

The John Graham empire continued to flourish. He employed more staff and had taken over the whole floor of the office building where he had previously rented only one large room, renting out space to fellow photographers Bob Tanner, Peter Cawson and fellow South African Viv Thomas.

All of these photographers shot magazine glamour sets, but they all had their own specific styles and areas of interest as well. Peter Cawson, like John, favoured big-breasted girls, while Viv Thomas was rapidly building up a name for himself as a premier photographer of top quality glamour pictures and video internationally. Bob on the other hand worked on beautiful Athena-style black and white nude prints in his darkroom which however he never seemed happy with, and would then throw them in the bin. I would often fish them out to try and take them home and frame them to put them on my wall, as I thought they looked great. But once Bob had caught me doing that, he'd slice them up as well so they were totally unusable. A real perfectionist, he didn't want anyone to see anything he's done unless they were what he regarded as perfect.

I got freelance work with both Peter Cawson and Viv Thomas. For Peter I edited some of his big boob videos, and, for Viv, I shot and edited a 'behind-the-scenes' style video of ex-Page Three model Gail McKenna for the Japanese glamour magazine *Bachelor*. They were producing a glossy coffee table book of Gail as well as a slick accompanying video.

As well as being credited in the book for the video production, I also got a picture of myself in the book, video camera in hand, behind Gail.

It was a strange experience meeting Gail, now a sweet and ordinary young mum, as she had been one of the Page Three girls that I had often looked at in the tabloids when I was younger, thinking of her as a big unattainable star because she was in the papers – and now here I was inches away from her naked body, and we were both just work colleagues doing a job together.

While at John's I worked with Lindsay again as editor for the Linzi Drew video *I Love Linzi Too*, a follow-up to her very successful title,

I Love Linzi. Lindsay had 'borrowed' John's suite and me as editor for the work.

I was credited as editor on the video as 'The Fabulous Ricardo' and, while we were editing together, Lindsay mentioned a new project that he was planning – a British version of John Stagliano's successful 'gonzo' series Buttman. Lindsay planned to take a camcorder to the streets and film a reality-style sex programme (or 'adult film noir' as he pretentiously called it). He planned to make an initial series of ten films to launch with and was looking for an on-camera sidekick to work with on the shows, and asked me if I was interested. I said yes, but heard no more until I eventually heard that the films had been released – initially with porn stud Marino as his sidekick and with Lindsay re-inventing himself as an on-screen character called Ben Dover. And for Lindsay, the rest was history!

As John's company got bigger it was clear that my tiny edit suite that consisted of two machines and sat in what used to be Bob Tanner's photographic dark-room was fast becoming too small for the job.

I therefore set about designing a state of the art multi machine editing system, with various play-in and edit formats and complete with digital effects, which cost several thousands of pounds to build and install and was a rival to any competitor of the time.

Once it was installed John would proudly show guests round, telling them how this was the same as a suite at the BBC. Completely untrue of course, but I was flattered that John thought my work comparable to the top broadcast quality of Britain's 'Auntie Beeb'!

I continued editing the Double D series and got quite a kick, and a certain amount of professional pride, out of walking into almost any video rental store that stocked adult material, and gazing at the rows and rows of titles of which I had edited.

Things came almost full circle as Dave Antony (the photographer I met helping Rex/Peter on my first ever shoot) also came to work full-time with John, and then John bought the entire back catalogue of Peter's old video titles when it appeared that Peter's business in Spain had no further use for them. John would then sometimes require a different compilation of sequences for an edit, and so I found myself in the strange position of re-editing titles I had originally edited the first time around.

John soon established business in all corners of the Globe and my monthly editing deadlines increased to include two compilation videos cut to British (BBFC) standards, one feature length movie cut to American standards, a German compilation and a compilation for Japan, all of which required a slightly different type of cut.

This was a lot of work per month for just one editor and, on top of all my other work commitments with Michael, Bill, Viv etc, I was soon working flat out – and totally exhausted!

So, to keep the porn machine rolling on, John hired another editor so that we could operate a shift system and efficiently keep the edit suite working literally around the clock; twenty four hours a day. So 'new boy' John Chalk worked days and I opted for the unsociable night shift.

John Chalk was an incredibly talented young man who had set up a video system transfer business with a half Italian, half British guy who is now better known as porn director David Lever, or by his on-screen 'nom-de-porn' of Jim Slip.

John Graham would use their system transfer company, whose main business was corporate tapes and domestic work, to transfer his PAL system tapes to the American NTSC system before sending them off to the States. David, who at that time had no active part in the adult business whatsoever, would take more of a personal interest in John's tapes with every visit I made to drop off more films, until one day he took me aside and told me that he wanted to have a go at making an adult film himself. So inspired was he that he folded up his transfer business and set up his own adult production company within the year.

He went on to make numerous programmes for the UK satellite TV station Television X, has acted as producer/director on a number of productions for Hans Moser, and, under the name David Donnozetto, worked as lighting director for Lindsay on several of his films for *Private* and *Helen Duval*.

In folding up the video transfer business however, it left his partner John Chalk unemployed, and so, having also come into contact with us through the original systems transfer business, he came to work for John Graham as the day shift editor, a move that was to change the career direction of his life, moving him totally into porn.

After a few years working with John Graham, John Chalk left to set up the highly successful adult production company Rolling Images with Viv Thomas. John now no longer works with Viv but as far as I know is still involved in the adult industry creating high-end big budget material.

What with these new personnel changes, it was clear that the top floor of the office block from which John Graham presided over his ever growing empire was clearly also fast becoming a breeding ground for new adult production talent, and I was proud to be right there in the thick of it.

Chapter Thirteen:
THE MAINSTREAM PORNO CREW

With business partners that he had met through his magazine connections in the United States, John Graham set up *Score* magazine, a premier big boob title of which John was virtually the sole supplier of material as well as a major partner in its profits.

Together with *Score*, John also set up the 'Boob Cruise', an innovative idea where amateur photographer fans of the American big boobed models could book a holiday on a luxury clipper yacht sailing round the Caribbean. Also on board would be professional photographers (John, Dave or Viv) to give the fans advise on how to take good glamour pictures, and of course a host of well known big boob stars who were there not only to be photographed by the fans and amateur photographers, but also to socialise with them throughout the voyage.

A dream vacation for most of the fans, each expensive trip sold out and of course each trip gave John and his team an ideal opportunity to shoot behind the scenes footage which would of course result in yet another video release that both the fans that had attended as well as those that hadn't would eagerly buy; more revenue for John!

As an editor, shut away in the edit suite in London, I of course missed out on all the Cruise trips and, apart from my New York editing vacation, I was always left behind in the office when everyone else would go abroad on shooting trips. However, all the extra shooting meant that I was kept as busy as ever in my editing suite. And, as well as my full-time occupation now working nights for John, other work continued to flow in.

My accountant introduced me to one of his other clients, who was keen to make a series of glossy adult videos for worldwide distribution.

Tim Milsom was an interesting man to work for; a television producer by profession, he naturally approached the concept of adult film-making in terms of total professionalism, and relatively large TV style budgets.

As a producer however he would also try to keep the 'large budgets' he had available to the absolute minimum to ensure greater profits for himself of course.

It was not an uncommon practice in those days, particularly in America, to shoot a major feature length porn movie in just one day. *Lusting London Style* for example had all been shot in a day, with one extra scene and some pick-ups shot a day previously. Really big budget features had the comparative luxury of being shot over a period of one week – still a ridiculously small amount of time by real film industry standards of course.

Tim asked me that, if it was possible to make one feature length adult movie in one day then, with two crews working simultaneously, would it not be possible to make two feature length films 'back to back' on the same day, thus saving on location costs, make-up artist's fees and model's fees by utilising the same girls available so that they alternated between films throughout the shooting?

'It's possible in theory,' I mused, 'But to my knowledge no-one's ever tried it before.'

'So let's do it!' Tim said.

I worked out a tight shooting schedule, which relied on critical timing, allowing models time between scenes to relax and get re-made up, and to make sure that each filming crew were never working in the same part of the location at any one time.

Two scripts were approved and ten models were booked: five girls and five guys. I warned Tim of the unreliability of glamour models, so we not only phoned each one of them the night before to re-confirm everything, but also sent out 'call sheets' through the post (unheard of at that time in the adult industry), which set down in black and white all the relevant information, including the location address and phone number, time to arrive, relevant portions of script, crew and cast list, and various phone numbers in case of emergency on the day.

Such pre-production work was second nature to Tim as standard to the television industry but unheard of in the adult world however where, as with John Graham, models were more used to being told to turn up at around ten o'clock in the morning only to find, once they'd arrived (probably nearer noon), that a script would then be thought up on the spur of the moment and most things would be improvised along the way with as much input from the models themselves as there was proper direction from the production crew.

I was to be quite involved in this project, acting as co-producer with Tim, directing one of the camera crews, and editing both films afterwards.

We had booked the same big house in Greenwich that I had worked in on *Lusting London Style* and a full crew had been hired for each movie; cameraman, director and sound man, with one make-up girl and one lighting director running between the two film crews.

I booked my old mate Mark as Team B's cameraman. He told me to call him 'Noodles' and, when I asked why, he told me that he thought it would be cool to have a nickname and that he intended to tell everyone he met from then on that his name was Noodles, and when they asked why, he would just say, 'Everyone calls me Noodles; I don't know why'.

To my knowledge however, to this day I am the only person he knows that has ever continued to call him Noodles after he'd told them this.

Apart from Mark (AKA Noodles), I booked Lindsay as Team A's cameraman, and the technical crew were all culled from acquaintances from the mainstream television and film world.

The lighting guy arrived with a lorry load of film lights and accessories, the lorry itself being about three times the size of the old van I'd used on *Apple Pie* which had contained my entire shooting rig, crew, props, and two models!

I thought, on the day, about just how far I'd come since that shoot where I'd accepted two unknown models who'd work for £50 each, which was my entire budget for the film.

None of the girls on this production were earning less than £400 each, and Tim and I had spent weeks looking through model cards, meeting prospective girls, and carefully casting each role.

Tim, however, had taken more interest in casting the guys for the film, as he was something of a rarity in the heterosexual adult film industry; Tim was gay, and involved purely from lucrative business motives.

I think some of the girls found it strange that, on the day, he didn't come onto them, as this was obviously what they were accustomed to on most other shoots, and were therefore half expecting, or as Rex/Peter used to put it, 'the director's perks'! One model once said of David Sullivan: 'It's blow job or no job!'

As far as I was concerned, I was just happy to be working in a truly professional environment for once, and producing something of hopefully both erotic and artistic integrity.

Lindsay had brought a male stripper friend of his along on the shoot to 'see what went on' and to help out generally as a runner, shifting lights and cleaning up. He worked under the name of 'Top Gun', because he would strip from the kind of full air force uniform that Tom Cruise wore in the movie of that name.

The female star of one of our films was Misty McKane, and she was instantly attracted to 'Top Gun', and took me aside to ask if she could do a scene or two with him in the movie.

'Well, he's not actually here to be in the film,' I explained, 'He's just a runner.'

Misty was so disappointed however, that I approached the guy, explaining that he had an admirer who wanted to work with him. I could tell that it would be a wonderful sex scene if he did agree – the sexual chemistry would be real and, if that didn't make for great porno viewing, then I didn't know my job!

'Well, I don't mind doing a little cameo role,' Top Gun explained, 'But I don't want to take my pants off.'

I explained this to Misty, advising her with a wink to 'try and get the most out of him'. She assured me that she would, a wicked gleam in her eye and sure enough, by the end of the day, he had not only performed two hard-core sex scenes with her (one in an orgy with all the other models also taking part), but the pair were inseparable thereafter, and the next time I saw them, they had moved in together and were making plans to get married. Tim and I felt like a cupid style dating service, and were almost tempted to waive her payment in lieu of our introduction fee!

Even though the owner of the location was used to having adult film crews in her house she decided to entertain some guests in her garden on the same day and so, quite bizarrely, was trying to make tea and sandwiches in the kitchen while Misty and Kerry Matthews (doing her first ever hard-core video sequence) were hard at it on the kitchen table!

For the orgy scene, which was set in the big drawing room of the house, we paired everyone up and then just roved around with the cameras, both Lindsay and 'Noodles' filming hard and soft angles of whatever they could.

Lindsay got a cracking soft-core shot in the large wall mirror, and proudly shouted out: 'Oh yes! That's fucking art that is!'

He also told everyone that no one was to ejaculate until he said so, and got very angry when one poor guy couldn't help himself and came too soon.

'You bastard!' he yelled, 'Right! That's it! No-one cums until I tell them to!' Such is the power of the hard-core video director. He can seemingly even dictate when natural emissions take place.

This was even more miraculous with the male star of one of the films who had the task of having to perform and ejaculate five times in one day – enviable or not? You decide. One might think that sounds like a dream job; having sex with five different girls to orgasm, but in reality even hardened porn studs would find it hard to keep that going – and this was in the days before Viagra! He did surprisingly well however, and I think we only had to 'stunt dick' one of his cum shots.

At the end of the day, after shooting nine sex scenes, we still had one more scene to film. Shooting out of sequence, the final scene of the day was to be shot in the main bedroom's en suite, of Misty taking a bath. The owner asked us if we really needed to shoot this, as it was gone midnight and we were in her bedroom, and she wanted to go to bed and get some sleep! Given her attitude earlier with the garden party, I'm surprised she didn't just go to bed anyway, and let us carry on filming around her! I debated whether we could get away without shooting it, but I knew that this scene was important in making the total time of the movie up to the required seventy minutes, and we were paying her handsomely for the use of her house as a location – and in cash – so I stuck to my guns and the scene was shot.

At the end of it all, well over twelve hours after we'd arrived, I got into my car to drive home, Misty fast asleep beside me in the passenger seat. I was giving her a lift back home, while she dreamed of her new 'Top Gun' boyfriend.

I breathed a sigh of relief. I had done it! Every single one of the ten models we booked had turned up (and on time!), and my shooting schedule was fairly well adhered to, with the two crews never disrupting each other, and only coming together to jointly film the orgy scene at the end of the day, a scene I anticipated would benefit from having two cameras film it.

I had completed production of two feature length adult movies in one day, and everyone seemed to have enjoyed working for me.

I felt absolutely exhausted however. As producer of the two crews I was in demand all day long, with everyone calling for me to check this or that or to ask what was required in a certain scene. The buck had stopped with me all day, and now I just sat in my car and, for the first time that day, allowed myself to relax, ready for the drive home.

I closed my eyes for a moment. The films were both 'in the can', and if the footage was as good as it had looked on the on-set monitor, then my next job of editing them together should be both easy and enjoyable.

Once again I pondered on just how far I'd come, from producing a VHS shot film for £100 to producing two feature length 'American' style movies for a budget of around £20,000 that would be shown in both soft and hard versions all over the world.

I credited myself as Richard Stern on the movie credits, while Tim and his partner Deric Botham called themselves The Ricotini Brothers, Deric taking the name Paulo Ricotini (and creating a whole visual image for himself of a sleazy looking 1920s style mobster to go with it) while Tim opted for Virgil Ricotini, named after the character in the TV series *Thunderbirds*.

The editing proved to be far more time-consuming than I had anticipated however. We ran short on the final running time of the UK soft edit of one of the films, and had to shoot a further scene in Tim's office in Wardour Street, Soho to make up for it.

While we were setting up in his office, the door opened and in walked none other than Sir Paul McCartney! He was recording some music in a sound studio downstairs and had got lost trying to find the loo! A few moments later and he may well have come face to face with a blonde model nakedly straddled over a chair with a banana! Who knows what music he may then have been inspired to go back downstairs and record; probably something a little raunchier than *The Frog Song*!

Even with this new added scene, it proved difficult to keep both films up to the required running time of seventy minutes, and Tim and I were forced to use a lot of slow-motion and special effects during editing in order to 'stretch' some of the scenes out to reach the required running time.

We were using an edit suite in Wandsworth in South London that belonged to a guy I used to work for doing wedding videos. A gruff down-to-earth man, he had clearly never guessed, despite all his conversations with Tim, that Tim was gay. One evening he came in toward the end of our editing session to lock up and, seeing Tim's leopard print jacket draped elegantly over a chair, exclaimed: 'Blimey! Who's is that? It looks like some poof's been in here!'

Tim and I exchanged glances, and finished off our editing in bemused silence.

The two finished video films, *The Erotic Dreams of Natasha* and *Lindi – A Study in Lust* went on to sell well worldwide, with *Natasha* regularly shown on U.K. cable television station The Adult Channel to very good reviews.

Tim continued to produce top quality porn films, employing Bill Wright (Frank Thring) to direct his next one, in Los Angeles.

Naturally enough, Tim soon turned his hand to making and distributing gay porn, becoming the sole UK agent for all material of top American bi-sexual porn star Jeff Stryker, and producing/presenting a weekly gay night on The Adult Channel.

Tim's co-partner on the two-film project that I'd worked on proved to be not only a lucrative source of future work for me, but also became a very dear and valued friend.

Deric Botham had been involved in various dubious adult ventures for many years. As a younger man he claimed to have acted as production assistant on the legendary 'pony sex' films of European animal sex star Bodil and, before he worked with Tim, he co-ran another company with a guy called Andrew, producing adult films for sale mail-order.

These however were about as low budget as Apple Pie and, if anything, even less exciting! Due to ingenious marketing however, of which Deric proved himself to be a master, the company did very well.

Marketing (and a good box cover) is in fact the key to the successful selling of any adult film, which is clearly why entrepreneurs like

David Sullivan have done so well.

In Britain an adult film was then bought either as a direct result of the customer being attracted to the picture on the box in a video store, or by very glossy advertising in men's magazines. Now numerous sales are done over the Internet, but often still based purely on representative pictures and box covers. And, of course once the video or DVD has been bought, it is then too late if those photos didn't accurately represent the film; the sale had already been made, and few are going to be bothered to send it back.

The Advertising Standards Authority's code of conduct rarely seems to be enforced when it comes to adult material, and so luxurious and expensive photographs would adorn a box cover, and yet in no way relate to the film inside or the actresses appearing therein. Advertising can trick you into believing you are buying the hardest German import sex film ever made, and you find yourself watching a tame '18' rated feature film made in the early 1960's, and showing less nudity than can be seen every day on Page Three of *The Sun*! Remember Sullivan's '*Horse and Hound*' scam?

Once the customer has made his purchase he will rarely complain as, obviously, the type of material he was hoping to buy would probably have been illegal in the first place.

Therefore, most customers would just put a rip-off down to bad luck and vow not to buy from that company again.

Deric's ex-partner Andrew made a lot of money out of this principle. People would be mail-shot and offered the chance to buy the raunchiest hard-core video imaginable. They would send their money and, in return, they would be sent absolutely nothing.

A few months later they would be mail-shot again by what appeared to be a different company offering a similar video and, incredibly enough, many punters would fall for it a second, third, and even a fourth time, sending off their money in the hope that this time they would receive the raunchy 'crystal clear film, imported direct from our suppliers in Amsterdam' as promised. An account was set up solely to accept these 'orders', but no product was ever sent out in return!

The company did make and sell a number of genuine films however, all shot on very low budgets and all perfectly legal and certificated by the BBFC. It was clever marketing that sold these films too. A range of videos featuring a static shot of a girl obviously in her twenties changing in and out of different school uniforms was marketed as a 'jailbait secretly filmed schoolgirl video'.

Finding there was a big market for Asian girls, Andrew hired an Asian visiting masseuse through an escort agency and, through a two-way mirror, filmed her visit to him, giving him a massage and 'extras'. He then sold that tape as a 'hot Asian girl sex video'. He made a lot of profit on the video and his outlay had been the cost of a massage!

Perhaps his most inventive coup however was a film featuring a fully clothed girl wandering around a children's petting farm. She then entered a nearby building where, supposedly inside (but actually obviously shot on a different day in a proper studio) we see a man lying on a bed. The girl strips off and they simulate sex. After which the girl gets dressed and goes back out into the little farm.

The film was granted a certificate under the title *Animal Sex Farm*, although the BBFC warned that they were fully aware what he was up to. The company made a fortune out of this film as they could legally advertise a genuine film they were selling called *Animal Sex Farm*, with all its implications of illegal animal sex acts. And if anybody complained? Well, there were animals in the film, there was sex in the film, and there was a farm in the film; the title wasn't deceptive; what was the problem?

Deric loved to get in front of the camera at any opportunity too, hamming it up as an a comedy actor, and he was also a very fast and prolific writer and so, on the two films we made with Tim, he had not only written both scripts, but he had written cameo roles for himself in both movies, playing Natasha's over-worked and sexless husband in one, and playing a Germanic psychologist, reminiscent of Peter Sellers in *What's New Pussycat*, in the other.

Deric was also involved in a corporate consultancy business, making training and sales videos for various well known companies and, after seeing how I'd worked on the two films for Tim, he was keen to utilise my skills in his corporate film work.

And so I became involved in making a number of films for various companies including London Electricity and Texas Homecare. Deric had a real skill at script writing and coming up with surreal comedy scenarios that he would then persuade the companies to let us film. Consequently our business films went from straight 'talking head' information shorts to weird surreal comedies where, in one film for London Electricity, the cast included a naked shopper (played by Jim Slip!) and even God Himself (Jim Slip again) complete with long white beard and wings!

For the London Electricity films, which were aimed at training new staff, we cast a young unknown British comedian who has since gone on to enjoy a very successful television and stand-up career, Terry Alderton.

Unfortunately what I didn't know until the first day of shooting was that Terry was dyslexic and couldn't follow the auto-cue very easily. This made for a lot of annoyance from Deric, and a lot of apologies from Terry but, with some very understanding coaching and encouragement from his friend and fellow actor Matthew Bawcutt, who had also appeared in some of the training videos for London Electricity, he pulled off a memorable performance, starring in a series of programmes as the well meaning but incompetent salesman

Kevin Lustcombe.

I chose my crew for these films entirely from the porno world, using spanking Michael's assistant John Thomson as my production assistant, one of the sound-men that I had used on the *Natasha* shoot, and Jim Slip himself on camera. At one point I had even asked Lindsay if he could do some camera work for me, but he was getting too busy at that point planning his fledgling *Ben Dover* series. If only London Electricity and Texas Homecare's head offices had known that their sales training videos were being shot by the people behind most of the country's top porno films!

It was ironic really – I'd used crew culled from the mainstream film world to make porno, and now I was using porno people to make mainstream videos. I even tried to get Misty McKane to do a cameo role on a London Electricity shoot playing the part of a pregnant shoplifter but, ever true to model behaviour, she didn't turn up on the day of the shoot and had all her phones on voice-mail.

The only exception to my porno-based crew was a wiry South London guy called Jason who came on many of the shoots as production assistant. Very much an individual who didn't take being told what to do very well, he would roll joints while driving one handed along the motorway and melted the plastic surround of a television set in a London Electricity store by placing a hot filming light too near it on one shoot. He then had the cheek to ask the store owner, as it still worked and if they were only going to throw it away, if he could have it!

Once, when we were filming late at night in a closed London Electricity store in central London, a group of Japanese tourists, clearly attracted by the lights and cameras through the store window, stood at the window of the store gazing in – right in the back of my shot behind Terry! Despite all our waving to them, they refused to go away.

'I'll sort them out' Jason stated and, grabbing a realistically looking toy gun, a prop for one of the more zanier scenes that Deric had dreamed up, he ran at the window pointing the gun at them and, looking like Sid Vicious in the *My Way* sequence from *The Great Rock'n'Roll Swindle*, he screamed at the top of his voice for them to 'fuck off'!

To save on costs, all our crew had cameo roles in the business films we shot, and, possibly true to character, we cast Jason as a deranged shoplifter, blatantly carrying out a television set from one of the stores right under the nose of the security staff.

I myself appeared, complete with a stetson hat, as 'Cowboy Dave', an 'Arthur Daley' type of character who was in every way a 'cowboy' operator, with John Thomson as his assistant Nibby.

Deric, a middle aged man in a suit, always played the store manager as well as the main customers, and we utilised the brilliant comedy actress and voice-over artiste Caroline Bernstein, a well known face on all the *Beadle's About* sketches on Jeremy Beadle's TV show, as his wife.

Deric and I also mocked up two 1940's gentlemen for a very successful black and white safety at work sketch, inspired by the 'Cholmondley-Warner and Grayson' characters from Harry Enfield's TV series.

On another occasion, Deric, wanting a new shed for his garden, persuaded Texas Homecare to erect one at his home for filming purposes, part of the deal being that he got to keep the shed after filming was completed.

For this particular production, Deric had written himself two cameo roles; that of the generic 'husband' (Caroline Bernstein playing his wife) who purchases the shed, and that of the husband's aged grandfather. For this role, not wanting to splash out on the fee of a make-up artist to make him look older, Deric had simply gone out and bought an 'old man mask' from a joke shop. Made of rubber, it fitted completely over the head with holes for the eyes and two small breathing holes in the nose area, and resembled something you might wear for Halloween if you were trying to look like Freddie Kruger! The rubbery flesh was fat too yellow in colour to look natural and, once on Deric's face, looked nothing like the real skin that protruded from the sleeves of his jacket.

Deric stared at me through the eye-holes and then said, his rubbery lips not moving as he did so, 'Does it look real?'

Deric was paying my wage, so I delicately told him that it looked quite good. However, ultimately Texas Homecare was paying Deric's wage and, if the resulting film looked rubbish, Deric would blame me as the project producer. So, with no other option available, I set about putting make-up on the rubber mask to try and match the skin colour to that of Deric's hands.

It didn't look great to be honest but Deric, ever the optimist, told me to go into the garden shed where the other actors taking part were waiting, and tell them that 'the old man has just arrived'. Deric believed that if he told them that they were looking at a different person, who was actually an old man and not really just Deric wearing a rubbery old man mask, then they would all believe it. This incredible self-belief in his own abilities was something that I was certainly to see a lot more of from Deric in later years.

I duly went into the garden shed and announced quietly that 'the old man has arrived'! Deric then tottered into the shed and all the actors said, 'Oh hi Deric. Good mask!' I kept my head down and just got on with the camerawork!

Driving together to the Wandsworth edit suite where these corporate masterpieces would be put together, Deric and I would usually keep up a stream of silly banter, inventing little characters and sketches to amuse ourselves on the journey. We invented 'Young Theresa', a naïve uneducated teenager who gullibly fell for every pick-up line going from dirty old men and pornographers alike.

Two other characters that we invented were the dubious comedic duo Shagnasty and Muttley, rogue would-be pornographers and womanisers who were constantly foiled in their attempts at pulling women. As will soon be seen, Shagnasty and Muttley were to become a very real and familiar flesh and blood twosome later on.

During the 1992 General Election I corresponded with prostitutes rights campaigner Lindi St. Clair (the tabloid's 'Miss Whiplash') with regard to helping her budding political campaign.

She had launched her own political party, The Corrective Party, and asked if I would be involved in the production of her Election campaign TV broadcast. I would have loved to have done so, but by that time it was already too late to get anything filmed and edited before the Election took place.

Despite the attractions of numerous models and sexually oriented celebrities (including Lindsay's partner Linzi Drew) standing as candidates around the country for her Party, the voting British public decided to put the Conservatives back into power that year, and so Ms. St. Clair remained in the background of British politics.

I wrote to German porn mogul Hans Moser seeking work, and was actually offered a full time job editing his films. After much deliberation however I turned the offer down, as it would have meant a complete upheaval and re-location to Hanover in Germany, which, at that stage in my career I just wasn't prepared to do.

In some 'downtime', while at John Graham's, I re-edited my small masterpieces *Apple Pie* and *Young Girl Piano Lust*, into one video programme which I called *Home Shot Number One*. I got this certificated with the BBFC with an 18 rating certificate and began selling a few copies mail order again, my original £100 outlay still trickling in a small amount of on-going profit. I even offered it to David Sullivan to sell through his shops, as it was now a legitimately certificated title but, after sending him a viewing copy at his request, I heard no more.

While I was doing all this however; making bizarre corporate films with Deric, still working at night for John Graham, and doing my other freelance stuff, Lindsay had been getting by selling pirated hard-core videos mail order, along with his partner Linzi Drew, under the name Stephanie Perry. But all that was about to change quite dramatically.

Chapter Fourteen:
THE PRISONERS & THE CAVALRY

In March 1992, life changed dramatically for Lindsay and Linzi. They had been summoned to appear in court faced with charges of 'publishing obscene material for gain' and 'being in possession of obscene material' – the hard-core pirated videos that they had been selling mail order under the name Stephanie Perry, which was the female equivalent of Lindsay's 'nom-de-porn' of Steve Perry, the name he worked under as the producer of the 'Ben Dover' films, and that he had chosen after one of his favourite musicians, Steve Perry, the guitarist and former front man of the rock band Journey.

One of the customers on Stephanie Perry's mailing list was an undercover police officer who had been regularly buying videos for over a year. This seemingly slow and drawn-out investigation was apparently to make sure that Lindsay's business was indeed that – an on-going tax free profitable business as opposed to a quick one-off way of making some 'pocket money' cash on the side, which would supposedly have been looked at in a very different manner.

Because of their high profile in the adult industry, the Court was determined to make an example of Lindsay and Linzi and so, whereas a lesser-known couple may have been let off with a warning or a suspended sentence, Lindsay was sentenced to nine months in prison, and Linzi for four months.

Linzi was sent initially to Holloway Prison and was later transferred to Drake Hall in Staffordshire, while Lindsay was sent first to Brixton Prison, but was transferred after just five weeks to Send open prison in Surrey, just seven miles from his own home.

Linzi Drew was at that time the editor of a number of men's magazines Including *Penthouse* and *Mens Letters*. Her employers at *Mens Letters* responded to her imprisonment by making her the cover girl for the next issue and including a free bumper car sticker inside that bore the legend 'Linzi Is Innocent'. They also asked her to continue writing a sexy column for the magazine while in Prison, entitled '*Within These Walls*. Linzi agreed, but later said that it was a real difficulty trying to think up sexy things to say when surrounded by shrieking crazy inmates in the filthy squalor of a tiny cell. Hardly the sexually frustrated jailbirds acting out lesbian fantasies that most men would have hoped for!

Lindsay himself was apparently treated relatively well in prison by inmates and officers alike, who all looked upon him as a bit of a lad's hero and none of whom really regarded what he had done as a crime worthy of imprisonment.

He worked in the kitchens at Brixton, which got him out of his cell for more hours a day than the other prisoners, and at Send he worked in the gardens which, along with going to the prison gym, got him physically fit and gave him a sun tan so that, when I next saw him at his welcome home party later that year, he looked healthier and in better shape than I'd seen him look in a long while.

He was refreshed and renewed from his imprisonment and, rather than showing any signs of a remorseful reformed character from his spell in jail, he was ready to get stuck in to new porn projects, one of which he was already planning at his welcome home party, as I learned from one of the models who was there. Blonde Louise Lane was booked to do her first ever hard-core boy/girl sex scene in a film that Lindsay was going to shoot in a few weeks time and, later that evening, Lindsay asked me if I would join the crew as second unit cameraman on the project.

I was overjoyed at the prospect of working closely with Lindsay again and he filled me in on all the details.

With Bill Wright (Frank Thring), Lindsay had been commissioned to produce the first ever feature length video film for Private Pictures, the video division of Berth Milton's legendary *Private* magazine empire. *Private* now churn out videos and DVDs by the score, but back then they had only ever produced magazines, and this was their first ever foray into the medium of film, and I guess that Bill and Lindsay, two Brits, should have been honoured that they had been chosen to produce that legendary first ever video title for the Swedish based Company.

It was to be the first production, in what was to be a series of '*Anal...*' programmes, and this first one was to be called *Anal Academy*.

Produced by Lindsay and Linzi and directed by Lindsay and Bill, it had a multi-national cast, headed by French porn star Tabatha Cash, Dutch model Debbie Van Gils and genuinely bi-sexual British girl Louise Lane who, as previously mentioned, was doing her first (and I think only) hard-core boy/girl appearance.

The location was a large country house complete with gardens, outbuildings and tennis courts, that Lindsay had booked for a week on the pretext of doing a fashion shoot which naturally had to be kept very private and top secret as he was 'previewing the next season's fashions'. On this basis he had made sure from the house rental company that there would be no unannounced gardeners or staff turning up, and that, if there were, they could expect to see a lot of female models in various states of undress as they were changing in and out of costumes! I had to admire his ingenuity!

Model Debbie Van Gils immediately paired up with Louise and the two stayed that way for the duration of the shoot, sharing their bed at night as well as their time on-screen.

Ian Mitchell was also involved in the shoot – but this time he had been booked as location chef rather than the on-screen star. It seemed strange in a way to see someone who had played huge stadium gigs with The Bay City Rollers who were, in their time, the biggest band in the United Kingdom, now making sandwiches and tea for completely unknown porno actors. Such I guess is the fickleness of fame and celebrity!

I was sharing a room with Ian and, that first night over dinner, I thought what a great atmosphere it was – just like the old days of *Rock'n'Roll Ransom*; a good party atmosphere, with alcohol, anecdotes and Louise methodically building the longest joint I'd ever seen, and then, after she'd smoked it, methodically building an even longer one!

While we entertained ourselves in this fashion, Lindsay and Linzi went off to bed early, preferring to watch re-runs of old British comedy shows like *Blackadder* and *A Bit of Fry and Laurie* on cable TV. The male models too were professional enough to get an early night after drinking a protein enriched goodnight drink, made with several whole eggs, which were apparently good for producing thick gooey sperm in preparation for the next day's cum shot.

Studs seem to have their own ideas as to what kind of diet is good for them to have for the production of good healthy sperm. I remember, on one shoot I was cameraman on, two studs arrived at the location, breezed in and headed straight to the fridge to unload a parcel of fresh white fish, assuring the director on the way, 'Don't worry, mate; we've brought our own cod!'

Despite the protein enriched drinks the night before, however, the next day Lindsay began to have trouble with one of the studs he had booked: he could get it up on camera OK but had lost his erection for the cum shot. Problems already – and this was only the first scene of the first day!

As may be remembered from the *Natasha* shoot, Lindsay is not renowned for being sympathetic to actors who can't get 'wood' as it's called in the business, and so he dismissed the original actor and phoned a stand-by – a guy who had been wanting an opportunity to try out as a porn stud, but would be coming from literally miles away. He was asked to come and 'try out' on the basis that, if he couldn't do the scene properly including cum-shot, then he wouldn't get paid.

As it turned out, this guy could get it up and screw but he too lost it for the cum shot and, just like the old *Rock'n'Roll Ransom* days, Lindsay was again forced to ask any free guys not needed for a scene later if they could stand in as the stunt-dick.

The scene was being shot in a cold barn at mid-day sitting on prickly straw. I felt a bit sorry for the poor guy who had driven a long distance and was then expected to perform as his initial try-out in these uncomfortable conditions, but this is unfortunately what being a professional porn stud is all about!

Eventually, after several guys had tried to get hard and failed, or tried to cum and failed, one of the guys finally came all over the waiting model, with Lindsay commenting that he was like the Cavalry – coming right at the last moment to save the day!

In the edit however, *Private* left the stand-in actor's voice in the cum scene, so that anyone who looks and listens to the opening sequence of *Anal Academy* can easily hear that it's a different guy doing the close-up cum-shot to the one in the rest of the scene!

Bill Wright seemed to be like a frustrated actor himself and usually always wrote himself a hammy cameo role in every film he produced.

In *Anal Academy* he played the Principal of the Academy, and I even had a walk-on (or rather a walk-off) role as one of the lecturers at the beginning of the main orgy scene, where I'm taking tea in the main hall and wander off before any of the sex action starts. This meant that there was an extra person in the scene (at least at the beginning) for production value, but freed me up to operate my camera for the main action.

Having now made the initial connection with *Private*, and working under his 'nom-de-porn' of Steve Perry, Lindsay continued to work on the *'Anal'* series as well as other movies for *Private* but by this time Bill had moved on to other projects.

With *Private*, Lindsay was now ready to work on greater films with bigger budgets and shot in sunny European locations.

Although these days in the UK a big budget porno movie would cost much much more, in those days a big budget for an adult movie would be something in the region of maybe £5000 to £10000. Lindsay was then working on budgets for Private that were in excess of £30000; then a huge figure, and enough for him to fly an international cast and crew to sunny Spain, rent a luxurious villa as a location and buy some decent props, which he would then keep to re-use on other productions, having got Private to cover their initial cost.

I remained as second unit cameraman for him on these new projects and together we shot *Forbidden Desires* in a beautiful old manor house in rural Oxford, before moving out to Spain for the location shooting of *Lady in Spain* and *Money For Nothing, Chicks For Free,* which we shot in various villas that Lindsay rented from the millionaires who owned them.

For *Forbidden Desires*, Lindsay had blagged an old aeroplane interior as a set. This was built inside an old antiques warehouse near London's Tower Bridge and I had another cameo role as a snoozing passenger on the plane sitting next to a young guy while he was getting a blow-job from the 'air stewardess', Yugoslavian born porn star Draghixa.

The eagle-eyed that watch the final film may notice that the shots showing the exterior of the flying plane look very similar to the shots of a flying plane from the mainstream comedy film *Airplane*, and that is simply because they are exactly the same! Lindsay just 'borrowed' the footage from a rental version of the movie rather than pay the heavy fees for library footage when compiling the edit.

Lindsay made a cameo appearance in the movie as well – as a whistling milkman at the very end of the film.

Once again Lindsay had used the 'fashion shoot' scam while hiring the main location for *Forbidden Desires* in Oxford.

French porn star Lydia Chanel was flown over to perform in literally just one scene on immediate arrival before being driven back to the Airport straight after. Being a much in demand international porn star, she had made time for just this one scene in her busy schedule, and needed to get straight back to Europe to carry on shooting with other producers!

She was performing a boy/girl sex scene by the side of the indoor swimming pool, which was set in an outbuilding of the main house. This outbuilding had big windows that were in full view of the driveway, which was shared by the neighbouring villa. Lindsay had two members of the crew with walkie-talkies on the driveway to warn us should anyone unexpected turn up. Unfortunately the walkie-talkies weren't working properly and the first we knew of someone driving past the windows was when the crew members burst in and told us to pack up as someone had driven by, slowed down and clearly seen what was going on. I was on one side of the pool and, as Lindsay's first concern was to 'hide the evidence' (i.e.: the camera tapes that we had shot) he told me to eject the tape from my camera and throw it across the pool to him. Never great at ball games as a kid, I dreaded that I would throw the tape straight into the water, but nonetheless did as he asked. The tape sailed across the wide expanse of the pool, and I'm glad to say that, much to my relief, Lindsay caught it perfectly. Rushing off to hide the tapes, we cleared the equipment out of sight while Lydia and her co-star covered up their nakedness. Lydia's first language wasn't English so it took us a short while to make her understand why we were suddenly stopping the sex and covering everything up.

After half an hour had passed however, with no one showing up, we got the rest of the scene shot and hoped that the driver hadn't seen anything too incriminating. After all, it wasn't an offence to have sex in the afternoon in your own privately rented villa if you so wanted – just I guess a bit odd if you were having it professionally filmed by several crew with a mountain of video lights!

When the shoot was all over and Lindsay returned the keys to the letting agency however, he was informed that they were aware of what he had used the premises for and that he would not be welcome to use their services again.

However, he then received a further phone call from the actual owner of the property who had heard from the letting agency what had gone on but was ringing to let Lindsay know that he himself was fine with it, and if Lindsay wanted to hire the property for a porn film again, this time directly from him and by-passing the agency, that that would be fine – on the condition of course that he be allowed to stay and watch the action!

Consequently, the beautiful old manor house later became the on-screen home of Marino's character Dick Richards in the latter series of the Television X show *Superdick*, which Lindsay was to go on to produce for the Channel.

We shot the orgy scene for *Forbidden Desires* in a Grade II Listed

Victorian Folly in Kent, which the owner used for lots of private sex parties, and which was also used as a location in many sex films at that time, including as the exterior for the private gardens of Buckingham Palace in a sex series featuring Royal look-a-likes that was shot by Deric Botham for Television X, *Crown Chronicles.*

To introduce the *Forbidden Desires* orgy, Lindsay got the British based Russian glamour model Lana Cox to do a sexy strip tease. She didn't do boy/girl work herself at that time however, so left before the orgy proper got underway. Such was her fan base at the time that having her do a cameo appearance in the film could only boost sales when her name could be featured on the cover as one of the stars, even though she wasn't herself partaking in any on-screen sex action.

I had been contacted out of the blue by a guy who fancied his chances at being a porn star and wanted to know if I could help. I met him in an old pub in London, appropriately named Dirty Dicks, to get a photo of him, and his details. I passed these on to Lindsay, who was happy to try him out on the orgy scene as, if he turned out not to be any good (i.e.: couldn't get it up, or came too quickly), there would be plenty of other good stuff to film as there were at least four other couples all having rampant sex at the same time.

Perhaps a difficult thing to film, but something that Lindsay would always include in his films for *Private,* was a scene where all the stars had a big orgy and the two main cameras that Lindsay and I were operating would just rove around catching what action we could, but trying to both team up to get the best angles on any cum shots.

An orgy scene was a way not only of getting a great multi action scene which gave the movie good production value, but also of utilising all the models booked for their own one-to-one scenes in one big go.

The guy who had contacted me did all right in his orgy try-out, but as far as I know has never gone on to do any more work in the industry. Perhaps he was just fulfilling his own private fantasy that day – and getting paid for doing so.

Lindsay built up a core crew that he used for all the films he shot for *Private*; There was a professional photographer who was just shooting the girls for the box cover and promotional material, a professional make-up artist (usually female so that the girls could turn to her as a 'mother figure' if need be), Lindsay and Linzi were the producers, with Lindsay himself as director and first unit cameraman. I was second cameraman, Jim Slip (or David Donnozetto as he was credited on these shoots) was in charge of lighting, long-term friend and collaborator of Lindsay's, Freddie Morse was in charge of production and a lovely guy called Marc was not only in charge of sound but also stood in as a stud on the occasional scene and in all the orgy scenes, when he would set up a remote boom mike and then get stripped off to join in. Marc went on to a have a varied and successful career in the adult industry, working on many top class adult DVD productions and also as a producer on adult interactive cable TV stations.

Freddie Morse, who took his nom-de-porn from legendary mainstream rostrum cameraman Ken Morse, went on to work on the successful Tanya Hyde series of videos amongst others and, keeping it in the family, his son Will worked with Marino on his *Road Trip* movies and on many other adult film projects. And the father and son team have more recently worked together on the production of scenes for Bluebird Films UK.

Lindsay also took along a full time cook to provide a constant running buffet and hot evening meals, and at least one production assistant or 'runner' to help out with all the menial tasks of picking people up from the airport or station, getting the food shopping and stuff like that.

Lindsay regularly used the same porn stars as well; Yugoslavian babe

Draghixa, Belgium born stud Alberto Rey and, in complete contrast to Alberto's hunky physique, a very white skinned weedy looking British porn actor called Peter Allen, who would wander around the Spanish villas we'd be filming in, wearing socks with sandals and an oversized pair of shorts with the Union Jack flag emblazoned on them. Looking for all the world more like the Charles Hawtrey figure from the '*Carry On*' films, he couldn't have looked like a more unlikely porno star.

I once arranged to meet him at a well-known London fetish club, advising him to 'dress appropriately'. He assured me he knew what I meant, but turned up in smart jeans with a crease ironed down the leg, and a smart shirt and tie, as if he were perhaps going out to a trendy mainstream night-club.

On the shoots, Jim Slip and Marc would often come up behind Peter and get their dicks out as a joke just as a photo was about to be taken; this kind of humour was totally lost on alpha male Alberto, who couldn't understand why any male would want to get his dick out around another male – even as a joke! Having said that however, Alberto was very proud of his body and thought nothing of wandering around naked in front of all and sundry. I remember one evening when he chose to cook juicy pork bangers for us all on the barbecue and proceeded to do so completely naked! Needless to say, we were all careful when choosing our particular sausage!

Jim Slip and Marc meanwhile had formed what they called the T.Y.A – the 'Tight Young Arses Club'; a 'club' seemingly comprised of just the two of them in appreciation of young girl's bottoms!

When we flew out to Marbella to shoot *Lady In Spain*, I overslept and raced into the airport just in time to hear my name being paged over the loudspeakers. A stressed Lindsay was pacing up and down and ushered me onto the plane just in time, and we flew out to a fabulous villa, which Lindsay had procured for the shoot from a young millionaire who owned it.

There was a pattern to how Lindsay worked; it was all very professional. Linzi had worked out a tight daily schedule which included two main sex scenes, various 'pick-up' or continuity scenes, and a couple of extra scenes that Lindsay would shoot alone on one camera. These were additional scenes that Lindsay would sell on independently for extra income, his production cost being nil as all the talent were paid to be there anyway.

There was also time factored in where the girls would have photos shot by the photographer for the purpose of the video box cover. It should be noted that getting well lit and well set up photographs for the box cover was a very important task, rather than just getting a few snaps as we went along or downloading some stills from the actual video footage. It should be remembered of course that, as a rule of thumb, people in a sex store, or indeed buying on-line, are going to make that snap purchase decision by the pictures on the box cover alone, so the better they look, they more likely the producer will have of getting a sale. Once the video or DVD has been bought, even if the footage on the tape bears little resemblance to the pictures on the cover, few will bother to complain or ask for their money back. Not that the pictures Lindsay's photographer were taking were in any way misleading: we had beautiful women in a beautiful location performing hardcore sex acts; they couldn't not look great!

Although the whole production was being financed by *Private*, as just mentioned, Lindsay was using the paid-for location and models to also shoot some extra 'vignettes' which could then be sold on to other companies as separate works, costing him only his time and tapes as clearly all other costs were all ready covered by the *Private* commission.

On this basis, apart from any extra scenes that *Private* had commissioned, that were to be used on their new *Private Video*

Magazine series, a kind of magazine style video, Lindsay shot several short boy/girl and single girl scenes which he sold on to the UK adult video company Electric Blue, as well as a couple of scenes for the forthcoming video that I was to edit with him, *I Love Linzi Too*.

During an outdoor threesome for *Lady In Spain* between two guys and one girl, Lindsay told me to film some facial 'cut-away' shots. A 'cut-away' in this case was a close-up shot of someone's face for the editor to 'cut away' to visually in order to break up the visual narrative of the scene. So I filmed a little bit on all three faces but afterward Lindsay blew his top.

'You're meant to film just the girl's face!' he stormed, 'Who wants to look at a bloke's face when you're having a wank?'

After this incident, Lindsay didn't work with me again and it wasn't until a year later, after Jim Slip intervened on my behalf, that I got back on the team as second-unit cameraman on another film Lindsay was shooting in Spain for *Private*, *Money For Nothing, Chicks For Free*.

With his love of popular music, Lindsay had of course taken the title of that production straight from the Dire Straits song of the same name.

Once again all the familiar faces that Lindsay liked to work with flew out to Spain and this time I made the airport with plenty of time to spare.

Once more we were staying in millionaire's mansions, two of them this time, with the crew and cast spread out over both. Each had its own private pool and both were used as filming locations.

Our main star for *Money For Nothing, Chicks For Free* was the beautiful Kai Nobel who loved sex and was happy to do any additional scenes (on or off camera) that Lindsay could arrange. Naturally, Marc dropped his boom mike and jumped in for an extra scene for Electric Blue, where he shagged Kai over the villa owner's motorbike. Getting ready for his scene, and trying to look like a 'biker dude', he made us all crack up as he donned leather trousers, crash helmet and false handlebar moustache to do an impromptu impression of one of The Village People! As the villa we had hired was owned by a gay millionaire, Marc's camp impression probably didn't go down as well with him as it did with the rest of us however!

Once again, Alberto was at a loss as to understand our British sense of humour and why we would want to dress up and pretend to be gay men! In reality of course Marc was about to have very heterosexual sex with a beautiful porn star so, at the end of the day, what did a little fooling around matter one way or another?

A representative from *Private* would sometimes make an appearance on the shoots to see that all was going according to plan, on one occasion handing out prized T-Shirts to all us guys, bearing the Private logo on the front and the word 'CREW' on the back. These visits however were generally something that Lindsay hated, as his ideas on production were very different to the business-like ones of theirs, which certainly didn't include much humour, and humour was something that Lindsay loved.

When shooting a three-boy/one girl vignette, Lindsay opened the scene with a pan across all three boys reading porno magazines. The first two were reading *Private* magazines, but the third (to introduce an element of humour and because Lindsay was a big *Thunderbirds* fan) was leering over a book about the Thunderbirds puppet character Lady Penelope! True to form, Private contacted Lindsay when they came to edit the scene, asking him if he didn't have enough *Private* magazines to go round when the scene was shot!

English not being the first language of the *Private* organisation also caused some problems. Lindsay's original title for *Lady in Spain* was *Laid in Spain*, a title that got changed by *Private*, possibly thinking that Lindsay had spelt it incorrectly.

Shooting the films in Spain I began at last to feel as if I had really 'made it' in the adult business. I would wake up in a millionaire's villa and be driven down the road to another millionaire's villa where we would shoot hardcore sex with beautiful international porn stars all day by the pool, and then party into the evening with free flowing wine and half naked girls. One night, as I watched Jim Slip snort coke from the naked bottom of one of the girls, I mused that this must be what it was like to be a rich rock'n'roll star.

I ambled outside sipping a cold beer and gazed up at the clear night sky studded with stars. Lindsay and Linzi had survived jail and were once again living the high life of porno that they had been imprisoned for in the first place. To an outsider, and indeed to me at that moment, this was surely what 'living the dream' in Porno-Land was all about.

If one believes that one's destiny is written in the stars however, then those same stars that I gazed up to in Spain would soon be calling me back home to London and diverting my career path into a very different avenue of the adult business – and one that I not only hadn't yet tried, but hadn't even considered.

Chapter Fifteen:
REALITY BECOMES FANTASY

Linzi Drew had for several years been the Editor of *Penthouse* magazine, whose British franchise was then owned by Fantasy Publications, a company which was itself part of a larger more mainstream publishing group. Linzi's contract was due to expire and Fantasy Publications weren't planning to renew it as Linzi was, during their time of reconsideration, residing in nick at Her Majesty's Pleasure.

While Deric Botham and I had been shooting the corporate films, I had mentioned this to him as a bit of gossip, as Deric had got to know Lindsay and Linzi after working with Lindsay on the *Erotic Dreams Of Natasha* project.

Never one to miss an opportunity, and without even telling me what he was going to do, Deric wrote to Fantasy Publications applying for the job of *Penthouse* magazine Editor, more or less on the basis of 'nothing ventured, nothing gained'.

One had to admire his balls in doing so, as he had no previous experience of magazine editing, let alone a men's magazine and let alone what was at that time one of the most prestigious and internationally renowned mens' magazines of all!

Nevertheless, experience and reality have never held Deric back from having a go at something that he wanted to do, and so he wrote to Fantasy Publications a very convincing letter, bluffing that he had been the Features Editor for British men's magazine *Fiesta* for several years, and informing them that he thought the current style of *Penthouse* was poor and out- dated, but that he knew just how to make it better and how to make their sales increase.

Under the name Clarence Stribes, Deric had indeed been writing short pieces for *Fiesta* magazine, which was a lower grade men's mag compared to the glossy *Penthouse*, and published by a rival magazine company, but my understanding was that he had been just a freelance monthly contributor, not their Features Editor at all.

He wrote an article in *Fiesta* about the making of *The Erotic Dreams Of Natasha* and *Study In Lust*, with much reference to me and my involvement in the making of the films. They published the two page feature complete with a cartoon that was a spot-on caricature of my face, something that either had happened by pure chance as no one at *Fiesta* magazine had ever met me, or by Deric having described me so vividly in the article that their cartoonist was able to draw my likeness so well. I of course like to believe it was the latter and got in touch with the cartoonist after I had seen the piece in order to buy the original artwork as a souvenir.

Deric continued to write anecdotal stories about me in *Fiesta*, basing these stories on truths or half-truths, but building my image up in much more detail, and making me out to be some sort of laddish playboy, incorrigible in a never-ending search for nympho babes to seduce and conquer in the name of porn.

Deric stylised my private life, making it out to be one constant sex orgy, something at the time that I found quite amusing, flattering, perhaps even mildly embarrassing but actually quite harmless. Little did I realise however that he was giving a kind of life and image to the character of 'Ric Porter' that was to become associated with me for many years after, whether I wanted to shake off that image or not.

In his letter to Fantasy Publications, Deric argued that the glossy out-dated and sanitised images of the women portrayed in *Penthouse* magazine were no longer relevant to the 1990s and that people now wanted to see naked girls who looked like the ordinary girls next door, rather than the unattainable and airbrushed 'perfect tens' usually portrayed in magazines like *Penthouse* and *Playboy*.

Based on this letter, the bosses at Fantasy duly called Deric in for an interview and so Deric, who had dabbled in the world of porn film-making but was in reality earning his living making training films for blue-collar British corporations after having been a sales executive for the electrical retailers Currys, now found himself sat round the boardroom table with the company bosses of British *Penthouse* magazine who were seriously considering giving him free reign to run one of the most prestigious and high-profile adult magazines in the Country.

Looked at it that way, it was against all the odds, but very much due to Deric's amazing ability of self-belief and self marketing as well as being able to generate enthusiasm in others for his ideas, that he persuaded Fantasy Publications to give him the job of Managing Editor of not only the British edition of *Penthouse*, but of the whole 'Fantasy' group of magazines; at that time around thirty top shelf titles that included *Asian Babes, Big Ones, Electric Blue Magazine, Black & Blue, Big & Fat, Over 40*, and many more mostly niche titles, as well as the more prestigious *Forum, Penthouse Letters* and *Video World* titles. This was a dream come true for Deric, who had clearly for a long time dabbled on the outskirts of 'Porno-Land' but was desperate to live and work in its heartland.

Deric loved to continually invent new characters under whose guise he could work and write and, following on from his Clarence Stribes character in *Fiesta*, he now became 'Doctor' David Michaels, a sex counsellor who, in an early issue of his *Penthouse* take-over, offered a sex advise audio tape free with the magazine. Deric himself, as 'David Michaels', in a photo surrounded by half naked girls, appeared in an accompanying double page spread, with pictures shot by regular *Penthouse* photographer Jeff Kaine.

Previously *Penthouse*, like *Playboy*, had aimed its market at the intelligent reader, littering its pages not just with airbrushed pictures of naked girls, but also with interviews with celebrities, car, film and restaurant reviews and short stories from well-known writers. Deric however had other ideas.

He adhered to P. T. Barnum's philosophy that one should 'never underestimate the stupidity or gullibility of the general public', and always aimed at the lowest common denominator but, also like Barnum, with as much style and pizzazz as a showman or fairground barker exhibiting a new fascination for everyone's delight.

Fascinated by pop celebrity, royalty, politicians and look-a-likes, in 1994 Deric persuaded the *Penthouse* bosses to let him commission Jeff Kaine to shoot a photo spread featuring look-a-likes of Princess Diana and Prince Charles naked. With the wisdom of hindsight, this now seems an incredible exercise in bad taste, but in the early 1990s Princess Di was regarded by many as an absolute babe who many lusted after and fantasised over.

The 'Princess Di issue' of *Penthouse* sold very well, and spurred Deric on in his belief that his ideas of taking *Penthouse* downmarket to the level of the tabloid reader rather than to those of the intellectual broadsheet reader was indeed the way to go.

Just as Deric had written about me in *Fiesta* magazine, he was still keen to give me exposure in the titles he was now in control of and, to that end, he arranged for me to be interviewed for a feature in *Forum* magazine as one of Britain's (then) few hardcore porno director/actors.

Forum was a small A5 sized magazine that had more text in it than pictures, thus making it something for those that took their erotica 'seriously' as opposed to those that just wanted a quick one over a picture of a pretty girl!

Their long time editor Liz Caldwell came to my edit suite at John Graham's to interview me, and I provided her with a photo to accompany the piece; a picture that Bob Tanner had snapped as I was leaving work one evening, in order to test out his new camera. Luckily it was one of the few that I had managed to get from him before he discarded it as being too imperfect!

In the picture I had a day's stubble, wore dark glasses and had long tousled hair and, when the article came out, Deric was convinced that I would be inundated with fan mail from *Forum*'s female readership. However, just as when Deric believed that he could affect people's reactions to him when wearing the old man mask by simply telling them he was an old man, his belief that his positive thoughts about the article would transfer onto the reader's actual reactions didn't work, and I of course received no fan mail whatsoever.

Now that Deric had to see his original proposals of sales growth of *Penthouse* through to fruition, and inspired by the success of the Princess Di piece, Deric proceeded to take the magazine downmarket, losing many of the air-brushed American models and replacing them instead with pictures of ordinary 'girl-next-door', even 'housewifey' types photographed in their own homes and wearing their own mis-matched bras and knickers, in photo spreads that were more akin to tackier magazines like *Razzle* and *Escort* than to *Penthouse* or *Playboy*.

Always a prolific writer, Deric now had a whole magazine to fill with his own ideas, and he revelled in the opportunity of writing every single article and review in the magazine, using various aliases, including of course the infamous sex counsellor Dr. Michaels. Deric now swapped the occasional celebrity interview and serious erotic book review that *Penthouse* had been known for, for amusing ponderings on women's underwear or how to have a successful affair without the wife knowing.

In an aim to find new and undiscovered British models for all the Fantasy magazines, Deric arranged an open competition for all housewives to write in to *Penthouse* submitting a snapshot of themselves, the winner receiving her own centre- fold spread in what was then Britain's most prestigious glamour magazine. This was unheard of – an 'ordinary' unknown girl getting a *Penthouse* front cover was at that time the equivalent of an unknown busker winning the Grammies or the Brits overnight!

Many aspiring models sent their pictures in, and the winner of the competition was 22-year-old brunette day-care nurse Rachael Brill-Edwards from Barrow-In-Furness, who made the front cover and centre-fold of British *Penthouse* when she won in 1994.

But while Deric was still 'searching' for his new face, he asked me if I wanted to become the official 'model contact' for *Penthouse* and all of The Fantasy Group's adult titles, building up regular recruits for the *Penthouse* model competition. Still working at John's, I agreed to do the job part-time, auditioning prospective models before or after my shift at John's began.

Not only was Deric getting good publicity for the magazine with his 'competition' but he was of course building a considerable database of amateur models that he could then call on for future photo-shoots for other projects, not least of which was a new title that he was working on.

Proving that he could increase the sales of *Penthouse* with more pictures of 'girl-next-door' type models, he had persuaded the Fantasy bosses to let him launch a new title that would be filled only with photos of ordinary looking girls naked.

The title of *Penthouse* gave the impression of a luxurious playboy's apartment filled with the world's most beautiful women. The title of Deric's new brainchild was to be called simply *New Talent*.

I got some business cards made at my own expense, which proudly displayed the world-famous *Penthouse* logo and my name as the official 'model contact'. I placed an ad in the free-ads papers for *'new girls to model for internationally famous men's magazine. No experience necessary. All ages, shapes and sizes accepted'*, and was soon inundated with would-be model's details – all ages, shapes and sizes!

I arranged to do a quick test shoot of many of them in my edit suite at John Graham's during my evening shift. The bigger breasted ones I also introduced to John, although I could see him cringing as I knocked on his office door with yet another ordinary housewife who, while she did have naturally big boobs, also had stretch marks and cellulite. I forgot that he was more accustomed to dealing with the top big boobed American models who, with silicone implants, fake nails, tans and bleached blonde hair all looked like 'perfect' Pamela Anderson look-a-likes, and not like my English housewife types!

I would pass on all my amateur wannabe *Penthouse* girls' details to Deric, along with their snapshots, and he would arrange to have them shot initially for *New Talent* by a team of cheap 'pro-am' style photographers he had found who were later to become known in *New Talent* magazine as the 'Wicked Uncles', but were better known to those in the Fantasy offices simply as 'The Scum Brothers'.

This prestigious title came about when ex-*Private* photographers Henry Fiskett and Ernie Taylor wandered in to the Fantasy building one day with no appointment, but with a portfolio of hard-core pictures, to see if they could get any freelance work.

The perhaps rather sensitive Group Managing Editor at that time went down to see them in the reception area and, after first being taken aback by their rather shabby appearance, and then noting the pride with which they displayed their hardcore portfolio ('Look at that cum shot – it takes real talent to get that' they told him), he scurried back upstairs to Deric and informed him that 'You'll have to deal with these people – they look like scum!'

Deric however welcomed these 'scum brothers' in with open arms, recognising a kind of talent that he knew exactly how to utilise, as they obviously had a nose for lowbrow, down-market sleaze, which was just what Deric was trying to introduce into *Penthouse*.

He employed them as 'house photographers', paying them pro rata but giving them the first option on almost every photographic job. The discovery of the 'Scum Brothers' meant that Fantasy could become less dependent on established expensive out-of-house glamour photographers like Jeff Kaine and start shooting with much lower budgets in-house.

Eventually 'Ernie Scum' left the team to forge his own career and 'Henry Scum' teamed up with a jolly roly-poly man who was to become known to us all as 'Peter Scum'. Peter Palmer was training as a video cameraman and so, with the new team in operation, the Scum Brothers could divide up the labour, with Henry shooting the stills, while Peter shot some accompanying video of the stills shoot, thus getting stills and video at the same time at no extra cost.

Determined to prove to the Fantasy bosses that he could not only get *Penthouse* selling more copies, but that he could save money in the process, Deric took his own snapshot camera and his own little VHS camcorder to the home of one of the women who had written in – a grey haired woman in her sixties!

Paying her just £30 as a 'test fee' he snapped away and returned with a bunch of stills and some useable, if very dark and grainy looking, video footage.

Although neither stills nor video footage ever actually made it into the magazines, Deric had proved a point – the days of expensive glossy looking glamour shoots were over. Deric and his band of 'Scum' photographers could take photos and video footage very cheaply and people would be interested in it actually because it looked cheap, home-shot and 'real'. The days of the aspirational glamour babe were over. The days of reality porn were just beginning. And Deric was at the fore-front!

The idea of low outlay (and therefore big profits) inspired Fantasy's chairman enough to let Deric run with the idea of developing a serious adult video division to the company, as now Deric and the Scums could get 'free' video footage while they were shooting a photo set in someone's front room.

In order to develop this new range of video titles, Deric was in need of employing someone to head it up, and he looked to me to do just that.

I was getting over-stretched at John Graham's, as his monthly video edit workload was just growing and growing, as John sold video edits of his scenes to more and more countries around the world, and so I went along to the Fantasy building in London's trendy Docklands area for a meeting.

There were several plus points to me if I took Deric up on the offer to go to work there – it was nearer to my home than John Graham's was, so I wouldn't spend so much time every day sitting in traffic, and it was more money than I was currently getting at John's. And of course there were more opportunities for promotion to greater things within the Fantasy group.

As I was shown round the building, I was welcomed like a familiar old friend, as Deric shouted out to everyone: 'Look! This is the real Ric Porter! You know – the one I write about all the time! This is him!'

I smiled meekly round at everyone who were gazing at me in awe of the outrageous character that Deric had been telling them I was. I knew however that once they got to know me, they would be disappointed that I wasn't the flesh and blood caricature of a porno mogul that Deric had been making me out to be.

Nevertheless, I was glad, in September 1994, to start work at Fantasy. I was to help out on the magazines, doing video reviews and odd bits of text while putting the video side of the company into operation.

For the first month, I left work at Fantasy at 5.30 every evening and drove straight to John's where I continued to work through the night as well, while I worked out my notice for him, catching a few hours sleep before driving in to Fantasy again the next morning.

Sometimes I got so tired trying to do both jobs at once that I would curl up under the radiator in John's edit suite and fall asleep for a while. John later told me that he had sometimes walked in on me in the middle of the night and found me fast asleep on the floor. Being the kind and considerate employer that he was however he never woke me up or shouted at me to get back to work, but would just creep out again and leave me to my dreams.

A month later, having sleepily worked out my notice for John, I went full-time at Fantasy as the official model contact, video reviewer, journalist and video editor/consultant. It seemed that, twelve years after I'd started out as a wannabe porn actor/filmmaker, I was in some ways only just coming into my own.

Chapter Sixteen:
NEW JOB, NEW TALENT

Deric continued to write about me at every opportunity, and his new magazine *New Talent* was going from strength to strength, thriving on reader interaction, with genuine letters and reader's photos and contact ads.

I was now listed on all the magazine's mastheads as the official company contact to send pictures into, and was involved in the production of *New Talent* in a lot of ways. I was the official model contact and, as such, I was the first stop for any aspiring models either sending in their pictures or phoning to make an appointment to come in and see us. I opened and answered all the post on behalf of the magazine, I reviewed the latest adult videos (a column that was also syndicated across to *Penthouse* and *Electric Blue* magazines every month), and I wrote two features for *New Talent* every month. All this, and yet I wasn't even actually employed by the Company! I worked simply on a freelance basis, invoicing every month for the work that I had done.

Writing articles for *New Talent* was the first time that I had ever tried out my skills as a journalist, but Deric told me not to worry, reassuring me that it was a 'piece of piss'.

'Just write down your thoughts in a chatty way, like you were talking to a mate' he advised me. And so I did. And, in my new role as *Penthouse* video reviewer, I made sure that one of the first videos I gave a glowing and very favourable review to, along with the price and address of where to buy a copy, was a little thing called *Home Shot Number One.*

Deric encouraged me to write articles too. I wrote a piece for *Electric Blue* magazine about my friend from John Graham's,

Dave Wells (AKA Lee Francis), and I began to write two regular pieces for *New Talent* magazine that were both part of a series on-going from issue to issue, *Porter's Portfolio* and *Making Movies.*

Making Movies was a light-hearted advise column on how to successfully make and market home-made sex videos, which I took over from Deric who had been writing it under his *Erotic Dreams* pseudonym of Paulo Ricotini. Deric, who loved to invent new characters to play out, had invented a whole background, history and image for Paulo Ricotini. He was one of the infamous Italian pornographers known as the Ricotini Brothers, the other brother being Virgil, and he looked like a 1920s mobster. Deric included a seemingly vintage black and white photograph of himself to illustrate the *Making Movies* articles, in which he wore a white tuxedo and black bow tie, hair slicked back, a little moustache bristling on his upper lip, as he posed beside a beautiful 1920s Rolls Royce.

Writing in these articles as Paulo, Deric had encouraged readers to build do-it-yourself makeshift lighting stands out of two-by-four bits of wood. I however concentrated on the production and post-production side of things: how to find girls to pose for you, shoot them successfully and then edit and market what you'd shot for a profit.

Porters Portfolio on the other hand was simply a two or three page column that, continuing with the 'discovering new talent' theme that Deric was now going all-out for in all of the magazines, highlighted amateur girls who had sent in photos wanting to become glamour models. We would print the photos sent in with the accompanying letter from the girl, or her boyfriend (whichever had sent them in), and I would then reply with encouraging remarks and usually requesting the girl to get back in touch and come in for a professional photo session with us; 'professional' in this case however only meaning that the photo session would be done by one of the Scums, probably in one of their sitting rooms instead of her

having more photos done in her own! The girl would however be paid for this shoot as well as sent a contribution fee for the original photos to be included in *Porter's Portfolio*, and we in return would have a photo-set of a brand new girl, and a page or two filled in the mag with the original amateur pictures – everyone was a winner!

Every photo sent in to the magazines for publication had to be accompanied by a 'model release' form for legal reasons, so we published a small consent form in every magazine we published, which every reader had to cut out and send in with any photos they submitted. The form had to be signed by the person in the pictures, not just the person sending it in. Hopefully this put off jealous ex-boyfriends sending in rude photos of their ex girlfriend, although of course there was no way of us spotting a forged signature, but legally we would be covered as we had done all we could in the circumstances in trying to obtain the necessary paperwork. Once or twice, people did ring in complaining that we had published pictures of them without their consent. In these cases, we would send them a copy of the consent form for them to see the signature, and put a note in our files that the pictures were not to be published again.

In the *Making Movies* article, we really did try to encourage readers to have a go with their video cameras and make some money selling their video footage. And how could they do this? By selling the footage to us of course! Deric had made contact with various

European porn companies and played the middleman by buying in footage from our readers and then selling it on to these companies, forwarding a cheque to the reader and of course taking a small cash percentage himself for his trouble.

In what he was doing, Deric was beginning to change the face of British adult magazines and videos forever. Prior to this, magazine editors just came in to the office and did their nine to five job, buying in material from professional

photographers to produce a magazine that the reader could buy and look at, but have no real interaction with. Deric however lived and breathed porno and, as in the old days of punk rock, he was a kind of porno version of Malcolm McLaren, encouraging everyone with a zealous enthusiasm to 'have a go' themselves – make a sex video on their camcorder at home with the missus – never mind that they 'couldn't play the instruments' or had no big budget or professional modelling talent; 'Just take some pictures of the wife and send them in to Ric Porter – he'll publish them in *Porters Portfolio* and pay you for the privilege!' Suddenly anyone could now be a published porno photographer, adult film director or published porn model! The roles of audience and performer were beginning to blur.

In America, porn filmmaker John Stagliano was doing something similar with video production. He was abandoning the idea of big budget studio shoots and simply taking his camcorder to the streets, inviting ordinary girls to strip off for his camera, while he talked to them from behind the lens and then got involved in front of the camera too, filming the action 'point-of-view' style. It was called 'gonzo' porn and was obviously a vastly cheaper way of making adult films as it involved no expensive sets, professional lighting and of course very minimal crew – in fact just one cameraman/director!

This certainly not only maintained the 'reality factor' but could also yield higher profits, as production costs were so low. It was a technique that Lindsay Honey, under the name of Ben Dover, was to emulate in Great Britain with fantastic success.

In writing for the magazines, Deric was very prolific. He wrote quickly and creatively and churned out article after article, virtually writing everything in every single Fantasy magazine single-handed. He would write serious articles containing poll surveys, and light-hearted video reviews, rating hardcore videos unobtainable in the UK with a star system. But the one thing that all his writing had in common was that it was all made up! All full of facts and figures, incredibly believable, and all made up! Even the videos he reviewed were made up, although I always thought it surely would have been easier to actually review real ones? But that of course would have meant that Deric would have to sit down and spend time watching one. Easier just to imagine what he'd like to see and write a review about what was in his head, finding a picture from the photo library to illustrate it!

One of the made-up videos that he 'reviewed' was called *Fuck Me Jacob Gently*. We got a letter from a reader asking where he could buy the video, and Deric then seriously considered making a video called *Fuck Me Jacob Gently*, not just so he could get at least this one guaranteed sale out of it, but because he could then legitimately make into existence something that he had dreamed up out of his own head. Deric loved the idea of this kind of thing and it maybe explained why, when he eventually made outlandish programmes for Television X using look-a-likes and crazy involved scripts (a porno extension of the mad films we had made for the corporate companies), it gave him so much pleasure to see something that he had dreamed up in his head actually take form and be broadcast on national television.

Deric had a knack of absolutely totally believing his own hype. He would tell me something one day, a story that he was planning to invent, and the very next day he'd call me over to his desk and read out what he'd written, telling me as if he'd just read this piece of 'information' himself for the very first time, and telling me in a way that not only presumed that I would believe it but actually implied that he himself believed it – even though he had just invented it!

He was at his desk one day when tabloid newspaper *The Sunday People* rang him. They wanted to do a piece on British women and pornography and wanted to ask him a few questions. Sitting opposite him, I heard him say, without pausing to think, that their timing couldn't have been better as Fantasy Publications had just completed a survey about women and porn and had discovered that a staggering 84% of all British housewives watched sex films and got turned on and that 54% said that they had a secret desire to appear in one, while 31% also said that they would like to have lesbian sex, and so on and so forth. When he eventually replaced the receiver, having also secured the job of writing the piece for them, I mentioned that I wasn't aware that we'd done such a survey.

'No, we haven't!' he beamed at me from across the desk, 'I made it all up just now'!

Apparently the article was pulled at the last minute but they still paid Deric a 'kill fee', which he later told me was enough money for him to buy a Jaguar car for himself!

Deric drove Jaguar cars, chain smoked imported cigarettes, wore bright designer suits and imported aftershave, and certainly played the part of the extravagant porn-baron to full effect. He would introduce himself to strangers on the train as the Managing Editor of *Penthouse* magazine and sometimes, much to the chagrin of the real Fantasy bosses, as the Managing Director of the entire Company. He would proudly hand out his business card to all and sundry and generally acted like a minor celebrity.

When he arrived at Fantasy, Deric had told the bosses that he could turn the profits of *Penthouse* around and certainly, if his enthusiasm was anything to go by, the magazine group should now be making millions.

He also rewrote the rule-book of how staff at Fantasy got paid. Prior to his arrival, everyone was on a salary and came in and worked nine to five just like everyone else did at any other job. Deric took a long hard look at all the magazine's individual budgets and realised that, as long as each mag appeared to come in on budget, then no one would question

how that budget had been reached, providing that all the paperwork was correct. As so much was now being done by the cheaper in-house 'scum' photographers and by Deric himself, there was a gap between what had previously been allocated for photography and contributor fees and what was actually now being paid out. Therefore there was a gap between the actual cost of the magazine's production and its budget. Deric advised all major contributing in-house staff, including myself, to set themselves up as a trading-as company and invoice for a little extra each month for various services (photographic, design, editorial etc). That way, it didn't look to the accounts department as if employees who were on the pay roll were invoicing for doing what was effectively only their job anyway. They would be getting an invoice from another 'company' for work apparently done, and which Deric would sign off.

Deric then gave these in-house staff members extra tasks to do (like writing more parts of the mag or extra design work) that they could invoice for separately, even though it was strictly speaking part of their actual job description anyway. The outcome however was that the staff were happy as they were getting a fair bit of extra money for the little extra work that they were being called to do, and it also gave them an incentive to do the job to the best of their ability and even stay late to get it done; something that, as we all know, is hard to achieve from office workers with a 'nine to five' mentality.

My salary at that time was entirely made up of little bits and bobs like that, that was all separately invoiced for from my 'trading-as' company, and it all added up at the end of the month to a nice little income; nice enough for me to finally buy myself a smart new apartment in London's trendy East End.

I took Deric to see it and he reported back loudly to the rest of the office: 'It's official – Ric Porter's a yuppie!'

A year after *New Talent* was first launched, we held a big birthday party at London's kinky School Dinners restaurant, where the waitresses all dressed in St. Trinians style uniforms and welcomed naughty diner interaction. Every photographer and model in the business turned up, and as many readers as wanted to come were invited to attend for free. This was Deric's way not only of saying thank you to our loyal readers but also of instilling the idea that we were a real interactive porn organisation, making the dreams of our readers to mingle socially with the porn stars a reality. And of course the resulting good public relations with our readers cemented their loyalty to our brand even more.

The queue went round the block, and we had to let people in Periodically as others left and made space. We staged a raunchy dance-show featuring among others top models Lynsey Dawn McKenzie and Sammi Jessop, which Jeff Kaine had arranged for us, and Deric had a beautiful cake made in the shape of the very first ever *New Talent* cover. He had also hired his Princess Di look-alike to cut the cake and pose with the revellers.

The Scum Brothers continued to be the 'staff photographers' at this time, but were soon joined by another pair of dubious adult photographers and filmmakers, Mark Matthews (then married to model Kerry Matthews, who had worked with me doing her first ever porno shoot in *Erotic Dreams of Natasha*) and his business partner, an older guy called Randolph.

They came in to see Deric one day and, as with the original Scum Brothers, Deric instantly recognised not only a perfect addition to the Fantasy crew, but also some porno soul-mates as Mark and Randolph loved their job in the same way that Deric loved his, and they were prepared to work flat out filming and photographing new talent in the same way that Deric and the Scums did.

Technically more experienced than the original Scums, their style of filming and equipment were both a little superior in quality to that of the Scums. And they bought their own style of comedy to the video shoots, keeping up a constant banter between each other as they did the filmed photo-shoots, one on a stills camera and the other on video in the same way as Henry and Peter worked. As soon as they had delivered their first tape, Deric decided to give them a new name – Shagnasty and Muttley! The characters that Deric and I had invented on our way to the South London edit suite when we were making the corporate films now had flesh and blood. Randolph's real first name was perfect for his character (Randy), and Mark had been wearing a T-shirt on the day of the first video they shot for us that bore the legend 'Stan The Video Man'. So Randy Shagnasty and Stan Muttley were born.

One of them would be doing the stills while the other one filmed the photo shoot, and they kept up an amusing repartee between them the whole time, which gave them a much stronger on-camera persona than those of Henry and Peter.

With all the video footage coming in from the filming of photo-shoots that the Scums and that 'Shag and Mutt' were doing, I was soon in a position to edit up a series of video films that Fantasy could get BBFC 18 rated and sell not only 'off the page' in the magazines and also through video stores. In the edit, I basically just let the footage run in real time while the models posed and the stills camera clicked. Quite boring to watch really, but Deric wrote the blurb on the box cover and, possibly recalling the scams he used to do with Andrew, he urged would be purchasers of the video to 'see the hardest debut shoot of this new young model' and to 'witness the actual moment that the model involuntarily orgasmed as the cameras rolled'.

We called the range *Home Made Video*, and while they were quite tame by today's standards, I made sure to give them glowing reviews in all the mags.

The marketing department of Fantasy designed a brilliant logo for *Home Made Video*, which showed the name forming the shape of a house. I had the logo printed on a sweatshirt which I would proudly wear to work, occasionally along with my old *Private* 'CREW' T-shirt.

Partly in order to justify taking me on as the one in charge of developing new video projects, Deric was the first in the adult business to realise the potential of putting a 'free' video onto a magazine, and I was soon busy editing up a thirty-minute video every month for an all-new title which Deric launched, *Amateur Video Magazine*. We would encourage readers to send in their video footage for us to use and, after buying it outright for £100, I would then edit clips onto the video. The magazine contained two photo-sets and pages and pages of advertising (mostly in those days adult phone-lines) but, although a very thin magazine in itself, it would sell for double the price of a normal magazine because of the 'free' video. Of course the reality was that the readers were paying for the video that had a free magazine full of ads attached to it! But it meant that, unlike straight sell-through videos, which had to be sold in video stores, we could now legitimately sell these 18-rated videos in every corner newsagents, as they were officially part of a magazine pack!

The governing body granting a legal certificate to all video productions, the British Board of Film Classification (or BBFC), provided us with guidelines of what should be edited out of our video titles that were so archaic that the girls in the videos could only wear big full-backed knickers; no g-strings or thongs. The BBFC had decided that any underwear other than a big full-backed knicker was in some way 'un-natural' and perverse!

Similarly, all sex toys were regarded by the BBFC as not to be shown (clearly they regarded it as 'odd' to want to pleasure yourself while on your own), and only two people could have sex at any one time as clearly the BBFC considered it an un- natural sin to take part in any kind of group activity sexually!

Consequently, if a scene we included in a video portrayed multiple sex partners, we would have to cut to shots only portraying two of the participants at any one time, after we had initially established the fact that there were more than two people actually present.

The BBFC would send a list of changes that they wanted done to the edit, once a particular title had been sent to them with a view to giving it a certificate. These lists would contain quite specific cuts, informing me that a shot should be removed from one particular point on the tape (the 'time code' of the shot would be specified) to another particular point on the tape. 'Big Brother' style, the BBFC were in fact telling me exactly where to make my edits, and how long particular shots should last. Seemingly, more explicit shots could only remain on-screen for maybe three seconds before the BBFC's cut-list would insist on its removal.

In general all sex acts were fine, but only as long as they were clearly seen to be faked! If anything looked too real, then the cut list would remove them, unless we could in some way prove that they were in fact faked in production!

All this made my editing job quite challenging – particularly as most of the material that the readers of *Amateur Video Magazine* were sending in were shot completely hardcore, let alone with or without big full-backed knickers!

Once bought outright for the nominal fee however, all this reader footage was not only used on videos, but also formed the basis for the entire early catalogue of programming for 'Television X 2'; the channel based on 'amateur style' footage. Television X would in time follow Deric's lead by inviting the viewers to send in their home shot footage for this Channel, paying them a similar nominal fee.

Amateur and 'pro-am' filmmakers alike found a home for their work with *Amateur Video Magazine*. It gave them the opportunity to do some filming and try out their skills, while getting the resulting footage paid for and published at the same time!

Amateur camera club owner Mick Brant also saw an opportunity here to diversify. He had from the early days been selling the odd photo to Deric that he had shot of various models in his run down camera club, Tower Studios, in London's East End. Now he saw that, for no extra cost or time, he could increase his revenue. So, he set up a video camera on a rickety tripod, set it to a static wide angle, and would then carry on with his normal photo shoot, while the video camera recorded all the action of the photo shoot; seemingly ideal footage for *Amateur Video Magazine*.

Except that Mick didn't monitor the shot that the video was recording and, consequently, because his models were often moving around his makeshift set as they disrobed and posed for his stills camera, what arrived in the Fantasy Publications office was a VHS tape proudly labelled up as 'The Mick Brant Photography Master Class', but when we looked at it, it was more often than not, a completely empty locked-off shot of a sofa or a bed, with just some shadows moving around in view, and the sound of Mick's voice encouraging and directing the unseen models, 'Yes, that's it! Lovely.

Now take it off!' etc. Very occasionally we would be treated to the model coming into shot during a fag break, or sometimes coming in to shot while posing but, as the video camera wasn't being manned, the shot may just have shown the top of her head or the side of her leg!

Classic stuff! I would however sometimes use a bit of 'Mick's Master Class' on the edit for *Amateur Video Magazine* and would of course put the cost of this video into the budget, which I passed on to Deric. When however I was one day packaging up a load of magazines to send out to contributors so they could see their published work, Deric stopped me from sending anything out to Mick.

'For goodness sake, don't tell him we've actually used any of his stuff!' he warned me! Clearly some of the budget set aside for reader's contributions were going straight into Deric's pocket!

Amateur Video Magazine was the first of many video titles that we produced, and it also spawned a host of similar 'video magazines' from our competitors. Deric and I even went on the then popular late night TV chat show *The James Whale Show* to promote the new exciting idea of Joe Public sending in his home shot adult video footage to us for us to then put it out in his local newsagent for all to see.

In this respect Deric was perhaps ahead of his time in realising the potential and popularity of providing 'reality porn' to the public, something that these days is the staple diet of much of the material on the internet.

At that time Deric was learning fast how to manipulate the media and he went on every radio and television chat show that he could, often taking me along with him both for moral support and also to sometimes appear alongside him, backing up his often outrageous claims and ideas.

We appeared on Esther Rantzen's daytime TV debate show, *Esther*, and I did TV interviews for *The Big E!* and *Eurotrash* among others. I did a radio interview for The Black Entertainment Channel with presenter Valley Fontaine and, when she filmed a pilot for a TV series *Deep Down With Valley Fontaine,* she called me in again for another appearance, which was set in a London pub with as much free booze as we could drink. I appeared coherent on screen but was glad of the taxi home afterwards!

I was also interviewed by Graham Norton for a radio clip about porn addiction, and woman's magazine *Marie Claire* published an interview with me as part of their 'men in porn' feature, persuading me to pose moodily in just my underwear for an accompanying photo. Although I felt the resulting picture looked a bit stupid and exploitative, I suppose I did better than Randy Shagnasty, who was asked to pose completely nude for his photo in the same piece.

Deric and I would do all these interviews for free to get publicity for our magazines, something that the Fantasy bosses obviously loved – in Deric they were not only getting someone keen to revamp their mags, but also getting a full-on one man PR machine thrown in.

The only interview that I did that I was ever actually paid for was for a programme called *The Sex Files* on the then satellite channel UK Living. I was only paid a nominal fee but they certainly got their money's worth as the interview was repeated countless times until, long after I had changed my look and even moved on from Fantasy, people were still telling me that they saw me being interviewed on TV the other night. I even had a girl run up to me one night in a restaurant asking for my autograph, recognising me from this interview. Normally I would have loved this kind of attention, thinking that it made me feel like some kind of pop star, but on that particular evening I was out for a meal with my ageing mother and so it probably wasn't the best time to go talking porn with a keen female fan!

When there was a live interview on TV or radio during office hours, the staff would all gather round in the office, listening in and cheering Deric or myself on.

Deric and I did a pilot for a late night radio phone-in show that BBC Radio London were interested in doing. Deric was to be the main host, with me as his sidekick. We mocked up some spoof phone calls to show what we could do, one of which was meant to be from male model Marino. He failed to call in on cue however, so Mark ('Stan Muttley') impersonated him for the purpose of the call instead. The pilot failed to impress however and the radio series never came about.

Deric at this time began developing his 'media tart' persona, courting the media in any way he could. He started dressing a bit like an outlandish TV quiz show host. He would drive to work in his Jaguar car, and then come into the office wearing loud brightly coloured suits topped off with a black fedora hat, and looking at times not unlike the character of Max Bialystock from the Mel Brooks' musical film *The Producers*, just as he is about to launch himself into 'Little Old Lady Land'!

A journalist from *The Guardian* newspaper asked Deric if he could come into our office every day for a week and write an article about us. Deric thought it would be great publicity for the magazines and possibly introduce a whole new audience of middle class serious broadsheet readers to our titles. When the piece came out however the journalist had written more about my 'lank hair', 'thin nasal laugh' and our deputy editor's weight problem than about how good our magazines were!

I became a little more wary about talking to the media after that, and even more so after going with Deric to take part in a live TV debate about porn. The producers insisted that they wanted a fair debate giving us the chance to show the 'good side' of our business and, eager to make sure we got to the Manchester studios on time, they sent a limo to London to pick us up. Minutes to go to on-air however, we found out that Deric was to be pitted against an elderly clergyman in the hope simply that there would be a good argument... and therefore good TV ratings. This was not after all good publicity for our mags.

Back at base however, in keeping with the image of me that he himself was creating, Deric had begun referring to me around the office as the 'Golden Haired Pussy Charmer', abbreviating it sometimes to just the initials, as in 'The GHPC', so that it sounded like an office moniker much like SEO or MD. One of the magazine designers made an excellent drawing of me cross-legged and flute in hand like an old-fashioned snake

charmer, summoning an erotic creature from a basket. However it was easier to liken a dick than it was a pussy to the traditional charmed snake, so that was what I was pictured charming from its basket; a snake with a bulbous penis like head, and unfortunately thereafter I was of course known around the office as the 'Golden Haired Penis Charmer' instead!

I was fast becoming a real integral part of the organisation, getting involved in the day-to-day running of almost every magazine. So much so was I now involved with Deric's premier 'baby' *New Talent* that, at one point, every month's edition of that magazine was entirely put together and written by me. I considered re-titling it *Ric Porter's New Talent,* but didn't really consider that that particular prefix would necessarily sell any more copies! Neither would a photo of me grinning from the front cover – there was already a very good cartoon likeness of my face illustrating the *Porter's Portfolio* page, which was even redesigned with shorter hair when I eventually had a haircut and lost my then trademark long golden locks!

I'd been wearing my hair in what was then regarded as a fashionable ponytail for some time, but decided to have it cut after some day trippers near our trendy Docklands office pointed at me, laughing at what they obviously thought was a perfect example of the stereotypical London yuppie of the time, complete with his business suit, mobile phone and ponytail!

The offices of celebrity gossip magazine *OK!* were at that time based in an office adjoining ours and we noticed that the girls that worked there became increasingly wary of walking through our office on their way to the ladies loo. They scurried through, trying to avert their eyes from the adult magazine covers adorning our walls and hoping that neither Deric nor myself would try and engage them in conversation as they passed! So wary were they of us that one of the senior members of staff there even came in and politely warned us not to flirt with any of her staff as they walked by! Needless to say, this only acted as a red rag to Deric and I who would then deliberately stop them and ask them irrelevant questions about which celebrities they thought might pose in the nude for our magazines.

I don't know if they felt worried that our seedy nudie material would somehow seep into their gilded world of celebrity? It didn't however stop one of our designers adding a snapshot of one of the female *OK!* Members of staff to his 'wall of babes'; a wall in the office he had covered with pictures of his favourite glamour models.

It was taken in good humour by the *OK!* girls however and, on their part, they added the *Marie Claire* picture of me in my underwear to their wall along with publicity shots of Tom Cruise and Brad Pitt!

On leaving *OK!* to do her own freelance work, one of their designers, Claudia Pattison, wrote a novel called *WOW!*, which was about life working for a fictional celebrity magazine. Clearly she was using all her experiences at *OK!* as the basic research for her book and, although I don't think that his personality was based on mine, certainly one of the characters in her finished book was even called

'Nick Porter'.

Celebrities were often shown around the *OK!* Offices and would be fleetingly ushered through our office on their way there. Our office chairs were on wheels and myself and colleague Dave Price would sometimes whiz around on them playing battle games in a short break from the work. I had unfortunately chosen the wrong moment one day to do this as, with my jacket hunched up around my shoulders like a superhero cape and scooting across the floor on my chair, I glanced up to see David and Victoria Beckham being quickly ushered past me! I got back to my desk as fast as I could and pretended to be on the phone as these royalties of tabloid celebrity glanced back at me, clearly bewildered.

Everything at Fantasy however was going from strength to strength, and we regularly attended model parties at London's Stringfellows night-club, socialising with other photographers and editors in the business and dancing the night away with the current circle of top glamour models, who were all in attendance in skimpy outfits, simpering up to anyone who looked as if they were in a position to give them some work.

Deric and I were often recognised in the street and asked for our autographs and, on the success of *New Talent*, Deric launched a sister magazine *Real Wives*, featuring '*100% genuine wives naked*'.

To ensure that the photos featured in this magazine justified this claim, Deric would only buy photo-sets where the models were actually wearing a wedding ring. He told all the Scum photographers to have a cheap wedding ring with them at all times so they could put one on the model's middle finger of her left hand if she didn't already have one or if she wasn't actually married. Sometimes, if they forgot but if the model was wearing a ring on the middle finger of her right hand, the pictures would be 'reversed' in the design so that the ring now appeared on her left hand. The only time this caused a problem of course was if there was a clock or a magazine in shot so that it could clearly be seen that the numbers or words were the wrong way round.

When asking the model to wear a ring, the Scums would explain that it was because they wanted her to look like a 'blushing newlywed' rather than the reality that she was to look like an ordinary dull looking housewife, or 'MILF' as it called today ('Mother I'd Like To Fuck'), which was the standard look of all the models who graced the pages of this particular title.

Real Wives appeared to be as successful as *New Talent* and we now had two publications in which to spread out the genuine pictures that readers were sending in – younger cuter looking girls going in *New Talent*, more ordinary 'MILF' types in *Real Wives*.

My next project was to oversee a video project that eventually became a series of vignettes I called the *Fantasy Chateau*.

The idea was to book half a dozen girls on one single day in a hired location. While photographer Jeff Kaine shot a photo set of one of the girls in one part of the location, I would be shooting a video sequence with one of the other girls in another part. We could also shoot one or two video sequences utilising more than one of the girls at once. That way, out of one day's work, Fantasy would get at least six video sequences and six photo-sets for minimal cost, as make up and location fees were all shared, as well of course as the model's fee, as she was being paid for the day rather than per job.

For a location I found a five-bedroom townhouse complete with indoor swimming pool and ballroom that was owned by the professional photographer Michael Joseph. It had been the location for The Rolling Stones' *Beggars' Banquet* promotional photo where the band are all eating a medieval style meal on a big wooden table. I booked this house as the location while Jeff booked all the models. They included Charmaine Sinclair, Lana Cox, Sammi Walker,

Natasha Lester, Shanine Linton and Eve Vorley, who was later to become David Sullivan's long term girlfriend and the mother of his two children.

I decided that I would simply be the video director of this project and booked Jim Slip as my lighting cameraman.

We shot a series of magnificent vignettes which included a leather clad Charmaine complete with bullwhip in the ballroom, Eve dancing against a stuffed tiger, a two-girl bath sequence with Shanine Linton, and a sequence in the swimming pool with Natasha and several of the girls.

We shot Charmaine's scene first, early in the morning with the sun streaming through the huge floor to ceiling ballroom windows. One of the Television X producers later commented on what good lighting we had achieved, assuming there was an HMI heavy duty lamp out on the balcony shining through. Well, yes, we did utilise a pretty heavy-duty light to get the sunshine effect – it was called the sun!

I shot all the sequences 'mute' and directed the camerawork ad-hoc as we went, watching Jim's shots on a monitor.

I had some original soundtrack music specially written, and I edited the sequences back at my old edit suite at John Grahams, hiring it out from him for a weekend.

I put in a lot of slow motion and special effects and tried to give it a modern MTV feel which I felt suited the visuals perfectly.

Toward the end of Saturday night I had been editing without a break all that day, blinds drawn and headphones on, locked in my own world as I cut image after image to the music. Deciding to have a break to eat and socialise, I left the darkened suite in a bit of a dazed state, and promptly fell over as I hit the air outside!

That evening I went to a launch party with one of the Fantasy designers, and mingled with TV presenters Terry Christian and Danni Behr (both then known for their presenting work on the TV music show *The Word*, Danni has since of course appeared on the reality show *I'm A Celebrity – Get Me Out Of Here!* in 2008), wondering firstly if it were worth trying to 'network' with any of these minor celebs, and secondly if any of them would want to 'network' with me when they knew what it was I did for a living, and thirdly if I could persuade Danni Behr to pose naked for any of our magazines!

The resulting edited sequences from my shoots with Jeff Kaine were eventually released on two videos, *Glamour Girls* and *Water Babes*. Under my original title of *Fantasy Chateau* the sequences were also shown on Television X in their first months of broadcasting and are still occasionally played out even now.

We planned to launch a middle shelf 'mens lifestyle' magazine to rival the then hugely popular *Loaded* magazine. It was to be called *Rogue* and we met with erotic photographer Ben Westwood, son of the notorious punk fashion designer Vivienne Westwood, in a pub near our offices. Ben snapped some pictures of us drinking beer and fooling around and I kept wanting to ask Ben questions about his father Sex Pistols entrepreneur Malcolm McLaren. Just as well I didn't however, as it was only later that I found out that it was in fact his half brother, Agent Provocateur co founder Jo Corre who was Malcolm's son, and not Ben!

After several planning meetings of *Rogue,* similarly spent in the pub, the planned magazine went no further!

With Henry and Peter Scum, Deric was now regularly shooting photo-stories that would appear in *New Talent* with bubble type speech balloons in the way that photo stories used to appear in teenage girl's magazines like *Jackie*, *My Guy* or *Oh Boy* in the 1970s – except of course that these photo-stories were aimed at men, and were far more explicit!

Deric would churn these pictorial epics out very prolifically using himself and anyone else in the office to appear in cameo roles as minor characters. I played myself in one such story, sternly telling off a junior member of staff. Peter Scum would often appear in cameo roles himself under the fictitious name of 'Bevvy Hughes', a name that Deric of course had come up with.

One such story concerned Bevvy making his fortune by inventing the 'Pantiscope', a device for looking up women's skirts which was basically a small mirror attached to the end of a bamboo stick. Deric took a full page in *New Talent* actually advertising the Pantiscope for sale just to see what kind of

response he would get, and on the basis that 'if we get enough orders, we'll bloody well make them'!

We received only one order, so sent the cheque back with apologies, although one interesting result of Bevvy's 'invention' was that I spotted a report in the tabloid newspapers some time later of the arrest of a man on the London Underground who had been harassing female passengers. Police reported that he had been hovering near women who wore short skirts with a device that appeared to be a small mirror attached to a bamboo pole! Coincidence? Or was the world of Deric's make believe really beginning to have an effect in the real world outside?

Chapter Seventeen:
FROM MIDNIGHT BLUE TO TVX – NOBODY DOES IT BETTER

Deric had made contacts with what was then the only late night satellite TV channel in Britain showing adult programmes, The Adult Channel. He had blagged a part time job with them doing some 'links' between programmes, getting the approval of the Fantasy bosses on the basis that he would try and drop in the names of some of our mags as free publicity.

I went along with him to their then tiny London studios on one occasion and we did the links together, improvising some chat and comments about the shows coming up.

Deric even shot a series for them called *Caught At Home* where he supposedly 'door stepped' genuine housewives and persuaded them to strip off for the camera, Ben Dover style.

Realising the huge potential of cable/satellite adult TV, Deric had for some while been trying to convince the management of Fantasy Publications to invest some money in launching their own TV channel as a rival to the monopoly of The Adult Channel.

One day I arrived at work dressed casually in a Bugs Bunny sweatshirt and jeans for what I thought would be a normal day opening the post and writing some copy or the magazines. I was however immediately whisked into a meeting in the huge management boardroom, somewhere I had so far never been.

I felt very out of place, wishing I'd put a suit on, as I sat there in meetings for the rest of the day with the suited board of directors of the parent company of Fantasy Publications, who had finally decided that it might indeed make good business sense to launch an adult TV station.

They sat there, tapping away at their calculators and their Psion organisers (these being the days before Blackberries and iPhones) and asking me questions about TV and video production.

As I was the only member of staff that had been employed specifically to oversee video production, the Fantasy bosses were looking to me to offer initial advise as to how to set up a TV studio with full editing suites. What equipment would they need, and how much would it cost to set up?

I felt way out of my depth but bluffed my way through, finally going home to do some serious homework and equipment research, returning the next day suitably attired in a suit and tie and prepared with budgets for further management meetings.

The new channel was proposed to go on air every day at midnight until four in the morning, sharing the same channel number (or EPG number) as the then existing channel UK Living. When UK Living's daytime programming ended, ours would begin after a short advertising 'free view' break.

Our proposed channel would be a subscription channel, operating on similar lines as The Adult Channel, showing bought in programmes and films. Deric and I were put forward to be the executive producers, setting the channel up and then effectively running it on a day-to-day basis.

Deric wanted to call this new channel Midnight Blue, not only clarifying the type of channel we would be and the hour we'd go on air, but also building on the already familiar adult name of Electric Blue, a groundbreaking adult video company from the early eighties that had been created by Roger Noel Cook, who had originally had some success in the late sixties as a writer for Doctor Who comic books.

Fantasy's boss however favoured a different name to Midnight Blue. He felt that Midnight Blue sounded too old fashioned and he wanted to call the station simply XTV, perhaps thinking of a combination of X-Rated and MTV.

And so plans for XTV went ahead. Filming studios and edit suites were built in an office block by the docks which had previously housed the Fantasy Publications Group, who had now moved to a huge office tower block a short walk away over the River Thames. The new parent company, Portland Television, renamed the old office building Portland House, and then even tried to unofficially rename the cul-de-sac that the building was on to Portland Place by simply putting that as the address followed by the correct postal code. The local authorities soon told them however that they could not just give existing roads a new name in that way, although I had to admire their guts in thinking that they could simply rename local roads in an effort to not only make themselves appear more powerful, but also attract free publicity to their company. A great marketing move if it had worked!

While another company was brought in to oversee the technical set up, Deric and I were given a free hand as to what programming we would show. We did a deal with Electric Blue and bought their entire back catalogue which, although much of it already looked very dated given that most of it had been shot around ten years previously, it gave us hours and hours of footage to use both as full programmes and also that we could re-cut to use as trailers and links for our new

Channel.

We did a deal with Lindsay to show exclusive newly filmed Ben Dover episodes, and Deric also commissioned him to produce another series, one of Deric's ideas, about a young man called upon to service frustrated housewives (always a popular theme with Deric). The young man was to be called Dick Richards but known by his nickname of Superdick. Lindsay had been working with porn actor Marino on Ben Dover and cast him as the 'Superdick' character. Deric wanted the suave Dick Richards to have a bumbling sidekick who the viewers would never actually see as he would be filming Superdick's escapades, and so the viewers would only ever hear his off-camera comments. The sidekick was to be the stooge to Marino's straight man and was to be called Reg. Lindsay played the part himself, verbally bouncing off Marino with amusing and entertaining off-the-cuff repartee.

The idea of a two-man cast, one of which was successful with a succession of women and one of which was a bumbling cameraman whose voice was only ever heard off-camera was repeated in another series that Deric commissioned, and one that finally gave full TV life to the Shagnasty and Muttley characters that we had invented to entertain ourselves on the way to editing Deric's corporate films all that time ago. The original title for this series was *On The Road With Shagnasty and Muttley*, and Deric explained to Mark and Randolph that they would be 'on the road' scouting for new talent, with Randy in front of the camera always managing to get the girl while Stan only ever filmed his antics and never managed to get lucky.

Mark and Randy became very inventive with this idea, filming in shopping centres and enticing young girls with ten-pound notes pulled along on bits of string, as well as mooning at would-be glamour models from a hired limo. They would actually approach real women on the street and ask them to strip for a few quid. These responses would be shown on their show before they then reached the set-up girl who really would strip for their cameras. She of course was a hired-in model booked for the shoot, but the inclusion of these real encounters added to the reality element of the show, along with the fact that, unlike Superdick, Randy looked like an ageing ordinary bloke as opposed to a porn star, and therefore not at all like the kind of guy one expected to see succeed with the girls.

On The Road With Shagnasty and Muttley became one of the most popular shows in those early days, making a star out of Randolph and getting him constantly recognised by male fans where-ever he went.

I think the appeal of this show was down to what one might call the Ron Jeremy factor. Male viewers, no matter how old, ugly or ordinary looking, could watch grey haired, out of shape middle aged Randy scoring again and again with beautiful young girls, seemingly picking them up on the street with the most ridiculous of pick-up-lines, and these viewers could take heart that if Randy could pull the girls, then there was hope for them too. I call it the Ron Jeremy factor because, as 1970s American porn star Ron Jeremy has got older and continued his career in the adult film business, viewers took heart that if even Ron, who will himself freely admit that he now looks like an overweight hedgehog, can get laid, then there was surely hope for us all!

With seasoned magazine editor and adult video reviewer Allan Bryce, we planned an adult video review programme called *Video X*, with Allan fronting the show with model Louise Hodges, chatting about new videos and introducing clips.

Allan was instrumental in buying in many of the full-length movies that we would broadcast on the Channel in those early days, including *Cruel Passion* starring Prince Andrew's ex- girlfriend Koo Stark, and *The Dinner Party*, starring Randy West, Debi Diamond and Asia Carrera, at that time the most expensive adult movie ever made.

The *Fantasy Chateau* series that I had made with Jeff Kaine was also now planned into the schedule for broadcast as a series.

As with his corporate films, Deric was keen to get involved in front of the camera as well as behind it, and so planned a show that he and I could host called *Deric Botham's World Of Sex*. This was to be a light hearted studio based programme with sexy clips and jokey interviews and was planned to be first broadcast on our third night on air. An example of the kind of silly things he had planned was one interview with an erotic photographer (played by Peter Scum) who kept a paper bag on his head as he didn't want his family to recognise him!

With one of the Fantasy Publications librarians, Deric planned a spoof sports programme called *David Dickie's Sports Night*, named after the then popular sports commentator Dickie Davies. The talented young librarian created the comedy character of 'David Dickie', dressing up in wig and glasses and commentating on sexy sports such as 'foxy boxing', jelly wrestling and topless table tennis, as well as inventing new 'sports' such as 'Olympic Muff Puffing', where he would try and manoeuvre a rice krispie cereal into a naked girl's belly button by blowing at it through a plastic drinking straw!

He would also promote ridiculous products in spoof advert breaks, such as the 'Wank-O-Matic', a false right arm that could stay in place while your real right hand surreptitiously wanked yourself off under your coat!

As one can see from this line-up of programming, the original idea for the Channel was much more of a mix of sex and humour than just blatant pornography.

We even planned a full-on live stand-up comedy series called *Anything Goes*.

I got back in touch with Matthew Bawcutt and Terry Alderton from the old corporate film-making days, and together we planned and shot the series, which I directed. It was hosted by Terry and produced by Matthew and myself, and featured many outstanding stand-up comedians of the time performing in front of a live audience in a comedy club in the coastal town of Southend in Essex. When I went there to do a preliminary reconnoitre (or 'recce') of the place, I watched Matt Lucas perform as the character Sir Bernard Chumley. Relatively unknown at that time, Matt was of course to go on to find immense success with his comedy partner David Walliams in TV's *Little Britain*.

Although Matt wasn't one of the performers we shot for *Anything Goes*, we did film some of Britain's best stand-up comedians of the time, including Scott Capurro, Ricky Grover, Mandy Knight and of course Terry Alderton himself.

I made the series with a hired-in mainstream camera crew, and a runner that was a friend of Matthew's who helped us out for free. I thought his face looked familiar when he turned up on the first day of filming, and after a while I realised that he was in fact the Asian actor Gordon Warnecke, who had starred in the 1985 hit film *My Beautiful Laundrette*. A nicer guy I couldn't have wished to meet and, despite his fame from that film, he was certainly no diva and now here he was helping out for free on a comedy show that was to go out on a porn channel!

We got a huge backdrop made for the club's stage, adorned with a cartoon figure with a microphone and the name of the show in huge letters.

We also shot a lot of exterior stuff in and around Southend-On- Sea for video inserts for the show, with Terry doing his legendary impressions (primarily of the boxer Chris Eubanks) which, along with the live stand-up acts, made this a unique and very entertaining show indeed.

After weeks of filming and many hours in the edit suite, piecing it all together, the series was ready for broadcast. However, it was only the first episode of *Anything Goes* that was ever actually aired, as unfortunately the boss of XTV, feeling that there must be some element of sex, and not just humour, to any of the Channel's programming, pulled the entire series from any more transmissions after only its first airing.

Needless to say I, along with Terry and Matthew, was very disappointed, as we had not only put a lot of work into making the series, but we were very proud of the finished result. However I was soon to learn that, even as an 'executive producer', final editorial and transmission decisions were not mine or even Deric's. We were playing at producing television, but with someone else's money and at the end of the day, it was the man with the money (Portland Television in this case) that ultimately made the decisions that would affect our television careers.

Other shows that Deric planned (some of which did make it to the screen and some of which didn't) were *Fly On The Wall*, a reality style show that filmed couples having sex with supposedly hidden cameras, *P.V.C*, a 'Q.V.C' style adults only home shopping programme (the P.V.C standing for 'Perversion, Vibration and Convenience'), and *Game For A Giggle*, a sort of adults only *Beadle's About* or *Candid Camera*, where hidden cameras filmed ordinary members of the public's reactions to set up stunts of an adult nature. This idea was not pursued as it was then regarded as an unbelievably risqué idea for television, but is now regularly seen on satellite TV in the form of programmes like *Sexy Cam, Naked and Funny*, and *Dirty Sexy Funny*. Deric clearly was coming up with ideas that were innovative and way ahead of their time. Similarly, *Fly On The Wall* was in itself an adult version of *Big Brother*, now one of the most successful reality-style programmes of all time.

A logo was designed for XTV, and T-shirts, baseball caps, mugs and other promotional material were all made bearing the logo, but it was only once this had all been done that Portland Television's legal department discovered that no one had actually done a copyright check on the name XTV. There was already a company called XTV in existence, and they weren't prepared to give their name up – we would have to re-think!

A relatively simple solution was to transpose the letters around and call the channel TVX instead, making a reworking of the logo easy, and so T-shirts. mugs and baseball caps were all re-ordered and Shag and Mutt were already wearing these items 'on the road' in front of camera in the recordings for their new show when the legal department discovered that there was also a company in existence called TVX, and we would have to change the name yet again!

Finally, before the final batch of promotional T-shirts and caps were ordered, the TVX name was lengthened to Television X, and an additional 'sub-name' was added so that, if we later found out that there was also a Television X somewhere in existence, we could always revert to the sub-name instead. And so 'Television X – The Fantasy Channel' was finally born, the new logo sporting a large X with the other words running across the front of it.

Although it seems strange to me now that the Television X legal department could let this happen at so late a stage, I must confess to making exactly the same mistake with this very book! It wasn't until I had the initial proof copy in my hands that I decided to check online that there wasn't already a book in existence called *Welcome To Pornoland*. When I did, I of course found out that there was not only a book in existence with the same title, a study of the International porn movie business by French journalist Paul-Jerome Renevier, but also a 2008 comedy movie with the same name! Fortunately there is no copyright in a title, so my British memoir could remain with its original title.

Jim Slip had already started calling me the 'Star Maker' due to my seemingly powerful position as casting director for now not just the Fantasy video and magazine range, but also for broadcast programmes for the new TV Channel.

So far however, despite all the planning, we still didn't have a definite on-air date. There was a lot of work still to do, a lot to get ready, and so I wasn't reckoning on anything happening before a few more months at least had elapsed.

However, I was at Jim Slip's edit suite in Surrey, editing another '*Home Made Video*' title when Deric phoned me in great excitement, and told me that we had the green light – we were going on air in just one week's time!

Two models had been booked to be the regular faces of the Channel, doing all the links and promos – Charmaine Sinclair and blonde Sammi Jessop. Another Page Three favourite Kirsten Imrie was also booked to do some regular links.

Sticking to his love of look-a-likes, Deric planned an 'opening ceremony' for the Channel, with a Princess Diana look-alike – the same one who had made an appearance at New Talent's first birthday party. We recorded this 'opening ceremony' at photographer Jeff Kaine's London studio, with John Thomson playing Di's security guard and with Princess Di going along the line and shaking hands with us all. This was scheduled to be the first thing aired on the opening night of our new Channel.

The day before we went on air, the bosses at Fantasy watched the planned first night's programming and I remember one of the management nervously asking if we had enough programmes planned to go on air with different shows the following night... and the night after that... and the night after that!

With the caption, 'Nobody Does It Better' branding all advertising, Television X went on air at midnight on Friday June 2nd 1995, with a line up that included *Superdick, Ben Dover, David Dickie* and a showing of the Koo Stark film *Cruel Passion.* There was however a last minute programme change two days later on Sunday June 4th June.

The programme that was to star Deric on camera, his *World Of Sex* show, had not been well received by the station bosses and, literally an hour or two before we went on air, I received a phone call in the transmission room telling me to replace the show with something else.

Deric arrived at the studio later that night after we had gone on air, unaware that his show had been axed. Deric loved being visibly involved in every show, so we all looked at each other, wondering who would have the courage to tell him that his face would not be on the Channel in its first week after all, except of course in the Princess Di opening sequence on Day One, in which Deric not only appeared as himself, but had also voiced a suitably reverent commentary as a 'royal correspondent'.

In September, after we had been on air for a trial three-month period, we had an official launch party at the BAFTA building in London's Piccadilly.

Stars of the Channel including Lindsay as Ben Dover, Marino as Superdick and Mark and Randolph as Shagnasty and Muttley were all in attendance, and the Channel had flown over notorious American prostitute Divine Brown at a reputed cost of around $20,000, to publicly launch the station's Autumn schedule. She had become something of a minor celebrity after having been arrested with the actor Hugh Grant when he had tried to pick her up on the streets of Hollywood where she had been plying her trade.

Divine, Charmaine, Sammi and Kirsten all arrived at the BAFTA building in an open topped bus emblazoned with the Television X logo, where they had been touring around Central London flashing their boobs to the delight of the British public and tourists alike – as well of course to all the invited press reporters and photographers!

Deric and I felt like two big kids who had been given their own TV station to play with, and for the first few months it was great fun and we could pretty much come up with any ideas we wanted and make them an on-screen reality.

But as the day-to-day problems and hard work of running a Channel became more intense, it became clear that Deric and I wouldn't be able to continue as executive producers full time but only in an advisory capacity, and so we returned to devoting the majority of our time back in the other building over the River Thames at Fantasy Publications.

When we celebrated *New Talent*'s second birthday, we aimed even bigger than the first party, hiring a huge warehouse of a night-club in East London and advertising the event for months in advance in all the magazines, with tickets to all our readers being offered on sale this time.

Once again we had a raunchy floor-show and this time around Television X were involved filming the event for possible later broadcast. David Dickie even made an appearance hosting a live naked Twister game, and Shag and Mutt recorded a special edition of their *On The Road* show, filming themselves supposedly sneaking in past the security guards after not having got an official invitation, only to land up in the models' changing room amongst the half naked girls!

Deric had invented another character for himself as the supposed editor of *New Talent* magazine; a jovial rogue named Steven 'Spiv' Eldridge. There was a certain amount of confusion at the party as there were some people there who knew who Deric really was and others who knew him, or were being introduced to him, only as 'Spiv'. One elderly lady was delighted to meet Deric in the flesh, but then insisted he introduce her to Spiv as well! He said that he would, just as soon as he could find him! I fully expected him to disappear off to the loo and reappear wearing the hideous old man mask he had worn on the corporate film, but fortunately on this occasion both Deric and 'Spiv' kept a relatively low profile and Deric stuck to his own look!

We also met one of the readers there who showed great interest in becoming a male model for us, despite the fact that he was well into his eighties!

Deric immediately saw the potential in this scenario and signed him up not only for a boy/girl photo shoot for *New Talent,* but also for a series for Television X in which he cast him as a retired military major, with Deric casting himself in the role of the major's batman.

Despite his advanced years, the old man put up a very good show and was no doubt very grateful for the opportunity of having sex with a young girl, albeit on camera for everyone to see!

The series *Major Cholmondley's Batman* was filmed by Peter Scum, although I'm not sure that it ever got as far as being screened, the managing producers of Television X by this stage having got a little wary of Deric and his crazy programme ideas, and not as keen to just let him run with them as he was used to in the early days of the Channel. They were more interested in making the Channel a serious erotic contender in the world of adult satellite television, and not just the fun plaything that Deric seemed to see it as.

Overall, *New Talent's* second birthday party didn't seem as well attended as the first party. We had maybe over estimated the number of people who might attend now that they had to actually pay for a ticket and, even though numbers may have been up on the first party, the enormous size of the club, made it look pretty empty even with everyone there.

It got a bit nasty toward the end of the evening when party guests who had travelled from far away were left on the street with nowhere to stay having missed their last train home when the club, despite assuring Deric that it that it would stay open all night for us, decided that attendance was below expectations and closed early.

As I left the club, Deric long since gone home, I was affronted by a group of angry attendees who had travelled from the North of England and now had nowhere to stay for the night. They demanded to know what I was going to do about it, and I felt lucky that they didn't actually get violent! I offered them a free visit to have lunch with us at the Fantasy Offices, and quickly drove off.

I confronted Deric the next day and he made sure that these people were indeed invited to one of the lavish 'Readers Lunches' that Deric had started organising.

As an occasional event, Deric would invite a handful of genuine readers to spend a day at the Fantasy offices for free to see 'how we put the magazines together'. A couple of scantily clad glamour models would also be booked for the day to accompany the readers as they toured around the office and also the Television X studios. Deric would let them roam our library of magazine back issues and give them a goody bag brimming with magazines and videos to take home.

The day would start however with a sumptuous silver service three course lunch in the management boardroom where the models would usually go topless and pose for photographs on the readers' laps. Needless to say, one of the Scum photographers would be booked to snap away throughout the day, and the resulting pictures would end up as a photo-story in *New Talent* magazine. Once again, Deric was combining a reality event with full media coverage with everyone's consent and at minimal cost. The result? Goodwill with all the readers, who were literally queuing up to attend these lunches, good publicity for the magazines that showed we actually had real interaction with our readers and helped them 'live the dream' of meeting the models, and of course Deric got free photo material to fill up the pages in his magazines.

Taking this idea one step further, Deric hit upon the idea of the annual Fantasy Road Show.

He hired a mini bus, had it decorated with both the logos and slogans of Fantasy Publications and Television X, and booked a bunch of models to travel around the country in it, stopping off at designated seaside resorts and doing impromptu shows at any night-club that would be happy to participate.

The P.R. department gave Deric lots of give-away items (pens, hats, T-shirts and old back issues of magazines) and, on the first Road Show, along with the models, Deric went on the road himself, taking with him Marino, and Randy Shagnasty as official photographer.

Once again, public goodwill was obtained, along with publicity for both the magazines and the Channel, and of course lots of free pictures of the girls posing topless all around the country with the happy smiling public – all great for use in the mags and as promotional pictures for the company.

The Road Show was a good idea, although the annual parties seemed to be waning in popularity. When it was time for our third *New Talent* birthday party, we advertised an event at one of London's top table dancing clubs, but the editorial staff of Fantasy Publications and Television X were by now all very conspicuous by their total absence from the event.

Chapter Eighteen:
THE LOOK-A-LIKES, THE ROAD SHOW AND THE DEAD BODY

Under Deric's guidance, Fantasy Publications and Television X both continued to grow in parallel with each other, and with a fair amount of publicity crossover.

We started to produce a Television X Video Magazine along the lines of the *Amateur Video Magazine*, but this one came complete with Television X listings, behind-the-scenes programme gossip and a 'free' cover mounted video comprising of cut-down teaser versions of many of the Television X programmes.

Deric continued to come up with ideas for new Television X shows, all of which were based on an adult version of some topical event or well known celebrity, and all of which contained at least one (and often more) major characters that Deric wrote in for himself to play.

When the Spice Girls were at the height of their fame in the 1990s, Deric and I watched them from our office window as they sped around on The Thames dock immediately outside our Docklands office on a speedboat, filming a sequence for their upcoming movie *Spice World*. When their film was released, Deric tried to cash in on their popularity by producing a series for Television X based on a similar all girl band called The Vice Girls. The series was called *Vice*

World, and Deric liaised with Shag & Mutt to cast and film it for him.

They got five look-a-likes to play the various girls and, using the skills of a local musician. Deric wrote a number of songs, which were then recorded using genuine singers, with Deric hoping to get the girls to mime to the playback of the songs on camera.

Unfortunately with little rehearsal time this proved to be an impossibility, and the resulting footage shows the girls badly miming out of sync. These musical sequences were only saved in the edit by lots of quick camera cutaways from their dancing bodies so that the lack of lip sync wasn't on screen long enough to be too apparent.

Just like the real Spice Girls had done, Deric filmed The Vice Girls in a sequence shot around the Docklands. By sheer coincidence, as they passed a local newsagents, the headline on a newspaper's board outside the shop read 'Vice Girls In Docklands!' My guess is it probably referred to an expose about local prostitution rather than Deric's fictitious badly miming look-a-likes!

Unconnected with this series, but very much inspired by the real Spice Girls, the idea came to Television X chiefs that it could be a very successful idea to launch a real vocal group like the Spice Girls but appealing purely to an adult audience. A group of Television X models were cast to front the band, who were to be called The Fantasy Girls, and a CD was launched using genuine singers doing a raunchy cover version of The Rolling Stones' song *Lets Spend The Night Together*. Despite a sexy video and a little airplay, the single unfortunately got nowhere and the project was abandoned. Perhaps, like Deric's *Game For A Giggle,* the idea was simply ahead of its time, when later on was to come raunchy music videos from genuine stars like Lady Gaga, Christina Aguilera's *Dirrty*, Madonna's *Erotica,* The Pussycat Dolls and Girls Aloud.

The next series that Deric worked on was *Crown Chronicles*, which saw him going back to his love of Royal look-a-likes. The series controversially featured Prince Charles, Princess Diana and Camilla Parker-Bowles (the Prince and Princess were in reality separated at this time) and, in an eerie foretaste of what was to come in real-life, the series ended with a car crash death – However it was Charles and not Diana that died in Deric's spoof TV show.

Years later, when Di actually did die in a car crash in Paris, the series was archived not, as far as I know, to ever be re- screened.

For this series Deric got Phil McCavity to film it, my old colleague from the days of working with Peter in Lincoln.

I had so far not been too keen to get involved in the shooting of Deric's films as he always wrote very wordy scripts with several characters and locations that needed quite a lot of planning in order to make them work successfully.

However, I did finally agree to film and produce Deric's next project which was *The President's Perversion*, based on the so- called 'Clinton-Gate' scandal of the then President Bill Clinton and White House intern Monica Lewinsky.

Deric sourced very good look-a-likes for both the President and Prime Minister Tony Blair, and we perhaps unfairly cast a rather oversized model as Miss Lewinsky. Marino (Superdick) put on a short-hair wig to play the President's randy aide, who took part in most of the sex activities while the Clinton look- alike himself just sat watching and egging him on. The look- alike himself did however take part in the infamous blow-job scene, complete with a re-enactment of the cigar insertion. The film ends with Clinton getting a phone call from Lindsay as Ben Dover who invites him to England to become a porn star.

Deric cast himself as a White House advisor in what was for him a more serious, almost dark, role compared with some of the comedy characters he had developed for his previous series.

This series was made into a video and we sent a copy to The White House for Bill Clinton's approval. Had we received a reply (even a standard compliment slip acknowledging receipt of the video) we would have published it in *New Talent* magazine and it would have made for good publicity for the video, but unfortunately no communication from The White House was forthcoming.

Deric wasn't the only one working on marketing scams at that time however. The official Television X marketing department came up with the idea of getting well known busty glamour model Linsey Dawn McKenzie to do a topless streak at a public event, making sure that she mentioned the name 'Television X' to any journalists who quizzed her about it afterwards. Television X would also have their cameras there to film the moment for screening on the Channel.

The event chosen was a charity football match held in an East London park. Celebrities taking part in the match included pop star Damon Albarn, then famous for his band Blur and later for The Gorillaz, actor/musician Chesney Hawkes, who had had a one-off hit in 1991 with '*The One And Only*', and Jarvis Cocker, then singer with the band Pulp.

When her moment came, Linsey made a beeline for Jarvis, throwing her arms round him and kissing him on the cheek.

'Backstage' after the event, the Television X cameras carried out impromptu interviews with everyone involved. Linsey, who by that time, had quaffed a lot of the free champagne, claimed she had done the streak as Television X's contribution to 'the charity' although, when pressed by journalists as to what the charity actually was, she clearly had no idea.

Chesney Hawkes asked Linsey if she hadn't run up to him because he 'wasn't as famous as Damon or Jarvis', and Jarvis himself recounted the moment that Linsey ran up to him, saying that her breasts were almost 'mesmerising' as they swung to and fro with her movements.

Possibly a fairly successful publicity stunt then. One of Deric's ideas however, didn't turn out to be quite so successful. He had the idea for Television X in conjunction with Fantasy Publications to launch their own version of the very popular Erotica sex exhibition, a public event where ticket holders could attend a kind of Ideal Home Show of sex! Deric suggested it be called The Fantasy Show.

Right next door to London's famous Wembley Stadium was the Wembley Exhibition Centre, and this was booked for the three-day weekend long event from Friday through to Sunday, and plans were made as to just what we would fill the venue with.

On the main stage was to be a continuous striptease show, interspersed with chat from Deric and Marino who, acting as MCs, would throw out goody bags into the audience. There was to be a 'Real Wives' stand and an 'Only 18' stand with free back issues of those magazines handed out by topless models dressed appropriately to those genres, the Only 18 models on roller skates, in tiny skirts and, with hair in bunches, they would be sucking on lollipops and blowing bubbles.

There would be a stand where you could have your photo taken with a top model, as well as a stand where you could try out as a porn director, directing a video shoot, under the watchful eye of one of the Scums.

There was a David Dickie's World Of Sport section with topless girls in tiny skirts challenging punters to play snooker with them, as well as demonstrations of live Jello Wrestling that were provided by an outside company who specialised in that particular 'sport'.

All of these events came at a separate price for the punter, which was in addition to their initial entrance fee.

My involvement? I was to run a mini cinema room with video clips from Television X programmes and Fantasy videos constantly playing on a loop onto a big TV screen.

On paper, the event sounded good, but the reality was that it cost far more to put on than we took in by way of ticket prices and entrance fees.

We had almost every glamour girl in the business booked with us for that weekend but, because each day was a very long working day for them, by the third day many of the models booked were getting exhausted and ill but nonetheless struggling in as they had been told by their agent that unless they completed the full three days they would not get paid at all. This was because the agents themselves had been told exactly that by us and, to make sure of it, Fantasy bosses were checking each and every model in and out at the beginning and end of each day with a clipboard! The agents were trying to sneak some of the girls out after they'd been checked in to give them more regular breaks, making sure however that every girl was back at her post by closing time in readiness for checking out!

The Scums took each girl aside during the event and shot an impromptu photo-set on site which could then be used in the magazines and for future promotions but, apart from this, there was little that came out of the event of long term value to the company and The Fantasy Show was not regarded as a huge success and there were no plans to repeat it.

The next summer a young long-haired guy joined Fantasy Publications as a general admin assistant. I met him for the first time one lunchtime at the pub. When he heard that I was also involved with Television X he showed great interest, and I promised to show him round the studios sometime. The assistant editor of *Penthouse* warned me not to steal this new employee for the Channel, but the truth was that adult film- making would eventually prove to be much more suited to Jack Bedford than working on the magazines.

Deric had planned a live broadcast on Television X on General Election night 1997 with several spoof pre-recorded sketches to be interspersed with our regular programming, topless girls keeping the viewers abreast of the latest results live. Deric thought that this might be a way to capture the politically concerned viewing audience that night who might otherwise be glued to the BBC or ITV Election Night Specials.

One sketch that we recorded for the night had Deric and I recreating the 1940s type roles that we set up for the London Electricity corporate film. In a short sequence lasting just a few minutes, Deric and I played two gentlemen replete in suits and trilby hats, advising on sexual matters from a supposed 1942 government health advice film.

One of the Television X editors did a fantastic job editing the sequence in black and white, complete with jumpy vision and constant on-screen old film style negative scratches, for which he wrote a specifically designed computer programme.

It was a very funny sketch with Deric tapping his pipe out on a prostitute's rear end only to find that a previous client had written a phone number there as an 'aid memoir', the number being Whitehall 1212, which had been the old telephone number for Scotland Yard.

On the night of transmission I was also to play my 1940s character from this sketch live in the studio, being pompous and shocked by the naked models that were in the studio with Deric who was playing himself. My own long hair was slicked back under my trilby hat (which, on loan from a costume hire company, had apparently once been used by the comedian Les Dawson as his name was still stuck in the lining!) and, because of his huge interest in the workings of the Channel, we employed Jack Bedford that night as a production assistant.

Jack's interest in adult television was fired up that night and it wasn't long before, as the *Penthouse* assistant editor had feared, he had defected to Television X and was working as a full time production assistant there, cutting his teeth and gaining the experience and insight that led him to eventually set up his own production company to make many hugely successful (and outrageously titled) programmes for Television X, including *Cum On My Great Big Tits, Mature Momma Meltdown* and *Layla Jade's Spunk Sucking Sluts* among others.

Before he got to that point however, he worked in-house for another ex Fantasy Publications employee who had also gone on to work as a Television X producer.

Known simply as 'Big Jim', he employed Jack as the director of his series *The Strap-O-Gram Girl* which starred big boobed blonde model Katie Ann Day, and I was taken on as both lighting cameraman and editor for the first series.

Having found that he had a talent to direct, Jack started to shoot his own programmes for Television X, working closely with me as his lighting cameraman.

I made mistakes while working for Jack, but he was always very forgiving. Once when shooting an anal scene on a snooker table upstairs in the well known Soho pub The Intrepid Fox, I lined up a fantastic shot from below of model Kelly Aris having a hard anal sex session. The shot went on for several minutes with Jack watching on the monitor and congratulating me on the framing, angle and lighting of this particular shot. It was only afterward, once he was back home and starting to edit, that he realised I hadn't actually pressed the record button on the camera and that, for an anal themed programme called *Butt Monkey*, there was actually no close-up hardcore anal shots whatsoever to use in the programme!

It was with Jack that I finally really began to see how the mechanics of making television programmes made sense however, and saw how, budgeted properly, an adult TV producer could actually make some real money. Unlike Deric, who just had crazy ideas and then expected someone else to make them happen with never a thought as to what it was going to cost, Jack had a totally professional understanding of how to produce a show, something that he later proved when making a mainstream one-off television documentary for Channel Four about the Cannes Porn Film Festival.

With Jack, I also gained more insight as to how far we could allow shots to develop for TV showing. Ofcom (the body set up to monitor and regulate all British television output) were more forgiving than the BBFC, although we still couldn't show a lot. What we could show on television however, that we would never have been allowed to show on video, included cum shots over female faces (as long as the actual dick was not in shot), front on pussy lips, and of course lots of, so far BBFC prohibited, dildo and group sex! On Television X, the girls could even wear G-Strings and thongs!

All this was fantastic for what I was now shooting with Jack, although still of course caused some problems when I was trying to edit cut-down teaser versions of the programmes for softer BBFC rated video release on the *Television X Video Magazine*, so I would always have to put a teaser message up stating that 'You can see the full uncut versions of these programmes only on Television X, where we can show the hardest sex allowed on British television'!

I first worked with blonde Layla Jade on a girl/girl scene that Jack and I shot for his series *Butt Monkey*. She had written to me at Fantasy Publications in my then role as the model contact seeking advise as to how to get into the adult business.

I had written back a detailed letter outlining the ups and downs and warning her to be careful who she worked for. She told me on the *Butt Monkey* shoot that it was because of my good advise to her that she had decided to embark on her career in porn.

Jack and I went on to give her her own series for Television X, *Layla Jade's Spunk Sucking Sluts*, which was cleverly re-titled *Layla Jade's Cream Obsession* for the more modest EPG television listings, as they had to be 'clean' enough to be viewed by the whole family. Often these rewordings got a bit confused however; a series that Jack and I filmed called *Lesbo Chicks Do Boy/Girl*, a series showcasing a debut boy/girl scene from a model who had previously only ever done girl/girl scenes (we filmed Angel Long's first boy/girl scene for this series), was re-titled for the TV Listings by a Television X employee whose first language clearly wasn't English as *Sexy Chicks Go Transexual*, thereby changing not only the whole meaning of the show, but possibly attracting a different kind of audience altogether!

Layla Jade has since gone on to carve a successful on-screen career for herself on both sides of the Atlantic.

Jack also cast Layla Jade in *Bad Brother*, a porno version of the mainstream reality TV series *Big Brother*.

We hired a location for a week that we could split into two self-contained levels, with the cast of four girls and two guys living downstairs, and the crew living separately upstairs. Although we would be present to film and direct certain scenes, we shot a lot of the scenarios with set-up locked-off cameras, after having left instructions for a sexy 'task' in what we had set up as a 'diary room', where the cast could go at any time and give their thoughts on the other models and how good (or bad) they were at sex.

True to the spirit of the original *Big Brother*, we left provisions for the cast in the diary room where they then had to fend for themselves, making their own meals etc. We locked all outside doors and wouldn't allow any of the models to leave the house for the duration of the shoot, something that one girl, big-busted Scottish model Scotti Andrews, found a little more traumatic than the others. She took to staying in her bedroom, and refusing to take part in the sex scenes. Jack had quiet words of encouragement with her off-camera however and she then bravely persevered to the end of the shoot, which resulted in a very successful series, and the only adult one I think that has been made as closely to the rules of the original *Big Brother* as possible.

With Jack, I also worked on two series of what was a genuine reality style TV show, *Search For A Porn Star*. We renamed it *Porn Idol* for the second series, to tie in with the then successful mainstream TV show *Pop Idol*. Television X advertised widely that they were seeking a new male porn star for their Channel. Initial heats took place at the Television X studio where wannabe studs would come in one after another, after a brief interview by the likes of Ben Dover, Marino or Omar. These guys would then have to strip off and play with themselves (without ejaculating) until they were hard while a naked pretty girl did a lap dance for them. The guys that made it through this heat (five were picked) then went on to the second round where they each got to star in their own episode of the show and have full sex with one of our models. Some couldn't get hard of course or came too quickly or couldn't perform successfully. All their on-screen problems were also recorded so that the resulting show, although sexy, also showed the genuine outcome of their efforts, good or bad.

The man declared by Television X as the overall winner was rewarded with his own series for the Channel, for which he was paid the going rate for a male stud, and of course his work invariably led on to further work for other producers in the industry.

Successful past winners included 'Justin The Beast', whose winning series was *Jeff Gets Jiggy* and *Jeff's Jiggy Day*, both directed by Jack Bedford, and Brett Tracy, whose winning series was *The Brettish Empire* directed by Jim Slip.

A year after the first Fantasy Road Show, Deric planned to repeat the event but this time he was too busy to personally oversee it or to attend, so he volunteered me to go in his place, assuring me that it would be great fun travelling round the Country with some naked birds!

Initially I travelled down to Bournemouth to pick up the customised mini-bus and only then encountered the first problem; they wanted a security deposit before I could drive it away. Deric had assured me that everything was paid for and now he was away on holiday.

I had no money or credit cards with me, and neither did I plan to spend my own money on something that wasn't really my problem. A quick phone call back to Fantasy HQ however revealed that the Company didn't plan to spend their own money on it either, as no company credit card was available for immediate use over the telephone.

Annoyed that I had come all the way to Bournemouth from London to get put in this position, I told Fantasy that I would simply get back on the train and come back home then without the bus as Deric should have sorted all this out. Given this ultimatum the problem was soon sorted out over the phone by Fantasy, and I drove the mini-bus back to London where, for the few days before we set off on the tour, it was parked very conspicuously outside my London apartment. I lived in an exclusive gated development of luxury apartments and, if my rather conservative neighbours had been previously unaware of what I did for a living, there could now be no doubt as I parked a large white mini bus outside the building that bore the legend: *Television X – The Fantasy Channel. Beware! Naked Models On Board* proudly across its body!

Deric had worked out an itinerary that, over two weeks, took in many major holiday resorts around Britain, and he had booked us into various local hotels and B&Bs along the way.

The plan was that we would arrive at a resort, book into the hotel, and then find a night-club or bar that would be happy to host our live road show event for later that night.

We would then tour around the streets and beach fronts, the girls in tiny tight fitting Television X T-shirts and bikini bottoms, handing out promotional leaflets, baseball caps, badges etc. In the evening, after dinner, we would do our road show, consisting of the girls doing a raunchy dance routine and we would hand out more promotional material in the club. We would then go back to the hotel to sleep, and set off the next morning for the next resort where we would do the same all over again.

I booked the well-known British black porn stud Omar (known to his fans as 'Big Willy' due to his amazing thirteen inch manhood) to front the two week long jaunt, and took Jack Bedford along as our tour manager. He would be in charge of the bus, take photos and liaise with me over booking us into venues and arranging evening meals etc.

I had booked a number of models for the trip, a different pair for each week, that included blonde Welsh babe Kelle Marie, fellow blonde Leigh Brooke, and two other of the regular Television X presenters.

On the morning that we were due to set off, I turned up at the Fantasy Building where I was going to meet up with Omar, Jack and the two girls we were taking for the first week and load the bus up with all the promotional gear. I hadn't been in the office very long when I got a phone call; one of our girls was sick and was pulling out of the trip. We were meant to be on the road in under an hour and I needed another girl who was free to come on the road with us for a week and be free to do it within the next few minutes!

After several frantic phone calls, it became apparent that no other model was either free or willing to join us. I was at my wit's end, until Omar came up with a solution. He knew a big-busted blonde who had shown interest in doing some glamour modelling, and would I be interested in giving her a go? At this stage, I didn't really have an option and so, without even seeing a picture of this girl who had never even done any amateur modelling before, I agreed to take her along on the Road Trip as an ambassador of what was rapidly becoming Britain's premier adult entertainment channel!

We all headed off for Omar's Essex home, where she was to meet us.

As we drew near, Omar told me to park the Tour Bus round the corner so that his neighbours didn't see it, as he didn't want to draw any extra attention to what he did for a living. Omar was at that time one of the most well known faces in British porn and, if his neighbours didn't already know who he was in that respect, I would have been very surprised! However, I complied with his request and parked the 'Porn Bus' round the corner and waited while he went to get the new girl.

When she arrived I was glad that Omar had suggested bringing her along as a Channel representative as, although she lacked the posture and polish that more established glamour models have, in every other way she was perfect as a Television X girl – big silicone boobs, long blonde hair and a more than open attitude to all things sexual. She was fairly uninhibited and keen to do whatever it took to do well in this, her first opportunity at being a glamour model.

So, with the new recruit loaded on board, off we set, touring round the seaside resorts of Great Britain, parking the van up and handing out free T-shirts, pens and flyers while the girls were happy to flash their boobs and pose for photos with the public, and then in the evenings we'd take our off-the-peg road show to any local pub or night-club that would have us for an impromptu set.

We were almost mobbed when we stopped the van for the first time and started handing out free T-Shirts and flyers. Eventually the local police had to move us on as we were causing too much of an obstruction on the public footpath as the crowds gathered round us but, as we drove away, it appeared that the entire population, young and old alike, of the particular little seaside town we were in, were all sporting Television X T-Shirts and caps. Great advertising!

Strangely enough, considering that we were touring around with two very scantily clad busty beauties, it was Omar who seemed to get the most attention as we wandered around the streets. He would often hide his head in his hands to avoid being recognised as he was mobbed by yet another group of fans, both male and female, who knew him from his many porn movies, which he released under the name Big Willy. All they wanted was an autograph and a chat but, unlike Deric who seemed to love nothing more than being the centre of media or public attention, Omar, originally a professional footballer by profession, was a charmingly reluctant star, shy of all the attention he got due to the fact that he just happened to have a big dick.

This was the first time I had really got to know Omar and I found him to be a thoroughly nice guy. Far from being the boastful cock-sure diva one might have expected, Omar was just a normal bloke; shy in company and with a great sense of humour that kept me entertained throughout the trip.

When the tour was over, I worked with him as cameraman on many of his Television X shows, the hard versions of which were also made into DVDs.

I played the off-camera role of 'Bert' in many of them. Bert was a similar character to that of 'Reg' in *Superdick*; a bumbling cameraman sidekick who Omar looked down on with disdain. Over the years Omar has used a number of different cameramen on his shows but the character of 'Bert' has always prevailed. So, apart from my persona as 'Bert', the character has also been portrayed as having a gruff Australian accent, a British Northern accent (and as such, unlike my version, 'Northern Bert' got much more involved with the girls in front of camera too), and 'Bert' has even been played by a female camera person, but with hardly any vocal inter-action obviously.

Omar, like Lindsay, was a huge fan of television comedy, and we spent a lot of time when I worked with him, laughing over things like *The Fast Show* or *Harry Hill*. Omar always used to put in a comedy prat-fall or a comedic run-off at the end of his shows, similar to something out of *Benny Hill*. These comedic elements, something that the Television X managing producers didn't like at all, became a bit of a trademark in all of Omar's films.

But back to the road trip...

The town with the most lenient attitude toward us was definitely Brighton, where the girls wandered down the prom completely naked with hardly anyone batting an eyelid, and that included the local police!

The town with the strictest attitude toward us was Torquay in Devon. The hotel, not unlike Basil Fawlty's *Fawlty Towers*, asked us not to socialise with any of the other guests when they realised what we did. They put us in a very 'out of the way' corner in the restaurant near the toilets, and they asked us not to park our van in their car park, complaining that they were misled when we booked the hotel as it had been booked in the parent company's name of Northern and Shell. They claimed that they believed we would be from Shell Oil and that they wouldn't have taken the booking if they had realised we were a porn company!

The manager even tried to stop one of the girls signing an autograph to a fan who was also staying at the Hotel and who had spotted her in the Hotel's Reception, believing that she was somehow forcing her autograph on him!

The club we booked our road show into that night also told us that we had to be very very tame in what we did as they had had several visits from the local police and been warned that they could lose their licence if they hosted any sexy adult style entertainment evenings. It appeared that 'Basil Fawlty' was also on the local council!

We did our best to keep the evening tame but our girls were on top form, getting their boobs out and dancing erotically on the tables and with the customers. We were consequently accosted by the burley suited bouncers and frog-marched out of the club while the manager moaned that, thanks to us, he was definitely now going to lose his licence, and also possibly his club! We kept the video camera rolling however as we were literally thrown out, as it all made for good footage that we could edit into a programme for Television X when we got back.

The seaside town of Great Yarmouth was another very interesting resort for us. The hotel we'd been booked into had no parking facility whatsoever for not only our huge van but also for any other cars at all and, after we'd checked in, the manager took us all into his old fashioned parlour where we perched on hard chairs like naughty children while he started reading us the rules of the house; we were to be back by eleven o'clock each night or we'd be locked out. There were to be no members of the opposite sex allowed in the rooms, etc etc etc. The girls started giggling and exchanging glances. We explained that we were a porn crew and that we would be out late every night performing our show. The hotel manager's face fell, and the very next night we made sure to leave that place and book in to a different hotel with altogether more lenient rules.

We found a great venue for the stage show on our second night in Great Yarmouth however, even picking up a good looking girl on the way there who hitched a ride with us to the club and asked if she could help us handing out leaflets as well! All was looking good as we piled back into the van after the show and headed back to the new hotel.

Unsure of the way back, Jack turned down a side road and almost immediately screeched the van to a halt. There, in the very middle of the road, lay a man – completely dead!

Two of his friends stood on the pavement, understandably hysterical. We assumed that the corpse had been run down by a hit and run driver, but his friends were not making much sense. As they had called the police, there seemed little point in us hanging around, particularly as the dead man's drunken friends were beginning to get a bit jumpy with us. Our new recruit model, Omar's blonde friend, wasn't really helping either as she too was getting quite hysterical at the sight of her first dead body just after having stripped naked in a drunken night-club.

The dead body was right in the middle of the road and it would clearly have been unethical to move it in order to drive on. Jack started up the engine and, just as the corpse's drunken mates started to try and get in the van with us, shouting that we too were to blame somehow for their friend's death, he swerved onto the pavement, manoeuvring the van round the corpse and headed off back to the hotel for a stiff medicinal brandy from the min-bar in Omar's room.

The next morning, two police officers arrived at the hotel and we were all interviewed separately about the incident.

This in itself must have been interesting for them as they took our names, and then took the names again, as the girls had accidentally given their stage or model name as opposed to their real one.

We were told that the dead man's friends had commented in their statement that they thought that they must surely be in some kind of bizarre dream; they were returning from a night- club, happily tipsy, when their mate gets run over in a tiny side street by a hit and run driver, and then from around the corner, out of the dark, headlights blazing, screeched a huge white van complete with sexy scantily clad glamour girls and emblazoned with the sign: *Beware! Naked Models On Board!* They told the police that they thought they must surely be in some kind of surreal nightmare, unsure as to whether perhaps God Himself or The Devil was to appear from the van and personally whisk their friend off to the afterlife!

As we visited different parts of the country I was also able to meet face to face with some of the readers who had written in to *New Talent* and our other magazines, and Jack and I filmed some impromptu solo sequences with some of their wives and girlfriends in whichever hotel we were staying in at the time, which we could then use on both the cover-mounted videos and on Television X.

I don't know if the Road Trips were generally regarded as a success or not by the company we worked for but, when we finally pulled back into the Television X car park after a frantic two weeks of striptease, flashing at lorries as we drove along the motorways, naked streaks on Britain's sea fronts and, of course, witnessing the aftermath of a manslaughter, the van was to be returned without a view to it ever being called back into operation, or to ever reviving the Seaside Road Show.

Television X have since however made road-show style appearances at other events, most notably the '*In The Bedroom With Television X*' Roadshow at 'The Ibiza Reunion' party held in Skegness where ex *Neighbours* and *Joseph And His Amazing Technicolour Dreamcoat* star Jason Donovan met our girls, and posed for photos with them.

Deric's original idea of the Channel going 'On The Road' like Shagnasty and Muttley however has not yet been repeated.

Chapter Nineteen:
A TALENT TO ENTERTAIN

Television X and Fantasy Publications seemed to be going from strength to strength. Deric and I were now familiar faces in the adult industry, influential in giving models regular work. It was all going great; a kind of self-financing party where Deric and I could play with television and video production as well as magazine publishing as if all these things were simply our big boys' toys.

But things were changing. The parent company of Television X wanted to do more with the television bandwidth that they owned than just run a porn channel.

Television X was at that time only on air until four in the morning, leaving a two-hour gap of dead air time before the more mainstream UK Living Channel came back on air at six a.m.

Someone had a bright idea of how to fill these two hours with programming that would cost literally nothing to obtain and very little to actually put on air.

Deric and I were brought in to do a dry run for a new Channel, which was given the working title of The Talent Channel.

The idea was a simple one. This would be a public access TV station, with viewers submitting their own material for broadcast, whether it be comedy, music, poetry, or any other form of human entertainment, as long as it was copyright free.

A satellite TV station that got its programmes in for nothing was one thing, but one that showed the material at an hour of the day when no one would be watching it? My first question was 'Why?'

I was told to wake up and smell the proverbial coffee. Had I never heard of public access?

'People will send in their tapes and we'll put them on TV', I was told. Singers, poets, independent filmmakers, people just fooling around with a camcorder having a laugh; all this would come flooding in to us I was assured. People want to be on TV and we would be the home to the would-be celebrity and the wannabe pop star, as well as the more inane and bizarre independent filmmaker; a kind of televisual YouTube, except that this was in the days before YouTube.

Certainly such channels were common enough in America and some parts of Europe, but Britain at that time, used to the sombre lavish tones of the BBC, had never had much in the way of public access television. All that has changed now of course with the likes of You Tube, satellite TV station Sumo TV, and a plethora of reality style mainstream programmes all geared at providing a platform for would-be TV stars all seeking their 'fifteen minutes of fame', as Andy Warhol once put it. But way back then in the mid to late 1990s, the idea of launching a successful public access style television station was revolutionary.

I assumed that this planned channel would be funded from advertising. I was wrong. It was to be financed by subscribers. But who, in their right mind, would pay to watch a channel that only broadcast from four a.m. to six a.m. in the morning when most people were in bed?

'Video recorders' was the answer I got when I put this question to the Portland TV bosses. The idea was to encourage subscribers to 'time-shift' the night's programming and watch it the next evening with a few beers. And because it would all be genuinely made up from what viewers had sent in, every night's programming would be different. You wouldn't know what to expect. Just imagine; if a viewer with a camcorder records himself doing something weird tonight,

he could be watching himself on TV the very next week! Genuine public access – and pretty immediate too. What other channel was offering its viewers this kind of instant 'Andy Warhol' type of public exposure on national TV?

Not even the people submitting their material would be able to watch their work on TV without paying the subscription fee first however, and that at least should guarantee a minimum of subscribers – at least those that sent in their own material and would like to see it broadcast!

Another incentive to subscribe was that, if viewers wanted it, they would also get a Television X subscription thrown in for nothing. The plan here was that, at the end of their first subscription, viewers who perhaps had not liked The Talent Channel, would still decide to re-subscribe – for Television X. And of course they would have the perfect excuse to put to their wives who might not be too happy with them subscribing to a porn channel; 'Oh, I'm paying for The Talent Channel, but Television X just happens to come free with it'!

It was the seventh of July 1997 when Deric and I had our first meeting about setting up this new Channel. There was as yet no office to work from, no material to broadcast and no new staff employed other than an executive producer called Chris to oversee everything.

'How long do we have before the proposed on-air date?' I asked, thinking that two months would be tight.

'August the first' came the reply! Had I been told April the first I might have assumed the whole thing was an April Fools practical joke. But no, we had less than a month to go on air; the heat was on and, never one not to rise to a challenge, Deric and I got stuck in.

However as the Channel was not particularly adult oriented in its content, Deric took more of a back seat, concentrating on building the Dating section of the programming under his guise as relationship counsellor Doctor David Michaels.

I was taken on as full time producer/presenter, along with two other new recruits; Liverpool based Adam O'Brien, and a smart London girl named Anna. Adam had no experience in broadcast television before and none of us had any presenting experience. We were all given a crash course in how to do our own make-up for TV by Television X's resident make-up artist, who was then sharing a flat with the Page Three glamour girl Katie Price, then known, in her pre Peter Andre/Alex Reid days, by her model name of Jordan.

I cancelled all my involvement with the magazine side of things, except for *New Talent,* where I went into the old office once a month and wrote all the articles as per usual, as well as checked over the post in my still on-going 'model contact' capacity.

A makeshift studio was built in one of the small offices where the Television X edit suites were then housed in the Portland House building over the docks from Fantasy Publications. Television X itself was in the process of moving its main studio and offices across to the same building as Fantasy.

To keep costs down, Adam, Anna and myself would do a bit of everything; we would spend the morning trying to generate material, either by phone, post or personal visit, we would shoot recorded links in the afternoon in our tiny purpose built studio and, during the evening, when the Television X edit suites were on 'down time', two freelance editors worked on the new material we had sourced as well as on the links that we had shot that afternoon, editing up the programming that would be broadcast the next day 'as live'.

Adam, Anna and I literally sorted out our own production parts. There was no crew and no director. The lights had been set up as standard by the Television X lighting guys, and so all we had to do was turn them on. We would do our own make-up, and set the camcorder up on a locked-off shot on a tripod, which we could then watch on a monitor fed through from the camera. We would then simply sit in front of the camera and do the links, improvising our own dialogue as we went along. Our Channel production was quite literally a one-man-band operation.

Our producer Chris gave the Channel a crazy, bright kind of look, similar to that of children's Saturday morning television, with the studio painted in primary colours with little toys and brightly coloured ornaments dotted around on shelves in the background.

I myself made sure that I always wore colourful shirts when I was presenting and tried to be very 'up tempo', like some crazy late night DJ on speed.

We had just three weeks before our first transmission date, giving us hardly any time to do any real advertising. So just where were we going to get enough material to fill two hours a night?

We knew that previous attempts by other companies at putting public access on national television had only had a half an hour a week to find material for. At that time, Britons were not as renowned as their Atlantic cousins for being hungry enough for some TV exposure to send material in for nothing.

We put a few ads in a variety of magazines, including the actors' bible *The Stage*, and pretty soon the tiny office below Television X in which we'd set up with borrowed desks and computers, was filled with jiffy bags containing home-made video tapes from an amazingly varied amount of Great British talent.

Eccentric middle aged Scotsman Alex McMenace played a tartan guitar and a trumpet that sounded like a kazoo. He was accompanied by his drum playing wife who, when she wasn't behind the drum kit, was doing a jig to the rock'n'roll music that Alex played. In complete contrast, there were well- produced music videos from the likes of Indie rockers Loudmouth, and there was a Frank Sinatra look-alike Frankie Dickens, who came from the East End of London and billed himself as the 'Next Generation Sinatra' or 'Old Brown Eyes', his eyes being the wrong colour for a Sinatra look-alike, who had of course been known as 'Old Blue Eyes'! Frankie sang songs that the original Frankie had rejected, and was only visually a look-alike for the more mature Sinatra in as much as he was an ageing white man who wore a fedora hat!

A fantastic tape turned up from a cheery black guy called Saleh Mohammad, a comedian, poet and singer/songwriter who had simply set his camcorder on a tripod in his sitting room, plonked himself down on the sofa in front of it without first checking that the camera was correctly positioned on him, so that his head appeared at the bottom of the screen, and then told jokes to no audience and sang songs to no music. His 'act' was unintentionally hilarious, and he became one of our favourite contributors. He was full of self-praise for his talents and told us that he was also an accomplished actor, something that we all thought was a figment of his imagination until one morning when Adam ran into the office loudly proclaiming that he'd seen Saleh sitting in the Queen Vic pub on an episode of *Eastenders* the previous night!

It was all classic stuff and, as we sat in the office every morning, excitedly opening the next envelope, not knowing what kind of material awaited us, it made me realise that there were more potential stars out there than one would ever see on Saturday evening prime-time TV; bizarre comedians and unknown rock bands that outshone many that were currently enjoying mainstream success. But, more to the point, we were going to give them the airtime on national television to do their thing alongside more professional performers and filmmakers. It was the spirit of punk all over again – what Deric had done for would-be glamour photographers and models through his magazines, we were now doing with unknown performers and film-makers on television; anybody could now be on TV, no matter how bad or how inexperienced or unknown they were, and it wasn't up to some cigar chomping big-shot producer or some Simon Cowell to decide their fate; it was simply up to the Royal Mail to successfully deliver their video tape to us in time to put it in the Show.

And still those jiffy bags came pouring in – Yorkshire based comedians Rick'n'Nick performed elaborate sketches of what were effectively the kind of jokes you'd tell down the pub that were only funny if you'd had a bit to drink and were telling them to your equally drunken mates!

There was strange comedy film-maker Wayne Kerr (geddit?) who sent us hours and hours of well filmed and well edited sketches that included a spoof Spinal Tap type rock duo, a rodent super-hero called Mouseman and the diary of spotty anorak clad Young Wayne who, in one episode, built a rocket and actually went to the moon, all believably well filmed and edited with no access to Hollywood style special effects or CGI.

One of the Television X editors, a lovely guy called Giles, walked in one day with a marvellous fantasy style feature length film that he had shot on a shoestring budget while still a student at university. Called *Nameless Kults*, it featured warring saxons, raping and pillaging, was incredibly well written, well filmed, well acted and well edited. We played a chunk of it out every night as a kind of surreal home-grown soap opera.

This was clearly all material that amateur film-makers were putting together with loving care on a zero budget and, as such, they deserved a showing on national television – albeit at an unearthly hour in the morning when not enough people would be watching to appreciate them!

We weren't offering any payment for material, just the opportunity for exposure on television so, to encourage these talented would-be stars and film-makers to send in their work to us, we told them that we were giving free subscriptions to our Channel to television and acting agents, who would therefore be watching and likely to see all this amazing new material. Whether television and acting agents ever took us up on our offer of free subscriptions, I have no idea, but we could at least boast that 'viewers tapes may well be seen by influential agents' as an incentive for people to send their material in.

Of course not all the stuff that we got was as entertaining as Wayne Kerr or Alex McMenace – there were also all the Z-list wannabe singers, actors and proud Mums and Dads sending in videos of their kids prancing about to kiddie-pop records or shrieking like a young Lena Zavarone on a bad day. But our plan was to show it all, with no editorial judgement. As long as it was legal, decent, honest and free of copyright problems, then it was on our Channel!

The fact that we three producers (Anna, Adam and myself) were also the presenters of the show every night was basically a money-saver for the Channel, but it also seemed to work very well, and we all took our roles seriously.

Deric presented the 'dating' section of the night, which we dubbed Talent Connections, showing video clips that lonely hearts would send in hoping to meet mister or miss right. In the early days before we got any genuine clips sent in, Deric would mock some of these up by persuading all the office juniors to record a clip under an assumed name.

One of the Fantasy magazine designers also did a stint at presenting, and office junior Darren and his mate Liam virtually stole the show one evening when they had a go at presenting the on-screen links. They both decided to wear black suits with ties, and dark glasses and, because of their shaven heads and clipped East London accents, they both came across as tough gangland mobsters. It could only have been good for subscriptions however, as when these two tough looking guys looked directly into the camera and told you to subscribe, you were much more likely to obey them!

Every night's programming consisted of several themed sections. We had Reel Talent, which showed independent filmmaker's shorts, Tiny Talent, featuring under eighteens, The Talent Charts for music, Talent Arena for the Arts (painting, poetry, dance etc), and Planet Talent for comedy and anything that didn't really fit any other category. In between each category and each clip shown, we would cut back to the studio, as if live, where one or other of us would link through to the next clip.

To keep the links interesting, we three presenters would introduce silly running gags throughout the evening. One night was dubbed 'Cushion Night'. We started off wearing brightly coloured cushions on our heads like hats and, as the night progressed, more and more cushions were added to the studio until, by the final link of the night, the presenter was just a muffled voice coming from underneath a huge pile of brightly coloured cushions that totally filled the studio and the screen.

We did silly student-humour style visual gags as we introduced the clips, and we introduced ourselves with spoof names while our real names appeared in the on-screen graphic.

'Hello, and welcome to the Talent Channel.' Adam would say, 'My name's Adam No-Brain...' (Adam O'Brien would appear in the caption)

'...And I'm Peter Doubt (petered out)' I would then respond, my real name appearing in the caption.

One night I introduced myself as Keith Banana Boy Bubble while Adam, holding a badly drawn cartoon of a face pinned to a clipboard over his own face, became the 'world's first cartoon presenter', Steven Scribble!

One night we planned a supposedly 'live concert'. We were to pre-record all the acts invited to take part over a two day weekend, filming them in the Television X studio and utilising Television X's regular crew, camera and sound-men, and then Adam, Anna and I would record the appropriate links the following Monday, as if we were just to the side of the 'stage' and about to introduce the acts. The show would then be broadcast as if it were live, with dubbed on audience applause etc.

Every act that had agreed to take part did so on the basis that they would be paid no appearance fee, but would receive an edited copy of their performance for their own use.

It all seemed to go very well. The Indie rockers Loudmouth did a brilliant live set as did 'Old Brown Eyes' himself, and everyone arrived at Portland House on time.

We had a Michael Jackson look-alike turn up to perform his act, which turned out to be very amusing as he was not only white (it could of course be argued that so was Michael at that time!), but he also had short ginger hair and was quite out of shape. He made no attempt to put on wig, eye make up or any other type of costume other than a black suit, trilby hat and black tie, making him look more like one of the Blues Brothers than the self-proclaimed King of Pop!

He couldn't sing, had no sequinned glove and he hardly even made any attempt to mime to Jackson's music.

He did however do a passable moon-walk around the studio but that was about the extent of his tribute act!

Unfortunately, as we couldn't use actual Michael Jackson music on air due to copyright problems, our look-alike couldn't take part in our 'live show', but he did of course take away a copy of the tape of his performance for his own use. This was I think the main reason that he had turned up; to get a free professionally shot tape for his show reel!

As the afternoon wore on, we got increasingly worried about a pair of very young kids who were travelling to our East London studio all the way from Leeds; the other side of the country. They were running late and couldn't be contacted on any mobile number that we had for them. We were even more concerned when, on finally speaking with their parents, who weren't travelling with them, we learned that they had put them on the train several hours ago, and that they were meant to have arrived at Kings Cross Station in the centre of London a long time ago. Kings Cross is an area notorious for street prostitution and drug pushers. These kids were barely into their teens, totally unaccompanied and having never been to London before. Needless to say, we were all very concerned for their safety. More so than their parents seemed to be, who reassured us that they could look after themselves and that they would be fine.

Thankfully, the duo eventually arrived at the Studio, telling us that they had arrived at Kings Cross without enough money for a taxi to the studio and, not knowing how far our studios were from Kings Cross Station, they had just started to walk!

The journey from central London to where we were based in East London is the best part of an hour even by car or train, but on foot, with no map and having never been to London before, it was an absolute miracle that they had arrived at all!

However, they were safe, not too tired and both very excited about the prospect of recording their self-penned ballad in a real television studio. We however were just glad that they were safe, and immediately sat them down and made sure that they had a cup of tea and a rest before they went into our studio to finally record their song.

The two children, a boy and girl, were so shy and over-awed by being in a real television environment, that we could barely hear them when they tried to sing the lyric to their song over the backing track that they had provided. We tried everything to get them to relax in front of the cameras, one of our editors turned cameraman Giles proving a great hit in making them laugh but, when the red light went on for a take, they both froze like two rabbits in a headlight and could do no more than mumble their way through the song, their bodies doing tiny frightened movements in place of a dance.

After several unsuccessful attempts, we paid for a taxi for them to get safely back to Kings Cross and made them promise that they would phone us when they got home, so that we knew that they had arrived back safely.

We were still at the studio when they rang some hours later, still full of excitement and thanking us for a great day in a real television environment. The fact that they hadn't performed their song too well hadn't phased them at all; they had just found the whole experience the most exciting day of their lives.

I don't think that either of them ever went on to any great musical success, but they were our heroes that day for their perseverance in getting to us and for their unspoiled enjoyment of the trip.

I was working as 'gallery producer' on this 'live' recording and, as such, it was my first time working on a live event, and I found it very daunting indeed. Our executive producer Chris showed me the ropes and then, sitting beside me, just let me have a go. The 'gallery' is effectively a technical room situated next to the studio where the artists perform. The producer and technical crew sit in the gallery, recording the show onto video tape, watching the camera shots on a bank of monitors and talking to the camera crew and floor managers over 'talk back', seeing into the main studio through a soundproofed glass window.

As all the artists performed I was meant to direct the cameramen as to what shots to get and do it live as I mixed the vision through from one camera to another. This may sound easy but, if the cameras don't give you anything different to cut to, the shots all look 'samey' and, while you're talking to the cameramen and directing them to get more interesting shots, you're forgetting to mix through or cut the pictures on time.

I found it all pretty stressful and, in the end, asked the camera crew to simply keep finding and offering good shots up for me to use, so I could just concentrate on the vision mixing.

After two long and stressful, but very fulfilling days, we all went home, and the next day or so, Adam, Anna and I filmed each other doing the introductory links in the same studio, so it would look as if we were standing just to the side of the set when the entire show was recorded, giving the impression that the whole event had been filmed completely live and as it happened.

I was expecting to dress like I normally did for these links in my brightly coloured designer shirts, with my long hair flowing freely over my shoulders, but our producer Chris had other ideas. He greased my hair back, gave me a little dark eye make-up and dressed me in an tight-fitting 1950s tuxedo with huge black bow-tie, musty white frilly shirt and round dark glasses, making me look like a sleazy M.C. from some seedy 1950s strip club. He also greased Adam's hair into a quiff and plastered his eyes in dark make-up, making him resemble a sleazy teddy-boy type Elvis imitator.

The finished edit of the 'Live Night' looked suitably tacky in what I can only hope looked trendily ironic in a '*Phoenix Night*' kind of way, and I was actually very pleased and proud of the result.

As we left the studio that evening, traces of dark make-up still visible on our eyelids, I mused on how, in just a few short months, I had gone from being a well known figure in the adult industry through my involvement with Deric on the magazines, to becoming a presenter on a mainstream TV show that was being aired every single night of the week – albeit only reaching a limited audience of subscribers at four in the morning!

Adam, Anna, Chris and myself carried on with The Talent Channel for another half a year. We would hold production meetings in a tiny room next to the main production office, where Chris would bring in tea and cream cakes, and cockney wide-boys Darren and Liam would bring in ready rolled joints for those who wanted them!

The Talent Channel was fun. It was as much fun as Television X had been at the very beginning when it was as if we had been given a real TV station as a big toy to play with.

I even provided several clips to broadcast featuring myself fooling around.

Adam, Chris, Anna and I would think up crazy ideas and act them out in the links. And the viewers themselves never let us down in providing enough crazy material to fill the two hours every night between those mad links!

Then one winter evening, just as I was about to leave to go home, Chris got a phone call from Portland TV's boss. A decision had been made and our lovely funny makeshift Channel was to be axed. We had just one week left on air to go.

The late night timing of our show had resulted in poor subscriptions. The original idea of filling the two-hour gap between Television X and UK Living with cheap programming to make an easy profit hadn't paid off, and the Talent Channel was to close.

Still keen to try and make that dead two-hour time-slot profitable however, Portland TV was to launch another Channel in its place. This was to be the first incarnation of what turned out to be a thriving TV Station in its own right, an adult channel aimed at cashing in on the lucrative 'pink pound'. Gay TV was to get its first airing at four in the morning for two hours in between a heterosexual porn channel and a channel aimed at housewives and families!

On our very last night on air, after the final clip had played out, all the producers, including Chris making his first on-screen appearance, sat on a big bed in front of camera in our night-clothes. I wore an old-fashioned night-shirt, 'wee willy winky' style night-cap with a long tassel, and had a face pack covering my face. I held an old-fashioned night candle and explained that we were going off-air for the Christmas break but that we may return in the Spring. I guess none of us really wanted to say out loud that the Talent Party was over. We didn't want to say a final goodbye or to admit that the Talent Channel had failed. We all sang a farewell song, taking a line each, singing out the nicknames that Anna had given us all. I was Rico Schmico and she was Anna Spanner. I think Chris was either Miss Chris or Chris Piss! At the end of the song I announced that we were now all going for our long winter nap. We all blew out the candle and, as the screen went black, the only sound that could be heard for the last few seconds on-air were our collective snores!

And so my great foray from porn into mainstream TV entertainment was over. Adam went back home to Liverpool, Chris and Anna continued to work together for Portland TV, working on the new Gay TV Channel, and their relationship blossomed to the extent that they soon became a couple and Anna moved in to Chris' smart East End home. After their involvement with Gay TV, they went on to run the very successful British hardcore adult distribution company

Hot Rod Films, after which Chris eventually returned to Portland TV as production manager of Television X.

Me? I was at first at a bit of a loose end. Apart from still keeping up my involvement with *New Talent* magazine, I had given up all other work on Deric's mags, in order to go full- time for the Talent Channel. I now had to go back to the Fantasy bosses, cap in hand, and ask them for my old job back, which I'm glad to say they were happy to give me.

So I once again returned to work as the 'model contact' and features writer on all the magazines of Fantasy Publications.

But things were changing at the good ship Fantasy; the seas were becoming rougher, and there were storm clouds ahead.

Chapter Twenty:
THE LUNATICS ARE TAKING OVER

A new girl had now joined Television X as a production assistant and she, like Jack Bedford before her, showed great interest in making programmes for the Channel and indeed she had even done her thesis at university on pornography!

Whether she had ever heard of Anna's Talent Channel persona of 'Anna Spanner' I don't know but, when she eventually started making shows for Television X, she changed her surname to rhyme with her first name and called herself Anna Span. She was to go on to have a very successful career in the adult production business, taking part in various University debates around the country on women's place in pornography, and marketing herself widely as Britain's 'only' female porn producer, a title to which many other British female porn producers took great exception.

However, Anna's company, Easy On The Eye, went on to do very well, as Anna, like Deric, was very good as marketing. She pushed her company out there as one that was in touch with young people, making vibrant modern porn for a new age of liberated men and women alike.

In the General Election of 2010, under her real name of Anna Arrowsmith, she stood for the Liberal Democrats as Parliamentary

Candidate for the Borough of Gravesham in Kent. She came third place behind the Conservatives and Labour.

But back when she had just joined the Channel, across the dock at Fantasy Publications, things were still drifting along fairly smoothly, but there was a sense that Deric had taken the magazines as far as either he could, or wanted to.

The parent company of Fantasy Publications were getting more involved in mainstream projects. They now not only ran celebrity based *OK!* Magazine, but also a number of other mainstream celebrity magazines, and were negotiating to take over top British tabloid newspapers the *Daily Express* and the *Daily Star.* At that time they also produced a spin-off mainstream terrestrial TV show *OK! TV*, which was aired on ITV.

Wanting perhaps to distance themselves from the supposedly downmarket and sleazy image of the porn mags, Fantasy's bosses were keen to sell the Fantasy Publications Group of magazines, and suggested to Deric that, if he could raise the necessary finances, they would be happy to sell them to him.

The idea of now becoming a magazine proprietor was very appealing to Deric and, needless to say, he immediately started to make enquiries to try and raise the necessary cash.

The following weeks became a time when Deric withdrew himself more and more from the daily life of the office in his attempts to raise the money to buy the company, making sporadic appearances at his desk, sometimes falling asleep over his computer keyboard mid-flow, cigarette in hand, due to the exhaustion of trying to juggle his existing job running the magazines while at the same time striving to negotiate with financiers to build a solid backing from which he might be able to actually take Fantasy over.

I, in my turn, was at a bit of a loose end without my mentor around, and started seeking other areas of work to fill the void.

I started doing some freelance camerawork for Television X producer 'Big Jim'. We were using the private home of ex- page Three girl Karen White as a location and, on the very first day of shooting, I met Television X presenter Vicki Holloway. Vicki was operating the boom mike on the shoot and, as such, was required to work very closely with me, as she was connected to my camera by a short audio lead.

I quickly developed a rapport with Vicki, and I think we recognised something in each other that we saw in ourselves; a longing to develop what we were doing in the industry into something bigger, stronger, and with more longevity.

While on the shoot for Jim, Vicki told me that she had once before tried to shoot her own series for Television X with another producer which had unfortunately come to nothing.

As a popular presenter on the Channel, I suggested that together we approach Paul D, the station controller with the idea that she once again produce her own series. With Jack Bedford I had shot a series for Misty McKane who had put in a lot of her own ideas to the series. Surely Jack and I could do the same for Vicki, and create a series that included lots of her own scene scenarios and visual ideas. Effectively Vicki would be the producer, while Jack and I sorted out the technicalities to make it a reality.

And so Vicki and I developed a four scene series entitled, '*Vicki's Fantasies*'.

With Jack in charge of production, we presented the idea to Television X who were only too happy to put up the money and let us do it.

We shot two of the programmes back in Karen White's house and the remainder on location, one in a local strip club, and one in a car repair workshop. We were very pleased with the end result as all the episodes looked very good and were well received by Television X.

After this series was completed, Vicki and I started seeing each other quite regularly and realised that there was no reason we shouldn't do more productions together, this time however with Vicki taking more of an active role behind the camera, not only devising the scenes, styling and casting, but also shooting the promotional stills and directing me on the day from the monitor, much in the same way that Jack had done previously. He would sit behind the monitor watching my shots and directing my camerawork. From there he could objectively direct the whole scene in the same way that a mainstream director would control his cast and crew on a more mainstream type of film.

This was the same way that Vicki was now to turn her hand at directing and producing.

It was the first time that she had tried any kind of TV production, but she turned out to be a complete natural at it.

She bought a sophisticated digital stills camera and took it upon herself to do the stills photography on our video shoots as well as producing the shows with me, jointly planning and styling the shoots, casting the models and directing on the day of shooting, from behind the monitor.

Television X's station controller suggested we initially shoot a girl/girl series called *Natural Girls*, featuring models with natural silicone free boobs, and he provided us with a list of potential models that he would like included in the series.

As we had previously done with *Vicki's Fantasies*, we invoiced Portland for the entire budget of the series and waited until we had received the money. This then gave us the funds to go ahead and shoot. One might wonder why Television X would give us all the money before receiving anything in return? Well, we had signed a legally binding contract, and I guess they had known me for long enough to trust that I was unlikely to suddenly risk all future work with them for the sake of an immediate few thousand pounds.

Vicki and I had recently moved in together into a nice two bed-roomed apartment on an exclusive gated development in Essex, also the home to several local sports personalities and actors, including snooker star Ronnie O'Sullivan, *Eastenders* actress Patsy Palmer, and ex-Blue singer Simon Webbe.

To save some money on the production budget, we made plans to shoot *Natural Girls* in our new home rather than spending out on hiring a separate location.

Vicki also now started shooting photo-sets in our apartment and once again took to it like a duck to water. She seemed to know instinctively what sort of poses were required, as well as how many pictures to take, and of what sort – how many portrait, how many landscape, how many close-ups, wides etc.

Being female, she found it relatively easy to persuade her model friends to pose for her, and between us, we soon had a cottage industry going from the apartment where we lived. We would shoot shows for Television X and shoot photo-sets which Vicki sold back into Fantasy Publications, initially anonymously to Karen, the picture-buyer, as we didn't want Karen to feel any obligation to buy them just because they were from Vicki. It was important from the outset that Vicki's talents be recognised on their own merits.

Her first ever published set and magazine cover was an exciting day for us, even though it was actually only a very non-glamorous shot of an old woman on the front of an issue of *Forty Plus* magazine!

Mainstream women's magazine *New Woman* were keen to include Vicki in an article they were writing about women in behind the camera roles in the adult industry. The published piece included an interview with Vicki as well as many photos of Vicki and shots of some of the magazines her work had appeared in.

I became more and more proud of Vicki's achievements on the production side of the adult industry and I was very glad that, due to our chance meeting through Big Jim, I had met her, and that we now not only were developing a very close bond but that we also had the opportunity to work together in this way.

Deric in the meantime had tried to raise enough capital to buy Fantasy Publications but unfortunately he had not quite achieved it.

He told me later that he felt that, not having been able to raise the required capital, he had failed the company and was therefore obliged to, as he put it, 'fall on his sword' and quietly leave and go elsewhere.

Whether this was really what Fantasy expected of him I have no idea but the process of raising quite a substantial part of the required millions it would have taken to buy out Fantasy had made Deric realise that, if he did indeed leave Fantasy Publications, he could raise enough money to be able to set up and launch his own adult titles, effectively in competition with the very magazines that he had conceived and helped to launch into the marketplace originally.

And so Deric handed in his notice at Fantasy and began to make discrete plans to launch his own adult magazine company. He talked with several other members of staff, all of which he eventually took with him, to launch a series of down-market magazines, all of which were almost exact rip- offs of the ones he had originally conceived at Fantasy: *Forty Up* instead of *Forty Plus*, *UK Wives* instead of *Real Wives*, etc.

Deric's resignation however was to leave a gaping hole at Fantasy. He had arrived at a time when Fantasy's biggest selling titles were

Penthouse and *Forum*, and when sales of the magazines generally were decreasing. He had single- handedly not only increased sales to those titles, but also launched a whole new range of more down-market but very successful magazines into the marketplace. He had persuaded the Fantasy bosses to branch out into adult television, launching the very successful Television X, and he had launched an adult video range at minimal cost. These hadn't been hugely successful, but as they were a low business risk as very low costs were involved in their production, there was little to recoup before they showed a profit.

There could be no doubt that Deric had been very influential at Fantasy Publications, but now, with his resignation, there would have to be a new Managing Editor to run the Fantasy Empire. Who would that be?

Television X's station controller was appointed as overall boss during this changeover period, and I was both amazed and complimented that he now looked to me to be Deric's natural successor.

Certainly over the last few years that I had been working at Fantasy, Deric had seemingly been grooming me to take over, by letting me sit in on the important executive board meetings, by making me privy to how the magazines ran, by introducing me to all the key people and by letting me shadow him as he conducted every area of the day-to-day running of the business.

Perhaps subconsciously he knew he would one day have to leave and leave me to it... or perhaps this was always in his plan.

Either way, I was excited to accept the invitation and to become the new boss of Fantasy Publications, a magazine group unrivalled on the British 'top shelf', with now more than fifty titles in its arsenal, many of which I had had a personal involvement in launching or honing, including *New Talent, Real Wives*, and of course all the video (now DVD) cover mounted titles.

New staff were appointed to replace those that were leaving to join Deric's new company, and I was now the one interviewing them, and making the decision to employ.

Our long-term picture buyer Karen took more of a key role in the day-to-day running of the business, effectively taking over what had been my role in answering the many letters and phone calls from the public. As I took over from Deric, I initially shared the job in the early months with another work colleague and friend Kevin, until Fantasy felt that I was comfortable enough to go it alone as the new boss!

Apart from Karen as my new number two, we also had a new female picture buyer, two female designers, female staff in the 'Repro' department, as well as ad sales women, and Vicki was also working for us part-time, not only as staff photographer, but also writing a lot of the material for the mags. As such, we were probably unique among our then competitors as being a mens magazine company very much run by women; a thought that would probably in itself have been a big turn-on for a lot of our readers, particularly as all the girls in the office were young, attractive and broad-minded.

Even with all their help however, running Fantasy was much more time consuming than I had foreseen. As the boss, the buck stopped with me and so, when all the nine-to-fivers had gone home, I remained at my desk most nights until eight or nine o'clock, signing off designs, meeting deadlines and working with the night-shift staff in the Repro department (people I had previously only ever heard of in the old days when I too used to leave at five!).

However with this new position came even more credibility within the British adult industry, and the first time I saw my name on the masthead of *New Talent* or *Forum* as the Managing Editor, it sent a thrill right through me.

By sticking with the business, learning my trade and climbing the ladder I had risen from a bumbling wannabe to an in- demand video editor, to a mainstream television producer and presenter, and now to being in charge of one of Britain's most successful adult magazine groups.

Now I was the one meeting new wannabe porn stars like I had once been, both male and female, and being in a position to actually influence their careers and make a difference.

Male model Marino (Superdick) claims that I was the one to give him his first job in the industry, and he is now running his own successful adult production company, Spanking Tomato. I remember auditioning model Bev Cocks in the old Television X studio the first time she ever did anything at all in front of a camera. She went on to achieve international success as a porn star, including being involved in Britain's first IPTV venture with her then partner Jim Deans (AKA Phil McCavity). Porn star Layla Jade phoned me when she was trying to break into the industry and I sent her a letter outlining the ins and outs of how to do it; she is now a well- known porn star on both sides of the Atlantic.

Although the fact that I had helped shaped people's careers gave me a feeling of warmth and satisfaction, it didn't help much however when I was still chained to my desk at ten o'clock at night ploughing through the paperwork that needed to be done in order to get the next jazz-mag out on time! This unfortunately was the reality behind the Fantasy!

A reporter from the broadsheet *The Independent* got in touch with me wanting to do an interview over the phone about the porn mags that we produced.

The article began:

'Ric Porter takes a deep breath and, in the manner of a children's story teller, prepares himself to begin. "Well," he says, "in

alphabetical order, there's Amateur Video, Asian Babes, Best Of Big And Black, Best Of Big Ones, Best Of Electric Blue..." Porter, the affable, softly spoken editor of all these titles, continues slowly so as to make recording the list easier...'

At least this time I was 'softly spoken' and there was no reference to my 'lank hair' or 'nasal laugh'!

I was also now personally 'under fire' in the form of satirical jibes in the weekly magazine *Private Eye*. It was suggested by the *Eye* that I was to be Fantasy Publication's next 'sacrificial lamb' over a problem with our magazine distributors. Clearly scraping the barrel for insults to aim at our company, they even made mention of my partner Vicki, a 'blonde model', working as a 'sub editor' on the magazines in a rather scathing way. I telephoned the *Eye* office to complain, and in the next issue they made mention of my phone call, without actually making any kind of apology of course, although in the same issue they had also printed a letter from one of their readers who had taken the trouble to email in to complain that their *'comments about Vicki Holloway were a cheap shot (as) she's actually very bright and funny, not the blonde bimbo that your article implies.'* – Oh well, at least we had one person fighting our corner against the media's campaign against us – even if it was only because he was a fan of our glamorous sub editor!

Around this time I also got a few threatening phone messages along the lines of 'I know where you live, Ric Porter, you filthy sleazy bastard'. Needless to say none of these callers ever left a contact number for me to phone them back on, and none of them ever followed through on their empty threats.

Back in the office, the Fantasy bosses had had the good idea to launch a new magazine; one that would be top shelf but had aspirations that were aiming more toward the middle shelf! David Sullivan's *Daily Sport* newspaper had launched *The Adult Sport,* a bi-weekly colour magazine featuring naked pictures of celebrities, both paparazzi style 'up skirts' and so called 'nipple slips' as well as more professionally shot stills taken from nude appearances in films that these celebrities had done. And all this with a cover price of just one pound!

As publishers of what were now several mainstream celebrity mags, the Fantasy bosses felt that they were in an ideal position to bring out a rival publication to the *Adult Sport*, and I attended several board meetings about this.

Deciding on the name *Celebrity Adult Spy* for this magazine, a new company, Best Magazines Limited, was created to publish it and I was asked to be its Company Director.

I was tremendously excited. Within a short space of time I had gone from just a guy working in the office, effectively answering the phone and the mail on a freelance basis, to running the department, and now I was to be the official Company Director of a new publishing company!

I thought that it was a shame that Deric had left Fantasy before we published *Celebrity Adult Spy* as, with his love f or celebrities and look-a-likes, he would have adored working on this title, particularly as every issue featured a double page spread of doctored pictures of celebrities that showed them in the nude; not look-a-likes exactly, but certainly faked shots; pictures of the real celebrities heads cleverly grafted on to the body of a naked model using computer software like Photoshop. For legal reasons of course we had to plaster each picture with a big banner stating that it was a 'FAKE!'

We could put the picture on the front cover with the nudity censored out and a slogan telling readers that they could 'see everything revealed inside'! We couldn't of course say that it actually was the supposed star inside naked, and to say 'see this fake picture of somebody famous inside naked' wouldn't have sold many issues either! So, we used the fact that we had to stress the 'fake factor' to our advantage and would splash a big headline across the picture, along the lines of "Britney Spears' horror at nude picture hoax'" etc. Whether Britney Spears was actually horrified, or even knew of the picture or of our magazine was of course neither here nor there – it all helped to sell issues!

The magazine was a bit like *The National Enquirer*, with its mix of gossip, scandal, paparazzi pictures, film stills of naked celebrities, and humour. The first issue, which to match the *Adult Sport*, also cost one pound, featured original Lara Croft model Nell McAndrew scantily clad across its front cover, along with the tag line 'The Famous And Rich – Without A Stitch'! Inside we featured genuine nude and topless pictures of Halle Berry, Joanna Lumley, Emmanuelle Beart, Jennifer Lopez, Christina Ricci, Charlotte Rampling and Reese Witherspoon among others, as well as faked nude pictures of Christina Aguilera, Sarah Michelle Gellar, Jessica Alba and Anna Kournikova among others. There were also lots of regular pin-up girls, jokey news items and show-biz gossip. Sixty-eight pages that I felt proved incredibly good value for just one pound.

Celebrity Adult Spy became a joy to work on, and a premier title of the company, selling in numbers that would rival our current best selling mag, *New Talent*.

Freelance journalist and magazine developer Allan Bryce, who had for many years worked for the Fantasy Group, most prominently on *Video World* magazine and then on the *Video X* series for Television X, stepped in and helped create *Celebrity Adult Spy*, providing much of the material and doing deals with picture agencies to get photos of celebrities naked for us to publish.

Vicki and I had shot a series for Television X where we had worked with a charming blonde model called Sarah. I noticed while shooting her that she bore a natural resemblance to the singer Christina Aguilera, whose single *Dirrty* from her album *Stripped*, was then riding high in the pop charts. Vicki and I had the idea of making Sarah look exactly like Christina as she had looked in the *Dirrty* music video, emulating the way she wore her hair and the clothes that she wore. We then made a series about an un-named rock chick (not drawing attention to the obvious connection for legal reasons) who had lots of sex in places like a recording studio, a magazine photo-shoot, a night-club and a limo driving around London's West End.

Television X station controller Paul D approved the idea and even argued the point with nervous company lawyers that we should call the series *Dirrty*, complete with the double 'R'.

We paid for Sarah to have the same sort of hair extensions that Christina had, and the series was a great success with Sarah looking every inch like the 'X-Tina' version of Christina Aguilera by the time that Vicki and I had finished tailoring her look. When, during filming, our limo pulled up outside London's Planet Hollywood restaurant, I jumped out like the paparazzi to film Sarah, and crowds gathered round our limo, thinking her to be the real deal! They banged on the car window as we drove away, waving and asking for autographs. It was a fantastic experience.

Photos that Vicki had taken to publicise the series looked amazing, and one really did have to do a double take before realising that it wasn't actually Christina posing there completely nude.

It was a perfect tie-in for *Celebrity Adult Spy*, as these were not doctored pictures like many that we had to use and were forced to brand as fake. They were genuine pictures of a nude girl who just 'happened' to look like Christina Aguilera! We plastered Sarah all over the front cover of *Celebrity Adult Spy* and also in a three-page spread inside, advertising the series and proclaiming that these were the pictures that 'all Christina fans have waited for'. With that wording, we were making an implication that these photos were of Christina Aguilera, but not a statement as such and of course, by the time the reader had read the article and realised that the girl on the cover was only a look-alike, he had already paid his pound and bought the mag!

The *Dirrty* issue of *Spy* was one of our best selling issues, something that I was very proud of as, not only were the photos ours (Vicki's and mine), but the whole concept and inception of the idea had been ours too – Deric would have been proud of me!

Chapter Twenty-One:
OPENING A PORTWAY IN THE OVERCROWDED POOL

Busy as I was with running Fantasy Magazines, I still found time to continue building up the stills and video production business that I had started with Vicki.

Our Television X series *Natural Girls* had in many ways been more of a success for us than Vicki's Fantasies. In shooting it we had proved to ourselves that we could by-pass a 'Jack Bedford' type figure and do everything ourselves. Vicki would plan and style the scenes, we cast them together and, on the day of the shoot, I acted as cameraman while Vicki took on Jack's role of sitting on the monitor watching the shots and directing the action.

To save money on those early shoots, Vicki had also acted as make-up artist, although it wasn't long before we started working with professional make-up people in order, not only to get a more exact, controlled and professional look, but in order to free up our own time prior to shooting so that Vicki could work with me in lighting and styling the set.

A very helpful and lovely make-up guy called Rio who Vicki had met through working at a local photographic studio, soon became what was virtually the third member of our production team, not only doing excellent make-up on all our shoots, but also staying to help in any way he could, and eventually coming on set after he'd done the make-up to be the boom operator and even sometimes operating a second video camera as well. The strength and success of what we achieved in those early days definitely owed a lot to him.

We would work very much 'by numbers' when we shot a series, following a regular pattern that seemed to work for us.

One model would arrive at ten o'clock in the morning and go into make-up with Rio for an hour while I lit the set and checked the styling and look of it with Vicki. I would also go over the sex positions that we were going to film. Our second model would arrive around eleven o'clock and then she would go into make-up for an hour while we then went over the clothes that Model One was going to wear, checked her hair and nails etc and got her ready. We then did the same for Model Two and made sure that they had both looked at each other's STD and HIV Test certificates and that they were happy to work with each other. If models (male or female) are to have any kind of unprotected sex together, or share any kind of bodily fluid (so that would include kissing), then their STD/HIV Tests must be completely negative and have been taken within thirty days. All models participating in a scene must see the other model's Tests, and photographs of their Tests, along with their I.Ds (passport, drivers licence etc) to show proof of age must be taken. No respectable adult company internationally will buy any photo set or video film without this all-important paperwork.

Having achieved all this, we would then start shooting the scene. I would be on camera which would be linked to a monitor that Vicki watched, checking my focus, brightness, framing etc. Vicki would direct the shoot from behind the monitor, while Rio or another person employed for the purpose, would handle the boom pole on which our Sennheiser microphone was mounted. In the early days of shooting shows for Television X we just used the on-camera mike for sound but this had the drawback of inconsistency (if I was getting a wide shot the sound would be fainter than when I moved in for a close-up). It would also pick up a lot of 'handling noise' from the camera itself. After several editors at Television X repeatedly informed us that the audio was the one thing that really let our films down, we invested in a decent microphone on a boom pole. The mike plugged directly into the back of the camera initially via a long cable, and more recently wirelessly via a transmitter and receiver. This way, the sound recorded was at a consistent level no matter how much I moved around with the camera.

Our shoots would take around three hours to do, including cigarette, bathroom and tea breaks for the models, and we would work on a 3:1 shooting basis. That is to say that we would aim to get one and half hours on tape, that would actually edit down to between twenty and thirty minutes of good useable footage.

Paul D, the station controller of Television X, by his own admission never the friendliest of people, had always kept a wary distance from me in the early days, thinking me as no more than Deric's lackey and merely an extension of all the crazy ideas that Deric represented. Now, with Deric out of the frame and having proved myself able to successfully run the magazine department, as well as produce well-made programmes for Television X, he grudgingly had more time for me, and even became a bit of a 'father figure' to me as someone I could turn to for advice when things were tough in the magazine department.

Vicki and I got more and more commissions from Television X – a second series of *Natural Girls* followed, as did *Tamara's Teenage Tarts*, another girl/girl series starring Television X presenter Tamara Noon.

It would sometimes surprise me when the models turned up at our flat at ten in the morning just how 'ordinary' they looked in real life, after having maybe travelled for an hour or more on the train, hair scraped back and with no make-up on. After an hour in the make-up chair however and under our soft flattering video lights, they blossomed into the heart- achingly beautiful model girls that we were all used to seeing on our screens.

Around the same time that we shot the *Natural Girls* and *Tamara* series, we also shot two Christmas specials for Television X, *New Year All-Girl Gang-Bang*, and *Tamara's Festive Fucking*.

We then had the idea of shooting a fetish style series, *Fetish Girls*, and we got specialist rubber wear company Libidex of London to loan us some beautiful and expensive rubber costumes for the models to wear on screen. In exchange they wanted a name-check in the credits, and for us to supply them with a few stills of our models wearing their clothes for them to use in their own promotional material.

Although we weren't allowed to show anything too extreme on camera for Television X, we wanted to get the flavour of the real bondage/domination/sado/masochism scene for this series, and so booked models who were genuinely into the sub/dom culture. One girl we booked arrived with a completely shaven head and several body piercings. She even had her back pierced with a line of little metal 'eyes' either side of her spine, into which hooks could be fastened and ribbons or rope fastened to her body. This all looked fabulous on camera and she was also quite happy for us to pour hot candle wax over her naked breasts.

We were shooting her in a fetish sex club in London, which, no doubt by night had all the elements of excitement and sleaze as a club. In the cold light of day however, as we set up for our shoot, the sight of used condoms strewn carelessly around, as well as a condom pulled over the mouth of an empty beer bottle all seemed a little crude and ugly.

We quickly tidied them away however, and hoped that our models wouldn't notice or be put off by such things as we set up for our shoot.

The only problem we found with some of the models booked for this series was that, as they were genuinely into the sub/dom scene, they would argue the point when I asked them to do things on camera, explaining that a real sub wouldn't get her mistress to do that, or that a real dom wouldn't allow her slave to do this or do that etc. All this may of course be quite true, but we were working to a strict deadline, shooting two scenes in one day, and with a legal limitation of what sex acts we could actually portray, as well as working to a brief from Television X to ultimately deliver a titillating show that a sex channel would want to show. And so, like the story of the difficult actor asking what his motivation was for a particularly simple scene, we told the girls that it didn't matter what a real sub or dom would or wouldn't do – the motivation for doing it was that we all just wanted to get the film shot and go home!

We planned to do a series starring popular British Essex based model Karen Wood, to be called *Essex Wives*. Karen wasn't married; the title was simply to trade in on the publicity of a mainstream reality style TV series that had just been launched on ITV, also called *Essex Wives*. The ITV one however was to introduce Britain to a girl who was to go on to enjoy enormous tabloid celebrity success – Jodie Marsh.

Ours in contrast would have Karen Wood having girl/girl sex in every episode but, by the time we were ready to shoot the series, the ITV show had finished its run, but we were still hoping to tap into the tail end of their publicity by using the same name.

Another series, this time a drama, was just beginning on ITV called *Footballers Wives*, and at the last minute it was decided that the title of our show be changed to *Footballers Wives* in the hope of cashing in on publicity surrounding that series instead, and so we had to make a last minute minor change to the story-line to show Karen as not just an Essex wife, but the wife of a footballer as well. As all the sex was to be girl/girl it didn't change anything within the scenes too much, although we did manage to procure a genuine football club pitch and changing rooms for the first episode, which had Karen having sex with Welsh model Kelle Marie supposedly after a celebrity charity match featuring glamour models!

We didn't have access to anyone else to act as extras as the 'crowd' at the beginning of this particular scene, so the 'crowd' cheering as Kelle Marie and Karen run off the pitch are in fact just Vicki and our make-up man Rio!

Rio has in fact stood in a fair amount as a nameless extra in the background of a number of our shows, as a lap dance punter, part of a football crowd, a voyeur in a night-club and even as himself doing make-up on the models!

Jack Bedford's make-up artist Alisha had also made a few walk-on cameo roles; most notably where she came out of a toilet cubicle in a night-club to find two girls engaged in oral sex over the basins!

All our shows so far had been girl/girl but, after a while of 'breaking ourselves in' with these, Vicki and I thought it was time to try our hand at a boy/girl show, and, after shooting this one guy/one girl series successfully, we then went all out with our next series, which was called *UK Bukkake Party*, where each scene would include one girl and several guys.

Utilising a big cast of genuine models would have proved expensive however, so we tried to do it within our slender budget by casting the guys from the 'leftovers' in Television X's book of wannabes who had applied to take part in the *Porn Idol* series. This proved to be a big mistake as most of these guys, apart from not having a tanned muscular 'porn star' type body, weren't used to a professional environment and, as in *Porn Idol*, either couldn't get it up at all or had difficulty coming for the final 'money shot'.

One guy didn't turn up for the shoot at all, clearly having had cold feet at the last minute. When I spoke to him on the phone prior to the shoot he asked me to repeat what he was expected to do and, as I could hear other blokes laughing in the background, I got the distinct impression that he had turned his mobile on to loudspeaker so that all his mates could share the moment! A moment of course which never actually happened, as he didn't have the bottle to turn up!

Models, male and female, don't seem to realise how much they're letting people down when they choose to just not turn up on a job, as of course it's not just the producer but also other models, a location owner, a make up artist and other production crew who have all been booked for the day as well, and have all made the effort to turn up on time only to find that perhaps the shoot has had to be cancelled due to one model's change of heart because (as is often the case) she went out the previous night, has woken up with a hangover and can't be bothered to get out of bed!

It always amazes me that, even though we strive to make our productions as professional as possible, and the models themselves regard what they do as their 'profession', they often treat it with such disdain that, only in this business, would they get away with such behaviour and continue to work. Can you imagine a professional actress – even a lowly extra – not bothering to turn up on a film set because the call time was too early for her to get out of bed and catch her train on time? Such a person wouldn't last long in the real mainstream world of film-making, and in my opinion, neither should models who act the same way in the adult industry.

During all this time of shooting shows for Television X, I was of course still running the magazine group and, under my leadership, Fantasy Publications had built from what had been a relatively declining sales position to becoming a very strong force in the marketplace once again.

However, working all the hours to get nearly fifty titles out a month was taking its toll on the amount of TV production that Vicki and I could achieve for Television X and I began to consider that I might have to leave Fantasy in order to devote more time to building up our own business of producing photo-sets and adult programming.

Vicki and I had got to the point where we could go no further without one or both of us putting more time in to it – time that, at that moment in our careers, neither of us had got, unless we made a drastic change to our present work situation.

Real life events however hastened my decision to leave. The parent company of Fantasy Publications had finally found someone with enough money to buy the adult magazine group, and on the first of March 2004 Fantasy Publications was sold to the Remnant Media Group for a reputed £10.8m, amid much media speculation.

I had already been 'grooming' our old picture buyer Karen to step into my shoes in much the same way that Deric had prepared me to take over from him and, realising that I needed to devote more time to my growing business with Vicki, it was mutually agreed, with the help of a nice redundancy payment from Remnant, that I should leave Fantasy and move on.

I also privately had a growing concern that I was beginning to turn into the 'boss from hell' character David Brent from the hit Ricky Gervais TV series *The Office*!

The saddest part of leaving Fantasy for me was losing the day- to-day camaraderie of all the wonderful staff that I had working with me. Everyone that contributed to the many magazines that we produced over the years were fantastically talented professionals and I not only admired them, but treasured the friendships that I had made with each and every one of them.

On my last day, meeting everyone for champagne at the local wine bar, I was presented with a framed *Celebrity Adult Spy* cover which the designers had specially created for me. It featured my face on the front cover, along with inset pictures of all my staff, under the headline, 'Ric Porter Has Left The Building.'

Finally now having more time to devote to building up the business that Vicki and I had created, we set about our task in earnest.

Using parts of both our surnames, we christened our business PORTWAY, after PORTer and HolloWAY. We decided on this after rejecting the less attractive sounding HOLLATER or simply RICVIC as Dave Wells suggested!

We registered our Company with Vicki as the Company Director and myself as the Company Secretary.

The prestigious and exclusive RSA (Royal Society for the Encouragement of the Arts) contacted Vicki inviting her to become a member, as they were keen to have the support of more female company directors. Vicki of course was proud to do so.

We carried on shooting photo-sets for Fantasy which Karen, in her new role as Managing Editor, agreed to buy, and we carried on shooting programmes for Television X as we had been doing, although we now had more time to devote to developing not only more series, but also the production value of what we shot.

We now planned to shoot two versions of all our shows (a hard as well as a soft-core version), and the first series that we shot two versions of under our new company name starred the main guy who had managed to keep it up successfully in *UK Bukkake Party*, a very pleasant and amusing guy from Birmingham called Saul, who was to go on to help out Jack Bedford as his assistant on many of his future productions.

We shot soft and hard angles on one camera at the same time, as opposed to other producer's methods, which was to shoot the whole scene hardcore with one camera, and then get the model re-made up and ready to shoot the whole scene all over again, this time soft-core. More commonly, producers shooting a hard and a soft version of the same scene would shoot only once but use two cameras, one dedicated to getting only hardcore shots, and the other dedicated to soft angles only.

We found that shooting both angles with one camera didn't take an awful lot longer than just shooting soft as I could just move a few inches from a soft angle, and film for a further ten seconds, getting a hardcore view. The models were much happier that they were only doing the scene once, as opposed to twice!

We were so taken with one particular model who we met on this shoot that we decided to give her her own series on the next shoot that we would do.

By the time that we were ready to shoot it however, this girl had had a boob job and now looked much more like a real porn star! The second hardcore Portway Films production starred big boobed British model Donna Marie and was called *The Donna Marie Experience.*

Just as Lindsay, Omar and Jack Bedford had all done before us, we booked a nice detached manor house for a week through a holiday home company as our location and we moved all our crew and talent in to shoot the series for Television X.

We worked out a daily shooting schedule that allowed for filming two scenes a day, one in the morning and one in the afternoon. Like Lindsay, we were taking along a full time cook who was the flat-mate of the studio manager at Television X, who himself was acting as production assistant/runner on our shoot.

All went smoothly and according to plan, although we did have one scary moment when we began to film the only scene that we had planned to shoot outdoors in the secluded gardens of our rented home. We had all the paraphernalia of filming laid out on the lawn, including large video lights running off power cables that snaked back into the house, a monitor set up on a small garden table, as well as stills and video cameras standing by in readiness. We were to shoot a two boy/one girl scene and we had our runner round the front of the house with his mobile phone to warn us in the unexpected event that anybody should suddenly turn up. His sole job was to make sure that, if this did happen, we had enough warning to be able to pack everything up and get the models back into the house as quickly as possible.

Donna Marie had her boobs out and one of the guys was between her legs when the runner suddenly appeared round the corner of the hedge and, no sooner had he blurted out that the gardener had turned up, than the gardener appeared behind him driving round on a motorised lawn-mower! Just our luck that the gardener had been booked to mow the lawn on the only day that we had decided to shoot a scene outdoors!

He gave us a big grin, clearly aware of what was going on, as we scuttled everything back indoors and spent the rest of the day expecting a visit, or at the very least, a phone call, from the owners of the house. But seemingly we had got away with it as no visit or call came. Either the gardener wasn't bothered, or he hadn't told the owners what we were up to.

We finished shooting that particular scene indoors just in case there were any further unexpected interruptions, and eventually, by the end of our week there, we finished off the film and returned to our Essex home to begin post-production on what was not only our first successful shoot totally shot on location, but also what was to be the first series that we were also going to edit for the Channel. Up until this point, we had overseen all previous editing of our programmes, but the work had all actually been done 'in house' by the Television X editors, who were all absolutely marvellous at their job and always made our films look fantastic. Each editor gave himself a 'nom-de-porn' for the credits; there was Sid Van Krak, Carlos The Jackoff and Dick Shadow, although the best 'nom- de-porn' of all was from the editor Giles. a loose cannon who ranted, raved, thumped the monitors and shouted at all the producers about how he couldn't work with the shit that they were giving him. Despite this attitude, he was very well liked at Television X, even by Paul D, who was renowned for 'not suffering fools gladly'. However even Paul D took exception to the 'nom-de-porn' that Giles gave himself on early edits for Jack Bedford. Despite Paul's protestations, however he still gave himself the on-screen credit of Dick Shitcrumbs on the final version that got broadcast!

We had befriended a very good video editor at Television X called Nick, and he taught us how to use the non-linear computer based edit system Final Cut Pro.

So, armed with everything he'd taught us, we put together our first series for the Channel, doing absolutely everything ourselves, including writing all the soundtrack music, cutting all the visuals and editing together the title sequence. We outputted all the scenes back to tape and delivered the master edits to Television X.

The broadcast version had been commissioned by, and was premiered on, Television X. However, according to our contract at that time, we could do what we wanted with the hardcore versions of the programming, as long as Television X had first refusal on the broadcast rights of these.

So, we then set about editing up the hard versions of each scene and sourcing a distribution company who would be happy to release *The*

Donna Marie Experience as Portway's first hardcore DVD.

We went with the company that Jack Bedford was releasing his programmes through, Rude Britannia, as they were offering an appealing deal whereby they would author the DVD, design the sleeve, get the title certificated by the BBFC as well as handle all the marketing and distribution. For this, obviously they were taking a hefty percentage of the sales profit, but to us at that time, with no experience of DVD authoring or distribution, this seemed like a good deal.

Appropriately named, Rude Britannia specialised in distributing British made porn, often very amateur style gonzo shot sex parties, most of which however bore little resemblance to the higher quality productions that Vicki and I were striving to make.

Whether it was because of this or not who knows, but our expectations of quickly retiring on the DVD profits were soon dashed when our first cheque came in of only a few hundred pounds. This represented world online and in-store sales, and we had even done an in-store promotion at one of London's premier sex shops with myself, Vicki and our star Donna Marie doing a signing.

We released one more title through Rude Britannia before calling it a day with them, as royalties dwindled even further.

We have since released a number of DVDs through Erigo Distribution which turned out to be a much more satisfying deal, although on reflection I think that by the time we were ready to cash in on the DVD market, we were just too late to really make a killing, as that particular market was already shifting toward Internet downloads, video on demand and pay per view. Had I been more astute, I should have been making films to sell into video and DVD shops almost a decade earlier when Lindsay was planning his hugely successful Ben Dover series.

Unfortunately the story of my life is that I have been lucky enough to have fallen into most of what I have done that happened to have been successful. There has been little planning or forethought to it. And so I am now often forced to learn new technology because I was too late to cash in on porn with the old media. But that's OK. I have always been, and hope I always will be, an old dog that is not afraid to try and learn some new tricks!

And so, both Vicki and I were now quickly learning the basics of fast-turnaround non-linear editing, DVD authoring and quick production turnaround, while endeavouring to maintain as high a standard production quality as possible. Unlike the world of mainstream film-making, there are very small budgets available to make porn films, particularly in Britain, with producers and models often shooting scenes for free either because, in the producer's case, they want to have free sex with the girls and filming it enables them to do so or, in the model's case, they are doing a 'content share' with the producer so that they can both use the footage on their own respective websites.

In these days of ease of web design, most models now have their own website set up, often designed for them for free by an adoring fan who hopes to meet or sleep with their idol as some kind of payment for their work. The models get website content for free either by doing 'content shares' with other models or by simply doing free shoots of themselves with anybody who wants to participate; there's always a high percentage of takers! The models then charge customers a small monthly subscription fee to look at the content and this subscription is automatically renewed every month. It's easy money for a model, but for the professional producers among us, trying to produce quality sex scenes under contract with location, make up and crew costs, it was a different story.

As Vicki and I were fast learning, not many people were making a fortune anymore (if indeed they ever were) on the profits of DVD sales alone.

What with the increase of more easily available better technology and now that hardcore sex films had become legal in the UK, sold as they were in licensed sex shops with an R18 BBFC certificate, the floodgates had been opened for anyone to now go and buy a cheap but good enough quality video camera from their local store, shoot a gonzo style movie and legally release it through sex shops, or put it up on their own home-made website for people to download or pay-per-view. Rather than it being a good thing for the sex production industry, the rise and proliferation of British hardcore had meant that there was now so much competition that prices had fallen to the extent that now nobody could really make any good money.

Whereas I had once been, as a commercially trained cameraman and editor, a talented big fish in a small porno pool, I was now just one of a large and growing number of moderately talented fish who were all swimming in what had become an increasingly overcrowded porno pool.

Chapter Twenty-Two:
JODIE MARSH, THE CALLGIRLS, AND THE APPRENTICE

Despite our dwindling profits, but partly because I had now taken the plunge and gone full-time for Portway and was determined to make a go of it, Vicki and I carried on making films for Television X and keeping the hardcore versions aside for perhaps eventual DVD release if we could find a better deal.

We went away on location again, hiring another big manor house for a week, to shoot the Donna Marie sequel *The Donna Marie Experience Two*, although the soft-core version was called simply *Porn Shoot*, and had this very different angle to it:

I had often thought that people would be very interested to see not only how we shot our films, but also what really went on behind the scenes on a porn shoot. To this end, in addition to our make-up man Rio, Paul our runner, and our location chef Mark, we also took along a second video cameraman, Paulo Bruno, whose sole job it was to shoot purely behind-the- scenes type footage, while I shot the main scenes as usual.

In the edit we would intersperse the main sex scene, properly edited with music, with cutaways of the crew filming and giving direction etc, shot in a more gonzo 'handy cam' style by Paulo.

Originally I had planned, while making the series look more like a reality style show, to actually script everything in the behind-the-scenes footage, including creating both sexy and comedic elements, as well as playing out my role as 'Ric Porter' as a larger than life character. I had the idea of making the series something along the lines of a porno version of *The Larry Sanders Show*. However, the reality of what really went on behind the scenes on this series proved far more entertaining than anything I could possibly have written, and so in the end we simply went with what genuinely went on rather than playing any kind of behind-the-scenes scripted role.

On the first day, we had all arrived at the location and were just waiting for our main star Donna Marie to check in. I had told her to go to Hayes station, which was the nearest train station to where we were staying, and to get a taxi from there to the location. Donna Marie had seemingly misheard me and had promptly arrived at Hastings station, which was about forty miles away! Running late, she had arrived at the station at eleven o'clock that night. There were no further trains from Hastings that night and so she was forced to get a taxi all the way from Hastings to Hayes at huge expense, which I refused to pay for as it wasn't my fault that she had gone to the wrong place!

She didn't arrive until well after one in the morning but I nevertheless expected her to be up, refreshed and in make-up by ten o'clock the next day, which to her credit she was, as bright as a button and ready for her first anal sex scene!

The caretaker of the house we had hired came to see us on our first day there, and tottered into the hallway from the adjoining annexe where he lived, reeking of alcohol. He clearly hadn't bothered to tidy the house up much before our visit, as we found the outside barbecue greasy with the remains of rotting food and, worst of all, I discovered a dying black bat in the wastepaper basket in my en-suite bathroom as I cleaned my teeth that night! However, it was reassuring to see that the caretaker was a lazy alcohol soaked old man, as we reckoned he would probably keep himself to himself and not interfere with our daily shooting schedule. And if he did?

Well, we would probably be able to bribe him with a bottle of something to keep his eyes and mouth shut!

We shot our first scene with Donna Marie shagging Tony James on what was my bed in the house. During the frantic anal sex scene, Donna Marie came out with the immortal line, 'Fuck me like a £10 whore from Kings Cross'. It was difficult to hold the camera steady as I was shaking with laughter at this wonderful improvised line, which I was even tempted to make the title for the proposed DVD!

Next day blonde model Alicia Rhodes arrived for her girl/girl scene with Donna Marie, in which they were to have sex with a banana. We put the chosen fruit in the fruit bowl on set after having cleaned it and shaved off the hard end so that it would be comfortable for insertion. I couldn't believe it when I wandered on set before the shoot to find Rio, while putting the finishing touches to Alicia's make-up, happily munching away on the banana! I remembered Ian Mitchell eating Lindsay's cucumber on The *Rock'n'Roll Ransom* nearly twenty years ago, and mused on how nothing had changed over the years – nothing anyway except the model and the fruit!

I remembered Lindsay going crazy with Ian and how Ian and I had both thought that he should 'chill out' over it. I now however saw Lindsay's side of things, as I was now the one in charge, with someone eating my carefully prepared prop!

Fortunately our cook had bought a large bunch of oversized bananas from the supermarket that morning, and so all we had to do was choose and prepare another lucky piece of fruit.

As I watched this action going on, I was also reminded of Natasha using a banana in my first 'masterpiece' *Apple Pie*. And once again I mused that, twenty years on, and all we were doing differently was using better equipment, filming in a nicer looking location, and paying the girls more than £50! The scenarios were the same, which of course, if one looks critically at porn movie plots, they would inevitably be, as every sex scene can only ever be a re-working of a handful of tired old themes, all of which must have been played out hundreds of times with tiny variations, different models, locations and camera angles, but essentially all the same. For, at the end of the day, just as there are only so many ways that one can have sex, there can also only be so many plot-lines or sex scenarios in which to do it.

The next night, at Donna Marie's request, we all played a murder mystery game over dinner. It was great fun, and would have possibly surprised any porn fan who might have suspected that cast and crew spent their evenings having wild orgies on porn shoots. I remembered Lindsay and Linzi, who would go to bed early and watch comedy shows on TV on location, and here we were playing a murder mystery game before our early night! So much for the 'sex, drugs and rock'n'roll' lifestyle one would have expected!

On the very last day of filming, we were let down by one of the models who was due to shoot a girl/girl scene dressed as a French maid, but she had phoned in sick. Fortunately one of our studs Pascal White had brought with him a pretty French model, Anais, in-tow. Although she had just come along for the ride, this was now her moment to shine, and she made a perfect genuine French maid in a cracking girl/girl anal sex scene over the snooker table with Donna Marie. Anais didn't speak much English, but her murmurings in a sexy French accent added all the more to the scene.

At the climax of this scene, Donna Marie not only came for real but squirted all over the green baize of the table. Laughing with embarrassment, she told us that this was the first time that she had ever squirted on camera, which would have been a real coup for us to have had on film, had I not accidentally stopped recording at the very moment of her squirting, and so missed it! Fortunately Paulo on the behind-the-scenes camera had caught the action, albeit more of Donna's re-action than the actual squirt!

Donna Marie was being paid a set fee for the entire week, no matter how many video or stills shoots she participated in, so while we were at this location, we tied in an additional scene for Television X, which was to be a Christmas Special. It was a mild autumn evening when we were shooting the scene, but we had come prepared and, that night, we dressed a huge Christmas tree in the large sitting room, putting up festive cards on the mantelpiece and lit a roaring log fire in the grate. Donna Marie was dressed as a Christmas angel in front of the fire as a 'present' for our stud, Pascal.

This was the fourth Christmas Special that we had shot for Television X as, after the *New Year All-Girl Gang-Bang* and *Tamara's Festive Fucking*, we had also shot a New Year's Eve edition of the Dirrty series, called *Dirrty New Year*. We hired a snow machine for an exterior scene of Sarah, dressed as 'X- Tina', getting logs from an old outside barn, the story being that she then got 'snowed in' for the New Year with her sexy girlfriend Sascha. Although the hire company had assured us that the snow machine would last for hours, it had almost run out of 'snow' after turning it on for just a few preliminary tests! Fortunately, Sarah did her bit of getting the logs in one take and so, with the machine spluttering a few last flakes, we could pack the ailing thing away and get on with the sex!

The same year that we shot the *Donna Marie Xmas Experience*, as we called the scene with Pascal, we also shot another Christmas Special, our fifth – a one-off programme that didn't 'tie-in' with any previously shot series. *XXXmas Ghost Story* was a horror spoof based on a spooky Christmas Eve tale of a ghostly girl in an everlasting quest for her dead lover. She has sex with a young traveller in an old English inn before turning into a vampire, complete with fangs, and killing him (sorry to spoil the ending if you haven't seen it!). I wrote the script, such as it was, and for once it was me and not Rio that had a cameo role in this production; that of the pub landlord.

Immediately after we completed this shoot, nude reporter Lily Kwan from the cult Internet/TV show *Naked News* turned up – not to do a report about us however, but about the cult publishers *Vice* Magazine who the following week were buying the East London pub that we were using as a location. *Naked News* did however utilise our lighting set-up for their interview before we left.

Apart from shooting the shows for Television X and the photo- sets for Fantasy, Vicki and I were always keeping a lookout for new angles to further our business.

We were offered, and subsequently took over, a run-down photographic studio in London's East End and used it to continue shooting photo-sets for Karen at Fantasy, as well as making the occasional sale to American magazines such as *High Society* and *Juggs*.

We intended to start shooting video productions there as well, although it wasn't really big enough to build full size sets for video, as these needed to cover a wider area than one would need to build for a stills set, as a stills set could effectively be done in just one corner of the room, whereas with video, I needed to get 'reverse angles' and shoot upwards and across the room as well as just 'front on'. We needed a fully dimensional set with at least three 'walls' on which to shoot video, although we did utilise our new studio for a number of productions, most notably by turning it into an Arabian style tent for a girl/girl scene between Leah Jaye and Sahara Knite for our Asian sex series *Bollywood Booty.*

The acquisition of the studio however did mean that we could now store a lot of our props and costumes somewhere other than in the spare room at home, which had been rapidly getting very overcrowded with plastic maids outfits, rubber dresses, high heel 'stripper shoes', vast amounts of lingerie and all manner of dildos!

We supplemented our income by doing other bits and bobs as well. I did some freelance camerawork for other producers,

and Vicki still did some presenting and voice-over work for Television X and the Red Hot Channels, all owned by Portland Television.

Television X had managed, due to its tie-in with celebrity based *OK!* Magazine (as previously mentioned, the parent company of Television X owned *OK!* Magazine), to procure some British tabloid celebrities to present links on the Channel, including TV's *Big Brother* house-mates Michelle Bass and Emma Greenwood, as well as Page Three girl and tabloid favourite Katie Price (AKA Jordan), Abi Titmuss and the *Essex Wives* tabloid celebrity Jodie Marsh.

Television X were putting a lot of money into a new weekly live show that was to go out on Friday nights called *Jodie Marsh – Live and Turned On.*

They hadn't done a live series for many years, the last being *Ceasar's Rude Arena*, hosted by Radio DJ 'Ceasar The Geezer', and this had been in Television X's early years of broadcasting.

In this new show, Jodie Marsh was to host and, draped across a bed, was to interview other celebrities on the bed with her. These were to include Princess Di's ex lover James Hewitt, Bez from the 1990s Manchester band The Happy Mondays, ex goalkeeper Mark Bosnich, two members of the UK garage band The So Solid Crew and the real life gangster and writer Dave Courtney. She was also to visit sexy clubs and places of ill repute in specially filmed weekly reports and, along with another regular, Lindsay in his 'Ben Dover' role, she was to help judge a weekly live striptease contest.

All good so far. Rehearsals, plans and pre-shoots had been well under way for many weeks and the series was being heavily trailed on Television X and in *The Daily Star* newspaper.

It was the Friday afternoon of the day that the first live show was to be broadcast live at 10pm, when Vicki's phone rang.

We were both in our new studio, shooting some stills of a new model. With the luxury of our new set-up Vicki was investing a lot of time in shooting new faces for Fantasy, while I filmed the photo-set 'behind-the-scenes' should Fantasy or Television X wish to buy the video footage as well as an add-on to the set. If they did, then these solo girl photo sessions were proving to be quite lucrative for our fledgling company and, now that we had the rent on the new studio to pay for every month, we needed to make sure that the income kept coming in.

We had finished the photo-set and I was in the middle of getting the model to sign a release form when Vicki got the call from Television X. Apparently Jodie Marsh was unwell and had left the studio. The producers were unsure if she would in fact return or, even if she did, if she would be fit enough to host the first live show later that night.

Having been impressed with Vicki's professionalism and reliability on previous shoots when she had done filmed links and voice-overs for them, they asked her to come in that afternoon and have a full rehearsal in order to be on standby in case, at the very last moment, Jodie was too unwell to do the show and Vicki had to actually stand in for her for real, as 'the show must go on'. It would be a kind of *'Jodie Marsh – Live and Turned On... (But With Vicki Holloway Instead)'*!

Needless to say we were both quite flattered that Television X thought Vicki good enough to stand-in at the last moment for their current top star, and Vicki immediately set off for the studio to get rehearsed and ready should she be needed to go on-air later that night in Jodie's place.

After clearing up at our studio, I then went on to Television X too, and watched Vicki go through the rehearsals, flawlessly linking all the sections and reading off the auto-cue as naturally as if she had done this and nothing else all her life. She was as at ease in the television studio as if she had been brought up in it. Nothing was stressing or fazing her and, even though this was the first time she had seen the script or the show schedule, she was relaxed, unflustered and professional. Everyone was very impressed.

It was now eight o'clock at night and there were only a couple of hours to go to the live show. If Jodie didn't turn up within the next few minutes, it would be too late for her to get made up and do a technical run-through, something that the producers felt was essential on this, the first night of her live show.

There was no sign of Jodie, and no phone call from her. The producers were congratulating Vicki on so professionally and calmly stepping in and saving the show at the last minute. They were getting her ready to go into make-up and some members of the crew were even quietly whispering that she was more of a professional to work with than Jodie herself.

There was a buzz of excitement that Vicki was going to save the day, and then the doors to the studio burst open, and Jodie Marsh herself strode back in!

Vicki was immediately ushered into a tiny back room while everyone gathered round Ms Marsh to see how she was feeling and to find out if she would indeed be well enough to actually present her own show.

One of the production team came in to see Vicki and told her that, although Jodie would be presenting her show that night, they wanted Vicki to stay on 'just in case', but that she mustn't be seen by Jodie and that it mustn't be known to Jodie that they had had this back-up plan ready to swing into action; apparently Ms Marsh's fragile ego wouldn't have taken the news too well that she was actually replaceable by a relatively unknown glamour model who come in at a couple of hour's notice to front her own show possibly even better than she had been!

Vicki hung around in one of the edit suites with me while they broadcast episode one of *Jodie Marsh – Live and Turned On* and, at the end of the night, the production crew were thanking Vicki as much as they were thanking Jodie, for being there and for helping make the show a success.

Although she wasn't in front of camera on that first night, Vicki did go on to appear as herself in later editions of the Jodie Marsh Show, without Jodie ever realising that the glamorous girl posing in the background of her set had almost been her replacement on the opening night.

Jodie Marsh – Live and Turned On was generally regarded as a success, although it had been quite expensive to produce. It was therefore considered too costly for Television X to plan repeating anything similar too soon, with Jodie, Vicki or anyone else fronting it.

Vicki's brief involvement with that live show however must have impressed station manager Paul D enough for him to consider her for what was to come some time after.

We were once again shooting in the photo studio one day when Vicki got another intriguing phone call on her mobile from Television X. They wanted her to go in for a meeting with Paul D to discuss a couple of new projects.

I went with her and sat in on the meeting, although it was clearly Vicki that they wanted to talk to, and not me. I sat in the background and occasionally interjected something, when everyone would look round at me as if suddenly remembering that I was there and then look to Vicki to see what she thought of what I had said.

She had clearly impressed them on the first night of the Jodie Marsh Show with her calm professionalism and ability to get on with the job in hand under pressure. And so, they had now come to her with a request that she get involved in a new live show project that they were planning – but this time with her on the other side of the camera.

When Television X had started broadcasting back in 1995 they were the only rival to what was then the sole contender to the crown of adult oriented television, The Adult Channel. Now many other young pretenders had sprung up providing a completely different kind of interactive viewing entertainment from the likes of Shag and Mutt or Deric Botham. Satellite channels like BabeStation, Babe Cast, Sex Station and Live XXX (so called 'Babe Channels') provided top models nightly free to air live to viewers who could actually interact with them for real – they could phone or text them live on air – albeit at an expensive premium rate number, thus potentially running up a huge phone bill in the process.

Television X felt obliged to compete with the growing number of inexpensively broadcast live channels that were now all competing for the same adult audience as Television X.

Plans had already been put in place for over a month, with Television X producer Big Jim put in place to run this kind of live show direct from what was the old Jodie Marsh Show studio for three nights a week, on a Thursday, Friday and Saturday.

Just like The Jodie Marsh Show however, changes were made at the eleventh hour and, again just like The Jodie Marsh Show, Television X wanted Vicki to come in and save the day.

With only a week to go before this new show was to go live, Paul D wanted Vicki to take control of running the new enterprise, taking over from Big Jim. From her involvement with the Jodie Marsh Show he had clearly been impressed by her professionalism and ability to keep calm under last minute pressure; both vital traits when running a live phone-in show three nights a week!

Vicki was given a crash course in 'gallery etiquette' – that is to say, how to run a studio based show on talk-back from the 'gallery', which is the technical nerve centre of production. It's where, as I had done before on the Talent Channel's live event, the producer will sit and prompt the talent via talk-back, while the director is also prompting camera cues, and the vision mixer is cutting and mixing the pictures so that the viewer at home sees a seamless entertainment show with no knowledge of all the frantic goings-on behind the scenes.

And this is what Vicki, as senior series producer, was about to learn how to do.

Unlike its rival channels, who did everything on a shoestring budget, no expense had been spared for Television X's new live phone-in show, and a beautiful purpose built set had been made, as had a devil-horned logo of the show's name which was to be used as the ident for the new show, and which had been edited into a short fast paced intro sequence.

This new live programme was to be called *TVX Callgirls Live*, and was to go out initially three times a week on a Thursday, Friday and Saturday at nine o'clock in the evening free-to-air, with three to four models taking part, two taking topless live private phone calls, while the other two acted as presenters, reading on-screen texts from viewers who could interact with them, asking them to take off articles of clothing or perform sex acts on each other. Later on, all the girls would perform a twenty-minute fully nude sex scene only visible by subscribers when the Channel went encrypted at ten past ten.

It was surprising that, despite the array of sex toys available to the girls on-set, the viewers who called in would, more often than not, merely ask the girls to do things like 'sit with your legs open' or 'put the soles of your feet up to the camera'.

TVX Callgirls Live was to be shot by two cameramen, and Television X were hoping not only to make some money from the premium rate phone calls and texts, but also that their subscriptions to the Channel would rise with viewers wanting to stay on board and see the live sex show after ten past ten.

One of our favourite models, bubbly blonde Essex girl Karen Wood (the star of our *Footballers Wives* series), was hired as one of the three girls to launch the show on its first night, and she even contributed an idea that was to become one of the Show's on-going catch-phrases among both cast and crew, as well as being something that helped generate more in-coming texts for the programme than almost anything else. Vicki wanted one word or a short phrase that could be quickly tapped into a mobile phone by a viewer to signify that they wanted a quick flash of the model's pussy. One of our rival channels used the phrase 'Flash The Gash' or 'FTG' for short. Karen came up with the brilliant anachronism 'POP', standing for 'Peek Of Pussy'.

And so, within moments of going on air, viewers were texting in 'POP POP POP' by the score!

I went along on the first night to give Vicki some moral support, although she had made it clear to me that she hadn't wanted me to get too involved in this project as, as she had been asked to take it on personally, and not me or Portway, she felt that she wanted to be seen to be doing it without any help or involvement from me. And not that she needed it as, when I turned up on that first night, I felt for the first time as if I was now very much in Vicki's shadow. The camera crew and technical staff, who were all unknown to me, all knew Vicki to be the boss and I was being introduced to them simply as 'Vicki's partner'. They hadn't heard of Ric Porter and it struck me that clearly the tide had now turned, and that gone were the days when I was the one in charge, with everyone knowing my name and looking to me to run the show and call the shots.

But I was glad to see Vicki finally get the proper recognition that I felt she deserved for the talents I knew that she so clearly possessed.

In the television studio she was in her element, buzzing around, full of ideas, telling everyone what to do and making quick intelligent decisions on the spur of the moment. She was exactly the type of animal that one needed to have running a live broadcast. She put 110% into the programme, and not just that first night. The first few weeks of *TVX Callgirls Live* were a dazzling success, with the show going from strength to strength under Vicki's leadership.

All the models wanted to work on the show, as Television X were comparatively paying much more than any of the competitor channels, as well as providing the most professional and pleasant environment for the girls to work in. Girls were defecting from the regular so called 'Babe' channels that they worked for to come to Vicki's show, as well as introducing their model friends to her too.

Not content to simply utilise the set that Television X had built for her, Vicki frequently turned everything upside down in order to construct elaborate themed evenings which, while being great fun to work on, unfortunately did nothing to boost the ratings.

She filled the studio with bales of straw one night for a cowgirl style event, making sure that all the girls wore cute stripper style cowboy hats, tiny denim shorts and pink and white gingham-check shirts.

On another occasion Vicki got all the girls to wear elegant evening dresses. They draped themselves across the bed on a set which Vicki had dressed with white muslin and long white candles. The excellent cameraman Nik Kindon shot the show with a soft filter over the lens of his camera, so that the entire on-screen effect was that of a lavish and elegant ball – to which all our viewers were able to attend, albeit only by text and phone call!

Needless to say, Halloween and Christmas were also great times for elaborately themed sets.

Vicki also thought up a different theme for every single evening's show, from Rude Food to Hot Pussies, Group Sex, and Foot Fetish.

I was happy to step back from all this, as Vicki was now the one regularly seen in the Television X offices and being heaped with praise from Paul D and his staff.

I was still however as busy as ever with making the programmes for Television X that together, as Portway, we were producing, and Vicki still found time to co-produce and direct these with me.

Around about the same time that Television X asked Vicki to start producing the *Callgirls* show for them, they also called her in for another meeting, of which I too went along to 'sit in' on. I was by now becoming used to walking in Vicki's shadow, and merely sitting in on her production meetings to make notes on her behalf!

As we all sat in the boardroom in this meeting, Paul D asked Vicki and I if we had been watching a new series that had been launched on BBC television called *The Apprentice,* where a team of would-be apprentices to Sir Alan Sugar would be given business tasks by him and then one by one fired, until a final winner would be given a job in Sir Alan's employ.

Television X had the idea of launching their own porno version of *The Apprentice.* Four would-be porn directors would be given the chance to compete for being given the job of making their own series for the Channel. But first they must direct a one-off sex show under the guidance of one of Television X's producers. Paul D wanted to know if we fancied being the production team under whose guidance these nervous newbies could either show their abilities, or fail miserably – and all live on camera!

The plan was to advertise for these would-be directors on the Channel itself as well as in other appropriate publications. These potential apprentices had to submit an idea for a Television X programme. Vicki and I would then be allowed to whittle the shortlist down to the chosen four, whose ideas showed the most potential. These four would each then be given their own one-off programme, which would be cast in liaison with ourselves. We would then act as their production crew on the day, shooting the scene in our normal way, while a runner constantly filmed all the behind the scenes action so that, in the finished edit, the viewer would be able to see exactly how the apprentices coped with the work on-set. At the end of each show, viewers would be given the opportunity to vote on a premium rate phone number for the director that they most wanted to see win their own series.

Four lucky apprentices were chosen, and Vicki and I invited them to an initial planning meeting, which was to be filmed and included as part of the series. Rio our make-up man, one of the Television X producers, one of the porno models that we planned to use in the series, Vicki and myself all formed part of the panel that these apprentices needed to impress.

The initial meeting was to take place at our new photo studio in East London, and we were offering to pay all the budding apprentice's travel expenses, as many were coming from outside London. One of them however had a problem. He was travelling from Birmingham but, not having any current employment, he couldn't scrape together the train fare. After emails back and forth he eventually managed to borrow the amount from a relative but wanted reassurance that we were going to reimburse him in cash on the day. He also wanted to know if he could be known by the 'nom-de-porn' of Kam, in case any of his family heard of his exploits. Neither of these requests were of course a problem.

One other apprentice also wanted to be known by the 'nom-de-porn' of Jason Sanchez, although when he arrived at the studio, I recognised him from the original *Porn Idol* auditions where, under yet another assumed name, he had been trying out as a stud in front of the camera.

This time however he was going all out to prove his abilities as a porn director, and he had come prepared with a sheaf of scribbled scenarios, far more than we could ever film in a year. He was brimming with ideas and brimming with enthusiasm, much more than any of the other apprentices, and he made it clear that he was definitely in it to win.

He, out of all four of the apprentices, bombarded me with emails, asking for specific models and making sure that he was informed every step of the way with full details about his shoot. The other three were happy just to let me cast their ideas and turn up on the day to direct.

Not Jason Sanchez! He arrived on the day of his own particular shoot with yet another notebook brimming with notes and stage directions. He introduced himself confidently to all the models and, while he did allow Vicki and myself to guide him in the ways of directing a porn scene, he was very confident and trying to take control at every opportunity and assert his authority on set. If ever there was a budding director, then out of our four apprentices, he was the one who was certainly trying the hardest.

But the final result was up to the viewer's vote. Jason's scene was very hot, and in more ways than one. We were shooting on the hottest day of the year, in a studio with no air conditioning and, for the benefit of the soundtrack to exclude any erroneous noise, we needed to keep all the windows closed and all the cooling fans turned off! By the end of the two-girl/one boy sex scene, the duvet and all the models were literally soaked with sweat, and we had to frequently stop filming as the girls were beginning to feel quite faint.

It was a very sexy scene however, but would the viewers think that it was the best? Another would-be director had also done a two-girl/one boy sex scene which was also very raunchy.

Kam had a brand new 18-year-old blonde in his scene who had never had sex on camera before, and our final apprentice was working with established Eastern European porn star Jessica Loveit looking very sexy in a white doctor's coat with little underneath.

Under our guidance, our apprentices had scripted and shot four very sexy scenes, but which one would the viewers vote for as the best? Who would they vote in as the new Television X *Porn Apprentice*?

Several weeks after filming was complete, and after the programmes had been shown and voted for, the results were in and the winner was to be announced in the fifth programme, which was a kind of 'round up' of what had been seen so far culminating in the announcement of the winner.

There had unfortunately been no votes whatsoever for Kam. Curiously, he hadn't even phoned in to vote for himself! But then, judging by his lack of funds in barely being able to scrape together the train fare, possibly he couldn't afford to ring the premium rate phone number either.

The winner, unsurprisingly, judging by his zealous determination and confident attitude, was Jason Sanchez, who was then given his own series to make for Television X.

Curiously enough however, I don't recall ever hearing from him, or his planned series again. I hope he made his show, although I never heard about it in the Television X offices, neither did I hear of Jason Sanchez going on to become a renowned international porn director for Television X or for any other Channel. But, judging by his previous 'nom-de- porns', perhaps he has done it under yet another assumed name.

Chapter Twenty-Three:
THE SHOW GOES ON

Vicki's live interactive show *TVX Callgirls Live* was going from strength to strength. Within a few months it had gone from being broadcast live just three nights a week to filling the screens from nine till half past ten every single night of the week, free to air from nine till ten and then, following a ten minute break for trailers and ads, an encrypted girl/girl sex scene just for subscribers until half past ten.

At first Vicki's commission was renewed month-by-month until, eventually, it was just taken as red that the show would simply continue indefinitely, seven nights a week, 365 nights of the year!

Given that the show was to continue being broadcast live every single day now clearly posed a problem for Vicki. She couldn't possibly carry on producing it indefinitely on her own without a break. She would need to share the production job with a fellow producer, someone who had been there from the beginning, someone who knew the models and the crew, knew just how the format of the show worked, knew how the studio worked, and ideally someone who could liaise with Vicki on a day-to-day basis regarding that night's production. Who better to jump in as Vicki's co-producer than the man who had so far been known to the *TVX Callgirls Live* gallery crew only as 'Vicki's partner'? Yes, Vicki and I approached Television X and suggested that I came on board as her co- producer, a suggestion that they had apparently been half expecting, and that they readily agreed to. *TVX Callgirls Live* now truly became a Portway Production and, apart from the fees of the models and crew, we would invoice every month for everything else; props, dildos, condoms (for the regularly used dildos for hygiene reasons), drinks, snacks and of course our fee.

I initially sat in on several of Vicki's shows before the nerve-racking night when I took the chair in the gallery myself and did my very first shift as the night producer, first under Vicki's watchful guidance, and then totally on my own.

I had to learn the routine of jobs that needed doing before, during and after the show, and these were not only far more, but also far more varied, than one might have originally suspected.

I would get to the studio at about six o'clock in the evening, just as all the daytime staff were leaving, armed with a crate of bottled water, huge party size bag of crisps and loads of chocolate bars for the girls to keep them going. They would usually bring their own energy drinks and, even though alcohol was banned on set, they would often manage to sneak in bottles of wine or vodka as well.

After dumping the snacks and water in the make-up room and some water bottles in the studio for the crew, I would then turn on all the equipment and do a quick technical check in the gallery to check that all the kit was working correctly. Then I would get some blank professional videotapes and prepare them for recording the night's show in the Transmission (or 'TX') gallery. Every night's show was recorded and stored away in case, for legal, or indeed for any other reason, the night's programming needed to be reviewed quickly.

It also meant of course that segments of the show could be quickly edited up into trailers to advertise the series.

Having set up the tape ready to record, it was now up to me to think up a theme for that night's show, if I hadn't done so already, and then prepare the set accordingly, perhaps changing the throws and rugs on the bed, or putting relevant costumes in the make-up room if we were to have a themed evening along the lines of 'naughty nurses', 'sexy schoolgirls' or 'pervy policewomen' for example.

I also made sure that there were enough condoms, lube and baby-wipes on set for the girls to use as, although the sex scene at the end of the night was only ever a girl/girl one, we always reused the same dildos and often with different girls, and so for the sake of everyone's hygiene, we advised the girls to always put a condom on the dildo that they were going to use before insertion.

After having done all this, an hour might have passed and the girls and crew would start arriving. On arrival, I would get them to sign model releases for their performance that night, and go over with them what we would be doing in that night's show. If anyone hadn't turned up by half past seven, I would then need to get on the phone, finding out why they were running late, if they had in fact remembered that they were meant to be doing the show with us, and if they were indeed going to turn up at all! Often, if a girl had let us down, there then followed a frantic half hour or so of phoning round back- up models who lived close enough to our East London studios to see if they could stand-in at short notice as, come hell or high water, we were going to go on air at nine o'clock with a live show!

I would also need to find out which of our girls would need a taxi at the end of the night and pre-book these in advance.

The girls would do their own hair and make-up, and would have to be ready to do a dry-run rehearsal between half seven and eight o'clock.

This was more of a technical run-through than anything else, more important for the crew than the girls, as this was the only time before we went on air that we could find out if a piece of equipment didn't work properly, or if the timing of a particular piece was too tight to do live. All important to test it out now, as the next time we would be doing it would be live in front of the many Television X viewers.

After the rehearsal, the girls went back to the make-up room to continue getting ready, while the crew generally popped out to get a bite to eat before getting back in their places at a quarter to nine to get ready to do final technical checks and start production of the real show.

We had a crew of around six people, composing of a soundman who sat in his own audio gallery, mixing the various on-set mikes and background music as well as fading up the correct sound for trailers and idents etc.

We had a director/vision mixer who directed the cameramen via a talk-back system, and cut the shots live once we were on- air.

We also had a graphics operator who edited the on-screen texts that came in, making sure that inappropriate messages (i.e. ones where people had included their phone numbers or rude words) were edited out before he sent them on to appear on-screen. We had strict guidelines from Ofcom, the authority overseeing legal and moral standards of decency on British television, that included words that shouldn't appear on screen before the 'watershed' hour of nine o'clock. Later on, we could allow certain words to be spoken on-air and the girls could also go topless. The girls were not allowed to go nude until after encryption (an incentive for viewers to subscribe) although Ofcom didn't seem to mind our 'Peek Of Pussy' too much as I suppose it was very brief and unrevealing. It was also done in the spirit of fun and I think that sexual explicitness on television is also all about context. Therefore, one can see quite an explicit sex scene on a mainstream television channel for example, in the context of a drama, but the same level of explicitness would not be allowed free-to-air on Television X, as it would be shown in the context of titillation. In the early days of Television X we showed a sex education series called *Sex Talk*, which was presented by a genuine sex counsellor (as opposed to 'Doctor' David Michaels). We got away with showing erect penises and blow- jobs on this show as it was in the context of sex education, whereas we couldn't show such things uncensored on our normal programming in the context of titillation and sexual entertainment. Even though the actual models involved and even the camera shots would be exactly the same in both types of programming.

Apart from the crew of *TVX Callgirls Live* already mentioned, there were also two cameramen and an occasional runner. Our main cameraman, Nik Kindon, worked almost every shift, rarely taking a day off, and taking great personal care with lighting the set and making sure that every shot he took was inventive, creative, beautifully focused and framed, and yet of course always within the legal guidelines.

I would need to liaise not just with Nik, but with all these people before and during the show via 'talk-back'.

Ten minutes before we went on air I would need to get the girls in the studio, making sure that they had not brought their mobile phones in with them, as this would interfere with the sound system, apart from also distracting them from the job in hand. I would also phone the Transmission department ('TX'), which was based in a separate building elsewhere in London, to check that they were receiving our video and audio signal and were ready to switch us live at nine o'clock.

Final checks having been done, I would wish everyone good luck over talk-back, and the director would then count us down to on-air.

Throughout the broadcast I could talk to the girls via a tiny almost invisible earpiece that each model would wear. This meant that they could hear me and that I could prompt them to say certain things (giving out the phone number for viewers to ring in, how to subscribe etc) as well as warning them to move position if they were revealing too much to the camera, or to reveal more if the show was sluggish, and we would do a 'Peek Of Pussy' ('POP").

Many of the girls found this constant murmur in their right ear very off-putting, particularly when they were taking calls from the viewers. Our rival stations didn't use any form of talk- back and just let the girls get on with it themselves and, for many of the models, this was what they had been used to and what they preferred.

Given my understanding of how things are done in mainstream television, I knew how important it was that we were able to communicate with the girls while the show was live on air. I knew how steep the Ofcom fines were if one of the girls accidentally showed more than she should do free-to- air (many thousands of pounds) and, if for only that reason alone, I knew I needed to be able to communicate with them during the show. So I was very tough with the girls when they just took the earpiece out or pretended that it had just 'stopped working'. In their defence, the earpieces did sometimes stop working when the girls were in a position that put them out of the range of receiving a signal, but I knew what positions these were and knew when that had happened. So, for the girls that continually refused to play the game our way I took it very seriously and, after giving them several severe warnings, it was simple – they were off the show, no matter how reliable or how popular they were. I wanted them to realise that no one was indispensable.

Unfortunately, that also included a particular pretty doll-like model who was very important to us as she would always stand in at the last minute when other models had let us down. Time and time again she saved the day by turning up at literally the eleventh hour, often minutes before we were to go on air, and once or twice even arriving after we had already gone on air. But she was reliable. She always turned up. And she was very popular, and had a big fan-base with our viewers.

And so I turned a blind eye to the few things about her that irritated me. She would always have her mobile phone with her on set and, by the end of the evening, she would be continuously in a doggy position, ass to camera, and I knew that, at the other end, away from the camera, she was sending and reading texts while we couldn't see.

She also treated our viewers with a certain amount of contempt, but she did it in such a sweet cutesy little voice that no one could ever take offence with her. For example, one night she read out a text from a viewer that said 'I would love to stick my big one up you. From John'. Most of the other models would have replied, 'Ooh yes, I'd love you to do that, John!', but this particular girl just looked straight into the camera and said coldly, 'Well, that's never going to happen is it, John? I mean, I doubt we'll ever really meet!'

Yet she got away with more than most, because she was pretty, always covered the shifts of the more unreliable models, and was kind of quirky in a cute baby-doll kind of way. But even her good points didn't help much one night when she turned up looking really thin and drawn, like she hadn't slept for a week. She sat down on one of the sofas on set and started taking calls. A short while into the show I began to notice that she hadn't changed her position in the slightest for quite a long while. I spoke to her on talk-back and asked her to move around a bit. No response. I asked her to turn round with her butt to the camera. No response. One of the other models, who could also hear my requests on the talk-back, whispered that she thought this particular girl was asleep. As soon as we were on a commercial break, I ran into the studio and crept up to where she was sitting. Sure enough she was fast asleep! By this time, we were back from the break and live on air again. Not wanting to do anything that would disrupt the show, I slowly and carefully moved the camera that was constantly focused on her away so that it was pointing at one of the other models instead. I then quietly crept up to her and whispered in her ear, 'Wake up. It's Ric. You're in the middle of a live broadcast'. I'd barely got the words out when she jumped awake, clearly disoriented from her slumbers and leaped off the sofa and about three feet to the side of the studio, stating loudly, 'I wasn't asleep! I wasn't asleep!'

On this occasion, I just nodded and returned to the Gallery to carry on with the programme. I kept a close eye on her for the rest of the night however and took more notice on other occasions when, at any opportunity, she would sneak off to the loo and return looking even more spaced out than she usually did, her pupils wildly dilated.

Months later, I read an interview with her in a mainstream women's gossip magazine where she admitted having come though a dreadful drugs habit around that time. I'm glad that she has now recovered of course, but it was a shame that she was playing out her drama live on national television in front of all her fans.

When the shows were over, the final ritual of the night would take place – that of clearing up! I would go over the studio floor, picking up all the empty sweet wrappers and cans of Red Bull as well as the used wipes. I would remove the condoms from the dildos that had been used and give the dildos a wipe over before returning them to their on-set toy box.

I would then tidy up the make-up room, which the girls had usually left in a real state, and I would eject the videotapes that had made a recording of the night's show and leave them on my executive producer's desk. I would then turn out the lights and, at around midnight, drive home. Only to wake up the next morning and start the same round all over again, beginning with texts to the girls reminding them that they were working that night and to let me know if there was likely to be any problems. That was normally when the day's troubles might begin if a girl had texted back to say that she was ill or couldn't make it, and then would begin a frantic round of phone calls trying to find a stand-in for that evening's show. This call round other models might not be over until close to the actual on-air time, overshadowing anything else that I might have had planned for that day. I remember once leaving a restaurant briefly where I was having lunch with Vicki and our post-production consultant Nick Cliff, to take a call from one of the models who we were having problems with.

I marvelled at how Vicki had been doing this routine day after day for so long, and with such calm professionalism. The baton was now being passed to me on the nights that I was to be in charge, but even so, Vicki would still usually watch the show at home, just as I had done on the nights when she had been producing, willing it to go well and be a success.

And a success it was. The nightly show was going so well that, when Television X had a brand new state-of-the-art studio built on the same floor as their main office, instead of using it themselves for their weekly filmed links and promos as was expected, Paul D told Vicki and I that the studio was to be used exclusively for *TVX Callgirls Live*. We were over the moon as this meant that our technical gallery area was now twice the size of the one we had been working from and would look like something one would expect to see at the BBC, with a myriad of monitors and play-in video machines. Paul D even asked Vicki what ideas she had for the set; what kind of bed, sofas and backdrop would she prefer? In liaison with Vicki and Paul D, the set designer built a more industrial looking set for the new studio, which we were to move into just after Christmas. It would have a crimson red and chrome theme, with the bed reflecting the horned 'g' in the *Callgirls* logo with padded red leather horns either side. The bed itself was a different shape; more oval than the perfectly round bed that we had previously been used to. And the dildos were to get their own 'toy box' incorporated into the bed design.

Vicki and I were very excited about the move 'downstairs' to the new studio, and it appeared that, at least to our bosses at Television X, we could do no wrong. We were at that time like the king and queen of live adult television. Indeed, our executive producer Fleur even introduced us to some new crew members once as Queen Victoria and King Richard!

The series was being regarded as a great success. We were being given the station's new premier studio to work from, and the BBC itself had even approached us, wanting to include us in a documentary that they were making about niche digital TV channels. We were happy to agree.

Their producer/director/cameraman Richard Macer had, amongst other things, previously made several very well received and revealing documentaries about Katie Price, or Jordan as she then was, and he came in to film a couple of our shows and interview me, Vicki and some of the models.

Vicki and I were very wary of Richard at first, regarding him with a lot of suspicion. My earlier encounters with the mainstream media had left me with a feeling that they usually only wanted to find some hook that would show us 'seedy pornographers' in a bad light.

My suspicions were not confirmed however when the resulting programme, part of the BBC's *Welcome To My World* series and entitled *Porno, Preachers and Peddlers* was finally broadcast on BBC3 the following July. In the programme, Richard contrasted our station with a small budget evangelistic Christian channel and a thriving shopping channel. It was a very well made and hugely entertaining programme, and I now remain a big fan of Richard's production style.

During filming however he nearly came to blows with Vicki when, finding out if she thought that he could become a porn director himself, he made the mistake of suggesting to Vicki that her job wasn't exactly 'rocket science'.

Bearing in mind the long hard hours that Vicki had put into *Callgirls* with all the inherent day-to-day problems, Vicki took this very personally and curtly advised him to come in the next day and have a go if he thought it was that easy.

He came in the next evening and directed a rehearsal, visibly buckling under the pressure, and a few days later Vicki phoned him to inform him that they couldn't risk letting him direct an entire show live on air.

Richard later said in an interview about his documentary,

> '*I was full of preconceived notions about the standard of programme making (of porn channels). I thought all porn telly was very simplistic and "lowest common denominator". In fact, I learned that the complete opposite is the case. Watching Vicki produce the show, I was struck by how much direction and choreography go into the performance from behind the scenes. Vicki really knows how to direct women in live action so that it is erotic to the male viewer and at the same time stays on the right side of the law. That's quite a skill and clearly one that I don't possess.*'

Richard had been filming us over the Christmas period, before and after our move downstairs to the new studio.

During the festive period, we had a constant seasonal look to the studio, with a silver/white Christmas tree, and with tinsel and glitter adorning the bed, the walls and the sofa.

We began to train up other producers so that in time Vicki and I would be able to have more time off together. One of the designers that used to work for me at Fantasy Publications, a bright girl called

Esme, had always shown an interest in Television X, and she was soon acting as a more than capable producer, giving us some much needed time off.

My friend Mark ('Noodles') was also on board and, on his first night left alone as producer, Vicki and I took all the Television X staff and all our business colleagues to a lavish Christmas dinner at a local restaurant overlooking the Thames, and by sheer chance, as we all went inside, loaded with Christmas crackers, cards and gifts, we noticed that there was a boat moored outside the restaurant in the nearby dock that was appropriately named 'Portway'.

Both Vicki and I went in to work on the show on Christmas Eve. The staff and girls were paid double and we made sure that we had mince pies, sweeties and champagne on hand so that the fact we were working over the 'party period' might be made a little more bearable.

Callgirls had one day off air on Christmas Day and then Vicki and I both went back to work on Boxing Day night to go back on air, once again 'bribing' the girls and the crew with festive snacks and booze. These Christmas shows however had a great atmosphere for all of us that were there. New Years Eve was another 'party night' and then it was back to 'normal service', although we continued to provide free snacks and water for the girls and crew as we always had done.

One month into the New Year and Television X approached us with yet another proposal. Gay TV, the gay equivalent of Television X, and also run by Portland Television, was also about to launch their own version of *Callgirls*. It was to be a much toned down version however, with just one guy acting out what texts asked him to do and receiving live phone calls. There was to be no live sound audible on-screen however, as the 'show' was to appear in a small on-screen box as part of the main free-view screen before the Channel itself went encrypted. It was to only run for an hour or so every night and, with no production crew, was run with just one locked-off camera in a tiny room little bigger than a toilet, near what used to be our old studio upstairs.

The idea of keeping it so simple was that we would be able to oversee this programme from the Gallery while we were doing the main *Callgirls* show. It simply meant our making sure that our on-screen gay guy had arrived on time and that he was in position in front of the camera when his show went live, and that there were no technical hitches. While we were producing the main *Callgirls* show downstairs, we would keep an eye on a separate monitor that would be showing Gay TV so that if there were any major disasters, we could quickly run upstairs and sort them out!

I felt quite pleased and proud that Portway was now looked upon as the company in charge of all of Portland Television's live output. The extra work to oversee *Gay* on top of *Callgirls* was minimal, but the extra income we derived from it was comparatively very good, and now made all the long hours that we had put in well worthwhile.

Vicki and I were finally managing to take some time off together, although we were usually very tempted to tune in and watch when Noodles or one of the other producers we had trained up was in charge.

We hired our long term make-up man and collaborator Rio to work specifically on the Gay show several times a week, feeding the texts through for the guy on-camera to read and act out.

As the Gay TV nightly guy shared the same dressing room and facilities as the girls on *Callgirls*, he caused quite a stir with the regular *Callgirls* models, who all flirted with him outrageously, loving the fact that he was 'unattainable', although several of the gay models told me that they were in fact straight and only did gay work (not just solo stuff, but full-on boy/boy sex action) for the money, so called 'gay for pay'.

At first I found this a bit hard to believe, although I suppose in some ways this is really no different from every female porn model being expected to do full strength girl/girl work, no matter what her sexual persuasion was in her real life. The difference of course is that the guy must really be seen to be turned-on (i.e.: have an erection), whereas a girl can of course always just go through the physical motions, and fake her on- camera orgasmic pleasure. However, these days with the help of the miracle blue pill Viagra, maybe most boys can also do the same!

Our position as producer of the gay version of *Callgirls Live* was short-lived however, as the agent who was supplying all the gay models for the show approached Portland Television with the suggestion that, as he was not only the model's agent but also an experienced adult programme maker in his own right (he made several of the programmes that were regularly shown on Gay TV), he would in fact be ideal to take over the day-to-day running and producing of the show at relatively little extra cost.

Portland agreed, and what was effectively '*Callboys Live*' was set up in an adjacent studio, going from solo boy to full two guy sex action after encryption.

Even this exciting version of the show didn't last very long however, and the gay version of the programme that Vicki had so successfully established was soon taken off air and, at the time of writing, has not yet returned to screen.

The main *Callgirls* show however was still going very well and its hours were even extended still further so that more viewers than ever could enjoy the show.

All viewers watching via the Sky satellite had always been able to see the show, but those that had access to Television X through certain other satellite or cable providers could only watch the Channel after 11pm – not only half an hour after *TVX Callgirls Live* had gone off air, but completely missing all the free-view material.

So, for these viewers, and also to add something extra for the existing fans, the programme continued its usual time slot, and then went off-air for half an hour, giving both cast and crew a well-earned break, before coming back on-air at 11p.m. with a ten minute free-view where, with the girls now fully dressed again, they welcomed the new viewers and gave them a complete taste of what they had been missing for the last two hours, complete with taking phone calls, reading texts and of course the now legendary 'Peek Of Pussy'.

The adult television audience had so taken 'Peek Of Pussy' to its heart that girls working for rival stations reported that viewers were texting in 'P.O.P' to their channels too!

After this new ten-minute version of the show, there would be a two-minute ad break, where the girls would freshen up and get ready for another girl-on-girl sex scene for subscribers only, from ten past eleven to half past eleven.

Cast and crew got a little extra money for the extra hours work involved and, as lots of girls were missing their last train home by the time they had got changed after coming off-air at half eleven, Television X agreed to pay for taxi fares to local main line stations.

By the following summer however Vicki was beginning to tire of the constant routine of the show, which rarely allowed either of us any quality time off, and she made the decision to tell our executive producer that she wanted to stop.

It was a case of 'never say never again'. She may come back at some point, but certainly for the moment Vicki wanted to indulge in some time away from the constant pressure to keep an adult programme live on air night after night after night.

Television X were naturally very sad to hear Vicki's decision. It was she after all who they had chosen to launch the new live show, and it was she who had so successfully seen it through from an initial test run to the incredible on going series that it had now become.

However, with Vicki's decision made, the question then had to be answered, and answered quickly, as to who would keep the roller coaster rolling on every night.

Vicki and I had already sounded out Noodles to see if he wanted to take over. I would continue to share shifts with him but I didn't want to continue with the day-to-day running of the show without Vicki's involvement too.

Noodles was happy to take the project on, and Television X agreed, as they were already used to his involvement as a producer.

So, after just over a year on air, the tables were turned and I was now working for Mark, rather than he for us.

The programme carried on under Mark's regime for several more months until one day, Portland decided quite quickly, and much like they had done with *The Talent Channel*, that the show wasn't making enough money and that it would end within the month.

On the very last night, every producer and engineer that had ever worked on the series, along with many of the regular models, were all in attendance in the Gallery, the producers taking turns at producing the last night's show. The sound room was also being used as a place where drinks were stored, many people having brought in bottles of champagne or wine, and we all celebrated the final programme in the series in a big party in the 'Green Room' afterwards.

The final words of direction in the Gallery of course went to Vicki who, although herself never appeared on-screen on *Callgirls*, without a doubt she was the real star of the Show.

The studio continued to be used for shooting links at Television X, our familiar old set being used as the backdrop and, after a time, our studio was transformed into first a shopping channel, and then a gaming channel, all under Portland Television's direction.

Over a year later, Television X again ran a live show, this time with a very limited run and featuring some star names in the world of adult British porn that Television X had put under contract; *Antonia Backstage Live* featured Antonia Stokes, and *Lolly Live* featured Lolly Badcock. They were shot back-to- back, one after the other on adjacent sets, and broadcast live on two different channels.

The crew for these shows was very big, and I was happy to be brought in as a consultant.

Almost another year after that, Television X brought *TVX Callgirls Live* back on air. This time it was a much slimmed down version, with just one producer/director and one cameraman on the night, and two girls taking live phone calls while the viewers just heard bland muzak. The show lasted two hours free to air, with a twenty minute encryption scene for subscribers only.

Under different names, and on different channel numbers, the concept of *Callgirls Live* continues to evolve and succeed, and I continue to do regular shifts as a cameraman several times a month.

Adopting the nom-de-porn of Cherry Valance, Noodles continued to work freelance for Television X, shooting programmes periodically, as well as becoming a valued second cameraman to Vicki and I on our shoots, along with Dave Wells, who also now stood in regularly to shoot the dedicated hard angle on our shows. Dave was fast becoming an integral member of the Portway team, totally taking over the role of stills photographer on our shoots as well.

Having a hard angle being constantly shot, as opposed to just me with one camera, getting the odd hard angle that could only be cut in with the majority of soft angles, became an increasingly important part of our filming, particularly as the hard versions of our programmes began to play more of a part in what we could do with them on another new medium – the world wide web.

Chapter Twenty-Four:
PORTWAY'S PORTAL AND THE HORNY SURFERS

Portway had been very unsuccessful in several areas; we had been too late to market our material on video, had tried to do so on DVD but had not found a satisfactory distributor. We had tried to make our pictures and video clips available as mobile phone downloads, but the companies that we had dealt with had not managed to secure us anything very lucrative. The one area that Vicki and I hadn't yet tried to develop was the Internet.

A web designer called Scott was recommended to us by the main company that had been trying to market our material to mobile phones. We made a meeting with the amiable softly spoken Australian who bore a passing resemblance to the film star Johnny Depp. We gave him all the necessary pictures and company information and he got going on building our official website.

But he got going slowly. Very slowly.

Neither Vicki nor myself knew anything about web design and, as we were very busy with filming productions for Television X, and with doing *Callgirls*, we were content to just let Scott get on with it at his own pace.

Which he did – but it took nearly two whole years from our initial talks with him to our actually going live with the final website!

It has to be said however that it was not all Scott's fault by any means. We had many setbacks in deciding exactly what it was that we wanted to do with the site. We wanted it to be primarily a showcase for our company and everything that we did. So pages were designed that highlighted the photo-sets we produced, as well as a page showcasing the studio space that we owned in East London, and of course personal profiles of both Vicki and myself, as well as pictures from our films that linked to pages that showed video clips, and all of these could be accessed by category or film title.

This was the first website of an adult nature that Scott had ever built, all his previous work being for major mainstream companies. He did a good job in designing it just as we asked, but we were new to adult websites too, and hadn't done any research as to what would work best, and unfortunately Scott didn't have the necessary knowledge of adult internet either, and so neither us nor he knew how to build a site that could effectively generate both traffic and income.

It seems that all successful adult websites need to follow a similar pattern, and this pattern is really quite simplistic. The main area of a webpage needs to be centrally designed so that the viewer's eye is drawn in toward the action right there in the middle of the page.

Then there just needs to be a large illustrated title at the top, and underneath, starting with the latest update, a scrollable list of movie clips, with the options to watch a free trailer or simply subscribe to the site and download the clip. As most people have PCs as opposed to Apple Mac computers, the clips should be in Windows Media format, or at best as a Quick Time file.

This pattern works. Anything varying too much from this template will just confuse the horny surfer who is clicking around with one hand on his mouse and the other on his dick, keen to see something sexy as quickly as he can. Therefore, a familiar template helps a lot, otherwise he is more than likely to just click away and go somewhere else that looks a little more friendly.

Scott had designed our site according to our requests, but it looked more like a company website, with lots of menus and pages. It looked nothing like a familiar porn site. All the clickable thumbnail pictures were tiny, and the text was all far too small and polite. Nothing flashed or was too 'in your face'. We were a very 'British' adult website in that respect and consequently, although we eventually got a healthy amount of visitors, nobody stayed long enough to actually spend any money!

We also had some problems with the format and the way in which viewers could watch the clips of our movies.

Scott had told us that Real Media format was the best quality to use for our clips and, not knowing any better and not having done any real research, we agreed.

It may well have been true that Real Media would technically give us the best quality clips but, as both Vicki and I worked on Apple Mac computers, we had no idea that the majority of the porno surfing world had PCs and therefore easier access to WMV files. Why would they bother to download a different format, albeit for free, in order to watch our clips? This was just one more thing to cause the horny surfer to click away elsewhere!

And then, while we were deciding whether to do pay-per- view streaming or video-on-demand downloads, two British companies were heavily fined for outputting downloadable footage that hadn't been given a BBFC certificate.

These became test cases in which it was ruled in British courts that the word 'supply' in the Video Recordings Act had a wider meaning beyond the word 'sale'. Effectively, the legal 'loophole' that had so far allowed British porn producers to send out uncertificated DVDs back into Britain from Europe by post was now closed. Similarly, if a British based porn company was offering uncertificated footage to download and own via the internet, this was also now illegal, even if that producer's website was being hosted off-shore. Adult footage from a British based company had to be certificated R18 by the BBFC and had to be purchased only through a recognised legally licensed sex shop in the UK.

One Internet company had been fined £2500 and court costs in excess of £22000! There was no way that Vicki and I could risk putting ourselves in a similar position – we were trying to build up a fledging business and certainly didn't have that kind of money to put at risk!

We took legal advice and decided that video streaming would have to be the way to go. That way, no one could actually download any clip to keep and could only pay to watch it stream in real time. This seemed a way around the new ruling, and also of course meant that, if a customer liked the clip, he would have to pay to watch it again, whereas if he downloaded it to keep, he would only pay for it once.

At this time, rather than offering a monthly subscription to allow our on-line customers access to the whole site, we opted to go with a little known British company called PayAsYouClick who, as their name suggested, offered a service whereby customers could simply set up an account with them and then pay a small amount (in our case initially just $1) to view any one individual clip.

This seemed to us at the time a good idea. With the wisdom of hindsight however, it was foolish. Every other adult website in the world offered their customers a monthly subscription to gain access to the whole site, usually via the American based payment service company CCBill. This monthly subscription would take place on a recurring payment basis, meaning that customers who forgot to cancel their direct debit, would simply continue forking out $20 or so every month in perpetuity.

Many of the people who clicked at our site were based in America. The familiarity of a CCBill payment plan might have reassured them enough to subscribe. Having to give their credit card details to an unknown British based payment company that they hadn't heard of in order to spend $1 to watch just one clip in a format that they probably didn't automatically have access to either was clearly not only off- putting but was actually stopping people from spending their money with us at all, and encouraging them to click away to a different, more friendly looking website!

The name of our website may also have been unwelcoming to the horny surfer. Instead of it being called 'Sexy British Sluts' or 'Hot British Babes' or something like that, we opted for the more sedate 'PortwayEnterprises.com' and, as an afterthought, the slightly more risqué 'PortwayFilms.com'! Wow! With hot URLs like that, surely the horny Internet punters would be beating a path to our portal in their droves!

Because of our contract with Television X, Vicki and I effectively had footage that was all paid for by our commissions and that we were allowed to put up on a website of our own for our own gain, and our thinking therefore was that if we even made $1, then it would be $1 profit.

However, because of web hosting fees, webmaster costs and of course one's own personal time editing and uploading footage, it didn't really work out like that, and our website was soon actually losing us money.

Nevertheless, at the beginning Vicki and I assumed that we would of course make much more than just the odd $1 here and there. We were naive enough to simply believe that if we put a good looking adult website out there, then somehow, with no promotion or marketing whatsoever, people would not only find it, but that it would also magically start generating enough revenue for us both to live on.

Wrong! The marketing of a website is I would say as important, if not more important, than the actual design of the website or the quality of the clips thereon. A bit like the box cover design of a DVD or a video – make it good enough, make people want to see what's actually on the inside of that box cover, and you'll get the sales. The marketing of a website is the equivalent of the DVD box cover.

However, Vicki and I had not yet realised that and so, a full one year after its launch into the market place (that's three full years after its original inception), our website was still only trickling in around $20 a month – on a good month! This meant that it was not even covering the $25 a month web hosting fee it cost us to have it up there, and so was in fact actually losing us money!

Clearly it was time for a drastic rethink. Our Webmaster, the Depp look-alike Scott, had flown off indefinitely to Dubai to work for a large property development company. The first we knew of this was when our site went down one day and, in response to an email to him asking what had happened, he replied informing us that he couldn't look at it because all porn websites were blocked from viewing in Dubai, which was now where he resided!

Okay, so possibly a webmaster with no previous experience of adult websites and who had now flown off indefinitely to Dubai wasn't the best man to have on the job of resurrecting our new porno website!

We met with a number of webmasters all who, understandably enough, were keen to charge us for their time in redesigning our site and all saying that they could build us a new site in a week.

As we were now losing so much cash in the 'Portway Portal', rather than spend out any more in paying another webmaster for his talents, we were keen to find a webmaster who might be interested in working with us on a profit-share basis. We would have to share any profits our site made with him but, as we weren't making any profit at all at that time, the thought of making around 50% of at least something was surely better than our current position of actually losing money every month in order to have a 'web presence'!

And, if a webmaster was only going to make money if he put the work in, then presumably that would give him the incentive to actually get on with the job and not dither around, or pretend to have 'coding problems' that he knew we wouldn't understand anyway, while in reality he was off on the golf course or whatever!

Eventually we were recommended to a guy who seemed to fit the bill. Ben, like Scott, was another Australian, but Ben came from a tiny little village whose main claim to fame was that it had been the setting for the original *Mad Max* film. Ben arrived at our flat with his small daschund dog 'Banger' who ran around chewing up all the cushions while Ben joined us in a Chinese takeaway, which we paid for, and assured us that he too could build us a website in a week ('even a day' he said at one point) and showed us other sites that he claimed to have built along with proof of their amazing profitability. We loaded Ben up with CDs full of our photos and video clips and waved him and Banger out the door.

And of course we didn't hear from him again!

On the rare occasion that he did answer his mobile phone to me (and only because I with-held my number) he was in the pub or watching a rugby game on TV, with little or no intent of starting work on our website.

The guy who had recommended him to us said 'Oh no! Not again!' when we informed him of his (non) activity, revealing that he had done a similar thing to him when working on his website. We also found out that Ben was in fact in a full time job and could only therefore have worked on our site in the evenings and at weekends when, due to his love of sport, he would actually favour going off to Rugby matches instead!

As we hadn't actually paid him any money however, we thought we'd come off fairly lightly. We hadn't given him anything that we didn't have a back-up copy of and obviously if he tried to use any of our photos or clips without our permission, we could try and sue him.

None of this helped however with the on-going problem of what to do with our ailing website.

And so finally we decided to do a little belated research! I looked around at other people's websites and found that every model and every amateur photographer were running their own website as a sideline to their main business. They had downloaded some user-friendly software that allowed them to build a website immaterial of HTML knowledge and they were all making some money through these sites, most of them claiming to at least to be making enough to cover their monthly rent or mortgage payments.

And so the light began to dawn – how hard could it be? If every Joe with a camcorder he bought at Dixons could build a website, then surely so could yours truly; a master skilled craftsman of porno! I'd certainly have a go anyway!

And so I sourced various web-building tools, ending up with Dreamweaver, which needless to say I found very intimidating.

I would 'borrow' the code of a site that I liked the look of and try to re-jig it to work with my images and clips, only to find that, while it looked fine within Dreamweaver, when I previewed how it would look in a browser, the images had all jumped around and changed position, leaving me with no idea how to work the code so that they jumped back to where I wanted them!

And then when I uploaded clips and tried to open them within the site, they would take literally minutes on end to buffer, leaving the viewer staring at a blank screen instead of the sexy porno scene that would be expected.

I spent hours pouring over the manuals, and testing things out with the codes, eventually coming up with something that was beginning to look like what I wanted our site to look like.

But it was taking forever, and this would only be one website when, and if, I managed to get it successfully designed. The more successful website models that I noted offered free access to a large number of websites for one monthly subscription; an incentive that seemed to work with the horny surfers!

How on earth would I be able to have enough time to design, maintain and market several websites while still producing programmes for Television X? I could employ someone to do it, but there was no spare money to pay them. Or they could profit-share with us, but who could we trust to do it – I had not yet met anyone who seemed competent, able and enthusiastic enough to do the job.

What to do?

While I was searching online for new locations, I responded to a post on an adult video forum and came across a beautiful 400-year-old converted mill being offered for use as a location for adult movies.

When I got in contact, it turned out to belong to old friends John and Angie with whom I had lost contact, and our old friendship was soon restored as Vicki and I went over to see both them and the mill that they now lived in with a view to using it as the backdrop for our next series for Television X.

We went on to shoot at John and Angie's beautiful Essex home so much that we were worried we had overdone it a bit in terms of 'milking' the location, even though the interiors had made a superb 'hotel' setting for two series of *Demetri's Hotel*, starring cheeky Greek porn stud and our very good friend Demetri XXX as the flirty proprietor of a sumptuous hotel, frequently populated of course by lonely female guests, honeymoon couples, and of course many naughty French maids!

There was only one scene of the *Demetri's Hotel* series that we had not filmed at John and Angie's mill, and for that one we went to a disused television studio which in its heyday had been the location for *Noel's House Party* (the original 'Crinkley Bottom' home of Mr. Blobby!) and, in more recent times, as the police station setting for the brilliant comedy movie *Hot Fuzz.*

The caretaker of the studio had let us use the place as a location on a cash-in-hand only basis, but clearly he had not let the real owners know about this. He consequently spent the whole time we were there trying to persuade us to film using less lights, as our 4000 watt lighting system would obviously be using far more electricity than should be legitimately showing up in what was now effectively a disused building! I almost felt that the prankish spirit of Mr. Blobby was still there, trying to get us to film a sex sequence in total darkness!

John and Angie's two sons, James and Sonny, who were still schoolboys when I had first known them, were not only now all grown up, but were in fact now running a very successful group of websites based around the incredibly niche 'fetish' of watching girls smoke cigarettes!

Their sites featured girls smoking fags while giving blow-jobs and having sex, as well as simply lighting up in front of the camera, while fully clothed!

Being a non-smoker myself, this was a 'fetish' that I confess I had no understanding of whatsoever! Even less so, another site that the two brothers set up featured girls rubbing large party balloons over their bodies until they burst!

No doubt whatever your own personal turn-on, no matter how incredibly specific, there will be an internet site out there somewhere devoted to it, and that site will probably do comparatively well, compared to all the millions of adult sites out there devoted to more generic porn, because if you want to look at something very niche, then there will be less sites that you can go to to see what you want. Those sites will be cornering a market, albeit a rather limited one.

While we spent the best part of a year shooting various scenes at John and Angie's new place, we spoke with son James a number of times, and witnessed his success as a webmaster. He had started off building and promoting his one smoking fetish website while he was still working at his Dad's clothes shop. Eventually he was soon in a position to not only go full time on a number of websites he was building, but also to employ his younger brother Sonny as well.

By the time that the Portway website was clearly in need of some restoration, James and Sonny were renting a luxurious two bed roomed apartment from where they ran their burgeoning empire, and were planning to move to a luxurious Spanish villa.

Other people in the adult business were working solely on website production, but none of them seemed to flaunt the trappings of success. We had seen James grow from working on one very niche website part-time to now running a series of successful websites full time from an apartment paid for off the back of the sites, and with one full time employee. James had also invested in top of the range video and editing equipment, including three HD video cameras, state of the art lights and sound, and even a tracking system for smooth camera movement.

Portway meanwhile had a ragbag of ancient equipment which all required a much needed overhaul, and we were scraping by running a website that actually lost us money.

Clearly we could do with some Internet business advise, and to our eyes, James was the ideal person to give it to us. Not only had he a proven record of adult website success, but he was the son of a long-term friend of ours, thereby coming to us with a built-in personal reference.

After many months of informal discussions with James, it wasn't until we started hiring his apartment as a location for our shoots, having exhausted the possibilities at the Mill, that James and I started talking in earnest about some sort of business partnership.

James was an incredibly focused businessman who fully intended to become the biggest and best at what he did, and to build and build on his already growing adult website empire until it was the best in the World.

As such, our range of footage could be of interest to him, and his talents as a website designer, builder and promoter were certainly of interest to us!

The four of us met up (myself, Vicki, James and Sonny) and carved out a plan.

Instead of having just one generic website, the so far ill-fated Portwayfilms.com, that just showcased every scene we had ever shot for Television X in its original place as part of a series, we would create at least nine or ten websites, each with its own niche theme. We could then plunder our back- catalogue of scenes, splitting them up and spreading them out across the sites according to genre. So, if one of our series for Television X contained a girl/girl scene, two boy/girl scenes, a scene featuring an Asian girl and a group or anal scene for example, then that would be enough to update five or six sites instead of merely piling all the stuff into the same site.

We could then offer our on-line customers what would appear to be a much more appealing subscription offer – if they joined one site, they would get access to all the other sites included in their membership.

This was a template that James had seen work on his own group of websites, as well as many others, and so we were happy to follow his lead.

We carved up all our old footage to fit into ten new niches, and I went over to James' one evening where, over an Indian takeaway, and with Vicki on conference call on my mobile, we brainstormed some URL names, coming up with a generic 'bang my' prefix for all the sites except the solo girl one, buying up the appropriate URLs straight away.

Portwayfilms.com (now renamed Portwayfilmsxxx.com) would act as a 'parent' site, advertising all the new ten themed ones which would all have a 'dot com' suffix as I was told that anything ending in 'co.uk' was useless as it would only attract someone in Britain. In the rest of the Internet World (and particularly in America) if it didn't end in 'dot com' then it wasn't worth looking at!

I set about re editing all the sequences, old and new, to make everything ready for James, whose responsibility it was to get the sites designed and up and running as soon as possible.

James had built his own affiliate programme, HardGlamCash, which would offer independent webmasters the chance to link to our sites via their own and earn a generous percentage of any income derived through someone subscribing via their websites.

What income was produced from the Portway group of websites was to be split at source 50/50 between James and ourselves. We would provide the on-going footage, and James would provide all the necessary technical work to get the footage onto the websites and promoted via affiliates to the waiting wanking world!

Finally, with James at the helm, it looked as if Portway's presence on the world-wide-web might become something of a force to be reckoned with.

As I started work on re-cutting the footage for our new group of sites, I pondered on how in the past I had taken porn through every new media.

When I started in the business, I was using the then new medium of domestic videotape (VHS). I had then moved onto professional videotape (firstly U-Matic, then Betacam and now DigiBeta), then print medium while I worked for Fantasy, and then television via Television X.

Then had come DVD, and now here I was formatting High Definition porno images digitally, ready for Internet streaming, downloads, podcasting and downloads for mobile phones.

These days hardcore porn is so easily accessible through the internet and other modern media that even stuffy old Britain appears to be finally giving in and accepting not only porn's existence but also its part in modern society; a far cry from the BBFC's original no g-string policy!

Chapter Twenty-Five:
WELCOME TO PORNOLAND!

Over the next few years, Vicki and I continued to build both the Portway brand and its business.

Despite all this continued work and exposure for Portway however, our new group of websites continued to bring in very little income and we were still reconsidering how to resurrect them from what currently appeared to be a pretty lifeless state!

The worlds of minor British mainstream celebrity and porn began to blend as, in 2008 we were commissioned by Television X to create a series entitled *Calling The Shots,* where people previously not associated with porn were given the opportunity to cast and direct their very own sex scene for the Channel, under Portway's guiding hand.

In October of that year, Georgina Baillie, the granddaughter of television comedy series Fawlty Towers actor Andrew Sachs, had hit the deadlines as mischievous BBC disc jockeys Russell Brand and Jonathon Ross had phoned Mr Sachs live on air and left a rude message on his telephone voicemail with references to a brief fling that Russell Brand had had with the voluptuous Ms Baillie.

This phone call had cost the BBC a huge amount of complaints and a hefty fine from Ofcom, and had in fact cost both Brand and Ross their jobs.

It had also suddenly spun Georgina Baillie onto the front pages of all the national newspapers from her previous relative obscurity of performing in both soft core web clips and as a dancer/singer in a cult burlesque band called The Satanic Sluts!

Hoping to capitalise on Ms Baillie's current 'fifteen minutes', she was one of the 'celebrities' that Television X chose to direct their own sex scene.

Georgina chose a raunchy girl/girl scene between buxom blondes Michelle Thorne and Robyn Truelove in a paddling pool filled with messy brightly coloured sweets!

Another celebrity that we worked with was ex *Big Brother* house-mate Billi Bhatti, who had been in the famous Big Brother house for thirty-one days in 2007.

Billi was very keen to get fully involved in the porn making process and was very 'hands on', scripting the concept of his show, casting it and finding the location. So good and involved was he as a producer that Television X went on to give him his own series that we were happy to produce in co- ordination with him: *What Billi Did Next*.

This series proved to be a great success as, apart from managing to get some brand new girls to have full sex for him on-screen, he also got various other ex *Big Brother* house-mates to make cameo appearances of varying degrees in the series. These included Sam and Amanda ('Samanda'), Rebecca Shiner, Darnell Swallow, Amy Alexander and Eugene Sully, and even, from *Big Brother* series one, the notorious 'Nasty Nick' Bateman.

Amy had previously been the face of Television X on leaving the House in 2007. Rebecca Shiner was happy to get quite up close with the handy cam filming in her scene for Billi and in fact talked to the model who appeared in her scene about going on to do the live phone in show for Television X, which she did in fact go on to do, and more recently on other 'Babe' style channels too, proving to be a huge success with the callers as those famous *Big Brother* boobs swung out for the cameras once again!

Albino rapper Darnell proved to be the most game however, actually fully taking part in his scene and getting an impromptu blow-job into the bargain!

In 2009 Television X commissioned us to make a spoof look-a- like series based around the life and loves of ex face of the Channel Katie Price (AKA Jordan). It featured amusing scenes with attempted look-a-likes for Katie, Peter Andre, Victoria Beckham, Dane Bowers, Gareth Gates, Kerry Katona, Michelle Heaton and Sarah Harding.

As a nod toward Katie's autobiography '*Being Jordan*', the series was called *Being Whoredon,* which was the jokey name we gave to the character that model Kerry Louise was playing that was meant to be a spoof of the ex model.

This series proved almost as successful as our previous look- alike one, *Dirrty*, with spreads in the *Sport* newspaper as well as popular women's gossip magazine *Love It*.

In 2010 Portway were nominated in Television X's own adult SHAFTA awards ceremony (Soft and Hard Adult Film and Television Awards) and, as voted by the public, we won two 'golden cocks'; for the best interracial series (for a series we had shot with black babe Keisha Kane), and for the most outrageous sex scene (for one of the *Calling The Shots* scenes, featuring Daisy Rock and Damian Duke.

We also shot a bisexual series for Television X called *Cum Bi With Me*, each scene featuring one female and two bi guys.

The same year that we shot *Cum Bi With Me*, Television X also commissioned us to shoot another fairly outrageous series, which we called *Different Strokes,* the premise being that there are, as the saying goes, 'different strokes for different folks'.

Each episode featured someone who, to the outside world, may appear a bit 'different' but the reality was that they just wanted good sex like the rest of us.

And so this series featured the following: A couple of aggressive looking heavily tattooed and pierced punks, a transvestite, the fantastic transsexual Jo Jet, an adult baby, and a wheelchair bound disabled guy whose dream was to have sex with two of our models.

Pete, the disabled guy, was great. He had been in touch with both me and Television X quite a lot before the shoot, assuring us that, despite his physical disabilities, he would be able to perform no problem.

On the day however it turned out to be a different story. We had booked a location in Brighton, near to where Pete then lived, that was up a small flight of steps. We assumed that we would be able to push Pete in his wheelchair up these steps. When he arrived however we realised that his wheelchair was one of these high powered electric ones that contained a heavy car battery and that, consequently, there was no way that we would be able to get this chair up a small flight of steps!

We abandoned the chair by the entrance to the apartment and physically carried Pete into the building, laying him on a long sofa in the living room.

It then became apparent that, despite Pete's brave claims, there would be little interaction that he would be able to do with our two game girls.

Perhaps in his chair, the girls would have been able to mount him but, as it was, this particular shoot became a girl/girl one with Pete merely looking on.

Perhaps the most unusual shoot of this series however was that of the adult baby.

Neither my cameraman Dave Wells nor myself had ever had any experience before of the fetish of adult babyism and so were unaware as to quite what to expect.

The particular location we had booked looked very ordinary from the outside; a normal semi detached house, and the guy who let us in appeared like any other bloke.

We began to wonder if we had come to the wrong place when the owner asked if we wanted to take a look at the 'baby room'.

We both followed him upstairs and he opened the door to the spare room, saying 'Are you ready for this?'

The door opened to a small room where Dave and I saw an adult sized playpen, an adult sized rocking horse, an adult sized high chair and, perhaps to us the most strange thing of all, an adult sized changing mat complete with adult sized diapers!

Other than these surreal adult sized versions of baby things, everything else in the room was reflective of a genuine nursery: baby mobiles hanging from the ceiling, baby blue and pink wallpaper, teddies dotted around etc.

This was kind of weird and one of those moments where I felt like 'making my excuses and leaving' as the saying goes, but I was here to film a scene for *Different Strokes* and that's what I was going to do!

Dave and I had our work cut out however as we were shooting a scene that wasn't going to end up on a niche adult baby themed website but was ultimately going to be broadcast on a titillating adult TV station. Therefore the footage had to be entertaining to the average heterosexual male viewer who would be clicking away on his remote if the show didn't hold his interest.

'Adult babyism' is clearly of very specialist interest and, although my initial instincts, possibly like most guys, was to back away from it, I can now with a little thought, understand what would draw people to it; The pressures of modern living and high powered jobs could make the idea of letting go and returning to babyism very appealing. To take no responsibility for our actions and to just let a 'nanny' look after us for an afternoon while we played, fed and napped could indeed sound like a very attractive idea. In a way it's what many of us do anyway, except that we don't go the whole way and dress up as a baby to take part. Instead what we do is regarded as the 'grown up' version – we drink till we can't take responsibility for our actions while we're out 'playing hard' and then we let our mates look after us and take us home where they might put us to bed and let us nap! Whichever way you look at it, as David Bowie put it in the song *After All*, we're '*just older children, that's all*.

Through our MySpace site, we got in contact with various independent rock bands who were happy for us to use their music as soundtrack to our films in exchange for an on-screen credit, and of course for the wider exposure that their music would get via our programming being broadcast on Television X. With a number of great tracks available to us, we put out a CD called '*Soundtraxxx*' as a digital download – but, true to form, we have to date sold virtually no copies!

In 2009 I started doing regular camera work on a freelance basis for the British arm of Bluebird Productions, a company with an American division which was set up by a British multi millionaire businessman, entrepreneur and on-screen entertainer. Films that had the Bluebird branding were of a very high standard indeed, and even the *Private* organisation did a distribution deal with them at one point. Bluebird are probably the only British adult production company to have dedicated filming studios and shoot two to three scenes a day with their own contract girls, full time crew, make-up and wardrobe people. In this respect they are one of the few, if not the only, adult production company to follow what is the normal pattern of the American porn companies based in North Hollywood.

I also started doing regular freelance camerawork for Asphyxiation, a company that specialised in both sub/dom and in transvestite movies.

I loved working with the transvestites as they were all without exception really lovely people and so easy to please! As long as you respected the fact that they were making real efforts to look feminine, called them by the appropriate gender (i.e. in the feminine rather than the masculine) and told them that they looked beautiful, you were immediately their friend!

In doing lots of freelance work in addition to the programmes I made for Television X, I had now become a bit of a 'gun for hire', offering my services and equipment to any adult production company that wanted to pay me my daily rate and, as such, I remained relatively busy in an industry that was changing fast, and that, with the influx of so much generic free porn on the internet, meant that production companies and models alike were beginning to suffer a bit of a downturn in work opportunities, something that I never would have thought possible in the age old business of selling sex in all its forms and fantasies.

Models were now launching their own websites and doing free shoots and 'shared content' shoots with other models, effectively getting themselves free content for their subscription based sites.

Ordinary guys with ordinary day jobs would book a model in their spare time and film themselves having sex with her 'point-of-view' style. They too then launched inexpensive websites and made back the money they'd paid out as well as a healthy second income.

Making porno succeed in this manner was now becoming relatively easy to the new breed of 'new-media' savvy men and women, while I was still struggling to make a living, still thinking in 'old-media' terms of shooting 'proper' productions for established companies, as that had been my original route into the business, and that was what I knew.

In 2009 I spotted Charmaine Sinclair working on a rival phone-in 'babe' channel and called her on the premium rate number while she was on air to try and persuade her to come back and work for us at Television X.

It took a few months but, in early 2010, in time to coincide with the fifteen year birthday celebrations of Television X, we shot a 'return series' of Charmaine called *The Deadly Sins Of Mistress Sinclair*, fifteen years after she was the face that had launched the Channel way back in 1995.

Perhaps because of her original appearances as Samantha Spade, Charmaine now had a big following as a Mistress, and so our series with her reflected this fact with her taking control in every scene and gleefully wielding her bullwhip to men and women alike!

To my amazement, Charmaine looked virtually no different than she did when I had first met her in Lincoln all that time ago shooting with Rex/Peter.

Our series was very successful and was one of the highlights of the on-screen fifteen-year birthday celebrations that Television X broadcast.

The range of programming that Television X now put out was incredible; over seven adult TV channels, four 'babe' style live phone-in channels, websites, DVDs, and, through its parent company Portland Television, a sports channel and, most recently, links to the more mainstream Channel Five.

I remembered the early days when the managing director of Portland

TV had nervously asked me if we were sure we had enough programming to keep going for a second day, or even a week!

In November 2006 I had put on my black bow tie and tuxedo and attended the first ever British Porn Awards ceremony, a glitzy affair held at London's Hammersmith Palais.

Who would have thought in the early days of back-street illegal porn that such an event would now be publicly accepted, and held in one of London's most prestigious venues?

Most of the other attendees chose to ignore the black-tie dress code however and wore the accepted 'porn baron' uniform of dark black suit and black shirt, worn over Costa Del Sol suntan. The girls attending of course were all wearing the female porno equivalent of expensive yet revealing dress that combined both the elements of night-club chic and slutty street-walker!

Lindsay Honey was hosting the event, introducing the various nominees and, after the dinner interval, he was brought on stage to be given a Lifetime Achievement Award to a standing ovation from his peers and colleagues in an industry that had given him a career and a livelihood spanning over twenty-five years.

Dave Wells and Freddie Morse filmed the event for Bluebird Productions as I, along with Jim Slip, Marino, Big Jim, Anna Span and many other friends, colleagues and models from the industry stood up and applauded the man who had given me my first on-camera video job all those years ago in a hired apartment in London's West End.

Choked with emotion, Lindsay left the stage, and I resumed my seat, sipped my champagne and thought about my own personal journey through a Land that I had come to inhabit and know as well as I knew my own home town.

When I started in the early 1980s, Porno-Land was indeed another country, a Narnia that was accessible only to the few who knew how to contact its guides or who struggled hard enough to find its location.

These days anyone can access Porno-Land with one simple click on a computer mouse. The fact that it is a more open country now has proved liberating for the many men and women who have chosen to travel there, but time alone will tell if its unrestricted access will have a good or a bad effect on society in the long term.

One thing is certain – the route to Porno-Land is no longer a closed secret. Lap-dancing clubs, sex scandal celebrities, R18 DVDs, video downloads et al have contributed to the address of Porno-Land very much becoming a known and accepted part of all our own post-codes.

On every computer in every home in every town in Britain, anyone can now find out as much as they want about the Land that I once managed to stumble across like Lucy finding Narnia.

Nowadays anyone can download its guidebook. Anyone can now be its resident, and all are welcome. Welcome to Porno-Land.

Sample Chapter from Ric Porter's Next Book...

Chapter One:
THE PORNO YOUTUBE.

When the international multi billion dollar adult business that I shall refer to as 'Pornoland' fell under the swift and sudden onslaught of free online porn, my own area of the business crumbled and, forced into unemployment and bankruptcy, I moved from a swanky gated development in Essex to relying on the kindness of friends and acquaintances to put me up in the English county of Surrey.

Once the home to mansions that belonged to John Lennon, Cliff Richard, publicist Max Clifford and various celebrities, the area of Elmbridge in Surrey that I moved to was now populated by porn people. Ben Dover and 'Superdick' Marino lived there, alongside an assortment of Babestation models, and the area also became the base for eccentric multi-millionaire Paul Chaplin to set up the international production company Bluebird Films.

Lennon was dead, Cliff Richard had moved to Berkshire and had suffered a very public police investigation, and Max Clifford had been arrested and charged with indecent assault on various young women. He had died while still serving his sentence.

Whereas I had once been a big fish in a small production pond, the torrential floodwaters of free online porn meant that I was now a very small fish, floundering around in the rising international waters and wondering how to swim through to some sort of career buoyancy.

Ben Dover and other porn stars in the area were all doing the same as me: desperately treading water while working out how to make sense of the new situation.

For as long as we all could remember, porn was a licence to print money. To be the owner of sexy adult content meant that we would be financially secure: Production paid well, content was commissioned, bought and sold on DVD or, photographically, sold many times over as usage rights could be purchased per territory and per usage. A photo set of s model could be sold to an American magazine once for USA first usage rights and then sold again for USA second usage rights etc. And the same set could also be re-sold to each territory around the world in the same way, reaping in hundreds if not thousands of pounds for the initial outlay ofva few hundred pounds. And if a magazine re-used a set, even though they'd paid for its first or second usage they had to pay again!

And prices for professionally shot video clips or photo sets weren't cheap.

Working in adult production, we all carried on, never thinking that things could change. Why would someone ever NOT want to buy porn? Porn was a currency that was never going to de-value. Sex sells, we all know that.

And then one day in the late 90s/early 00s, a geeky guy from Germany called Fabian Thylmann had a brilliant idea.

If YouTube has become so successful in just a few years by giving everyone who had access to a computer the ability to upload video clips to the internet so that millions could see them for free, then surely a porn version of YouTube would work equally well... if not better!

In the 1990s, when only 17, he spent his time on forums on Compuserve, sometimes trading passwords to pornsites with others online, and the idea dawned that maybe trading free online porn could some day somehow possibly make him very rich.

By the late 1990s he had developed a software called NATS (Next-generation Affiliate Tracking Software), which enabled website operators to track user clicks on advertisements and links, so that they could be paid a commission.

He bought the existing online companies Mansef and Interhub, which included a fledging site called Pornhub and, under his own company name of Manwin and combining his NATS software, he launched Pornhub as his vision of a porno version of Youtube.

Now anyone with access to a computer could upload a clip (or an entire movie) of porn for free to share online for free.

But what if the uploader didn't own the copyright to the porn clip, as was often the case? Well, Manwin would of course immediately take the clip down once it was notified of a copyright infringement. But by that time, the clip had already been up and, notching up millions of views, had earned its money. And people uploading clips were faster than the producers of porn could keep a track of their product and complain. Within an hour, the same clip and more would have been back on Pornhub!

So almost any porn clip you want to see on any genre was now available to watch for free as easily as clicking through YouTube.

And for we producers of porn? Our currency had virtually overnight become devalued. Why would we spend thousands of pounds producing high quality scenes when there was no longer any guarantee that we would be able to sell it anywhere?

With its currency devalued, Pornoland was plummeting into a

worldwide recession. And guess what? Mirroring this particular niche trauma was the very real global financial crisis of 2007/2008.

Email Ric Porter to be kept up to date as to when this new book is available:
ricporter@yahoo.co.uk

Thank you.
Ric Porter 2019

Printed in Great Britain
by Amazon